CONSTITUTIONAL
HISTORY OF THE
AMERICAN REVOLUTION

CONSTITUTIONAL HISTORY OF THE AMERICAN REVOLUTION

THE AUTHORITY OF LAW

JOHN PHILLIP REID

THE UNIVERSITY OF WISCONSIN PRESS

The University of Wisconsin Press
114 North Murray Street
Madison, Wisconsin 53715

3 Henrietta Street
London WC2E 8LU, England

Printed in the United States of America

For LC CIP information see the colophon

ISBN 0-299-13980-8

For

Samuel W. Pringle

and

William R. McKim, Jr.
1930–1993

and their friends of Hastings Hall and Holden Green

WILLIAM D. WALSH
JANE GORDON WALSH
ALAN CLEVE SCHNEEBERGER
AGNES ANN SMITH

HERBERT F. ROTH
MACDONALD BUDD
DEBORAH JEANNE WALSH
HERBERT WASSERMAN

CONTENTS

CONSTITUTIONAL
HISTORY OF THE
AMERICAN REVOLUTION

INTRODUCTION

"The dispute between Great-Britain and her colonies is now reduced to a single point," a "Citizen of Philadelphia" reminded the American public in 1774. That question was, "*Whether the Parliament shall give laws to America?*"[1] All other constitutional issues dividing the American colonies and the mother country of Great Britain, including the controversy precipitating the crisis, Parliament's authority to tax the colonists for the purpose of raising revenue,[2] had become secondary. As the Philadelphian said, the constitutional controversy that commenced in 1765 with passage of the Stamp Act had since been narrowed to the "single point" of Parliament's authority to bind the colonies by legislative command in all cases whatsoever.

Our topic is why the participants in the American Revolution controversy could not find a constitutional solution to that "single point." There is no need to recount the legal issues argued by both sides as to whether Parliament possessed the right to bind the colonies by legislation in all cases whatsoever—the constraints of consent, the constraints of the original contract and the second original contract, the constraints of constitutionalism, the constraints of liberty, the authority of precedent, the authority of analogy, and the authority of custom.[3] There is, however, one feature of eighteenth-century constitutional jurisprudence that requires reemphasis.

3

It is the dichotomy of the two constitutions. The dichotomy was important enough to the revolutionary controversy to deserve repeated examination by people interested in the history of that time. Even more it merits attention because it is usually overlooked by scholars of the period. Even those who realize that there were two constitutions, perhaps assuming that only one constitutional rule can be law at a time, have missed what was going on. "[M]any of the ideas," stressed by American whigs, a writer recently observed,

> the right of resistance, the concept of a fundamental law, and the whole framework of political confrontation between rulers or prerogative powers and the people or popular liberties—predated the 1688 Revolution and harked back to the seventeenth century. In contrast, the ideas Loyalists derived from or shared with [Sir William] Blackstone placed them in the mainstream of contemporary British political theory. In emphasizing the supreme authority of Parliament, the independence and interdependence of the branches of the constitution, and constitutional means of redress, Loyalists spoke the language of eighteenth-century British constitutionalism.[4]

All very true except for the fact that American whigs just as much as American loyalists were speaking the language of eighteenth-century British constitutionalism.

Throughout the eighteenth century the British constitution was in a remarkable state of contrariety—not a state of transition, it is always in such a state, but a state of polarity. Constitutional theory in Great Britain was torn between competing constitutional superstructures which, without tearing the nation into impotency, existed side by side, each supported by tenable, familiar, aggressive legal theories. Indeed, the eighteenth century can be termed the epoch of two constitutions in both Great Britain and North America, with the mother country eventually succumbing to the convenient simplicity of one of the two constitutions, and the American states consciously selecting the other. If we wished to summarize the situation in two sentences, we could say, that the British imperialists who opposed the American whig version of the constitution were "looking ahead," away from the ancient constitution of customary, prescriptive rights, to government by consent, to a constitution of parliamentary command, in which government was entrusted with arbitrary power and civil rights were grants from the sovereign. The Americans were "looking backward," not to government by representational consent but to government by the rule of law, to a sovereign that did not grant rights but was limited by rights, a sovereign that was, like liberty, law, and the constitution, created by custom, prescription, and conventional practice. Perhaps they were not looking back to the ancient, Gothic constitution of the prehistoric Germanic peoples, but they were looking back to the constitution of Sir Edward Coke, to the constitution that beheaded Charles I and dethroned James II.

There were many differences between the two constitutions. None was more basic nor bisecting than the definition of law. Under the nineteenth-century constitution of parliamentary supremacy, legislation was command, the fist of power and the voice of sovereignty. Under the seventeenth-century constitution of customary rights, law was not power but restraint on power;[5] and people thought of government not so much in terms of sovereignty and command but somewhat optimistically as the rule of law.[6] In large part because they were defending a static, customary, prescriptive constitutionalism against a dynamic constitutionalism of will, power, and command, American whigs throughout most of the revolutionary controversy followed a strategy of constitutional avoidance, either by preventing parliamentary legislation such as the Stamp Act or the Tea Act from becoming precedents for Parliament's authority to legislate for the colonies,[7] or by ignoring an issue, especially by not raising constitutional defenses likely to get in the way of political compromise. With Parliament, which acted unilaterally in these matters, being the only tribunal competent to resolve disputes under the constitution of sovereign command, it was better, as a correspondent of a Boston newspaper told "the People of America," not to claim a "right."[8]

> Any kind of declaration of our rights and liberties, will bring the question of *American* rights into view, and make it the ye[a]st of a dispute, which can never be determined; for, it is certain, the *Americans* never will acknowledge the legislative and taxing power of the *British* Parliament, nor will the *British* Parliament ever relinquish that claim. All we can expect is, that the *British Parliament* will, on some prudential considerations, suspend the exercise of it; not that they will give up the principle. This question, therefore, ought, by all means, to be kept out of sight, because there is no hopes of it being settled, and any discussions of it will certainly widen the breach.[9]

The other eighteenth-century British constitution, the constitution of parliamentary command, spawned a more authoritative definition of law than did the constitution of customary rights. The fundamental constitutional theory, applied to the crisis with the American colonies, was outlined by Joseph Galloway of Pennsylvania in his address of reconciliation to the first Continental Congress.[10]

> The advocates for the supremacy of Parliament over the Colonies contend, that there must be one supreme legislative head in every civil society, whose authority must extend to the regulation and final decision of every matter susceptible of human direction; and that every member of the society, whether political, official, or individual, must be subordinate to its supreme will, signified in its laws; [and] that this supremacy and subordination are essential in the constitution of all States, whatever may be their forms; that no society ever did, or could exist, without it.[11]

The dynamics inherent to the constitution of parliamentary command were somewhat the opposite to those of the constitution of customary rights. Instead of a strategy of avoidance, Parliament by the constitutional need of maintaining its "right" was propelled to a strategy of active command. When the Massachusetts Administration of Justice Bill[12] was being debated in the House of Commons Edmund Burke warned that using force to coerce American obedience "will cause wranglings, scuffling, and discontent." The prime minister, Lord North, answered that there was no choice. "By what means is authority to be maintained, but by establishing that authority from parliament?" he asked.[13] North's constitutional theory was both understood and widely endorsed by the British public. "[F]rom the present disposition of the *Americans*," the House of Commons was warned by citizens of Nottingham, there was reason to "apprehend that the trade and commerce of *Great Britain* with her Colonies, cannot be effectually restored and permanently secured, without a due and proper submission and obedience to the laws and Government of this Kingdom." "[T]herefore," they beseeched "the House to take such measures as may seem most likely to secure and maintain the supreme authority, honour and dignity of *Great Britain*, enforce a due obedience to her laws, and restore subordination, order, and good Government in *America*."[14]

The strategy of asserting legislative command forced on Parliament by the dynamics of constitutional imperatives did not seek confrontation. It sought, rather, to remove constitutional ambiguities and quiet constitutional opposition. There were two sides to the strategy. One was to eschew most appearances of surrendering to American constitutional challenges. Even if colonial opposition to legislation such as the Townshend duties rendered a statute inoperative, it was constitutionally risky to repeal it unconditionally. The first tax passed for the purpose of revenue, the Stamp Act, had been repealed without a saving clause, giving legal color to American claims that the law had been unconstitutional. Parliament did not repeat that mistake. "I confess," the earl of Hillsborough told the House of Lords, explaining why he had voted against repeal of the Townshend duties, "I was of opinion, that unless we resolved entirely to relinquish the sovereignty over that country, by no means to consent to a total repeal. I saw the necessity of retaining a part of the duties, till America should recognize the right of imposing them."[15] The same constitutional imperatives informed the strategy of Lord North. "I do not know," he told the Commons after news of the Boston Tea Party reached London, "what is the proper time to lay a fresh tax on America; but this I know, that this is not the proper time to repeal one. We are now to establish our authority, or give it up entirely."[16]

North wanted Parliament to do more than reserve its right. The more assertive action was to exercise command by enacting legislation of supremacy. As the constitutional controversy with American whigs became more and more intense, Parliament attempted to reenforce its "right" by promulgating supremacy into the statutes books. Put more specifically, the primary purpose of some laws enacted by Parliament was to assert supremacy over the colonies, and, by enforcing those laws, to obtain precedents for the exercise of sovereignty.[17] In fact, it is only a slight exaggeration to assert that the Townshend duties had been intended as much for legislating supremacy as for obtaining revenue.[18] When persuaded by colonial opposition that it had no choice but to repeal the Townshend duties, Parliament preserved its claim to the right by retaining the duty on tea. American whigs then had to keep the tea tax from becoming a precedent for Parliament's claim to supremacy just as they had prevented the original Townshend duties from being a precedent. "It is not, I apprehend, the amount of the duties arising by this act that is the chief ground of the dispute, but the nature and purpose of them," Connecticut's agent in London wrote the colony's governor. "The principle upon which they are founded, alone, is worth contesting. A tax of a penny is equally a tax as one of a pound, if they have a constitutional right to impose the first, they may the last; and if they continue the one, with the acquiescence of the Colonies, though for the present, no more is pretended, I, who am no prophet, will foretell with certainty, that, upon the ground of that precedent once admitted and established, they will impose the other."[19]

The tea tax standing alone was no more successful in establishing supremacy over the colonies than it had been as part of the Townshend duties. With some hope of obtaining revenue, but chiefly to assert parliamentary supremacy, Lord North replaced it in 1773 with the Tea Act.[20] "All idea of any other tax but the Tea-duty was disclaimed," Henry Seymour Conway later recalled. "[B]ut still the Tea-duty was maintained; we quarrelled for the Tea-duty, fought for the Tea-duty," and, Conway added, eventually Parliament made war on the colonies for the tea duty.[21] The constitutional dynamics now carried the revolutionary controversy onto a new stage. To assert supremacy Parliament had drafted the Tea Act in such a way that American whigs no longer could successfully execute their strategy of constitutional avoidance. If they ignored the tax and boycotted the tea, the tactics with which they had brought down the Townshend duties and the subsequent tax on tea, Parliament still would have a precedent. The Tea Act provided that the dutied tea could not be returned to Great Britain. As soon as the ship carrying it came into a harbor the tea was legally "imported" and had to be entered at the customs house as a dutied product. It did not matter if no one purchased it. After twenty days the tea was seized and at auction some person acting for London might bid enough money to satisfy the duty. Parliament then would have obtained a precedent of colonial payment of a tax for purpose of revenue. Admittedly, the precedent would have been weak—very weak as a matter of law—but it was not intended to be argued in a legal tribunal. Its value was more political—in parliamentary debates and as precedential evidence to persuade the British public that the American constitutional argument was wrong. For whatever reason, American whigs took it seriously enough to decide that they had to prevent the precedent. Realizing that avoidance was now pointless, the whigs of Boston adopted open defiance. They staged their Tea Party to keep the tea from being unladen.[22]

The Boston Tea Party was the genesis of the events covered in this book. The same constitutional dynamics that had driven Parliament to promulgate the Tea Act left it little choice but to retaliate for the Tea Party. It struck back at Boston with more legislation of supremacy, the Coercive Acts, the topic of the first chapter, and the constitutional die was cast. The question being debated remained the same—whether Parliament could constitutionally bind the colonies by legislation in all cases whatsoever— but the premises of the revolutionary controversy had been changed irrevocably. Parliament had crossed an invisible constitutional line, not only legislating supremacy, but legislating it so emphatically that the claim of the right to legislate in all cases whatsoever could not be ignored. Either the colonies or Parliament would have to retreat or there could be civil war. For the first time American whigs had to confront the issue of parliamentary supremacy and the constitution of sovereign command.

The obvious question asked in the following pages is why the politicians of reconciliation failed to negotiate a solution to the constitutional crisis. A deeper question is whether the controversy had become too legal, and, beyond that, is the question whether law can really change the course of human events.

CHAPTER ONE

THE COERCIVE ACTS

The Boston Tea Party caused an even greater sensation in the mother country than had the Stamp Act riots. "There never was, since the [Glorious] *Revolution*, so important a crisis in the constitution of this country," a London newspaper told its readers.[1] Even the opposition in Parliament said something had to be done about Boston. There was, in fact, little disagreement about the need of hitting the town with a bill of pains and penalties.[2] Debate was over the nature of the punishment and its severity.

The bill of pains and penalties—actually a statute enacted into law by both houses of Parliament—withdrew from Boston "the officers of his Majesty's customs," and made it unlawful to unladen or to load nonmilitary goods in the bay called the "harbor of Boston." The port was to be closed to all civilian traffic "until it shall sufficiently appear to his Majesty that full satisfaction has been made by or on behalf of the inhabitants of the said town of *Boston*" to the East India Company for the teas destroyed in the Tea Party. Everyone understood the unstated purpose of the legislation. It was not only to punish Boston. More importantly, Parliament was legislating its claim to supremacy, a fact Lord North emphasized by insisting that the money Boston was ordered to pay the East India Company was damages or compensation. It was not to be referred to as a tax. "I trust we are not now upon any question of that kind," he told the Commons. "We are upon a question wherein we will agree whether the right of British subjects should be asserted, whether their property should be protected, whether their injuries should be redressed, and not whether it is right or wrong to lay a tax upon the colonies."[3]

North stated several purposes for the Boston Port Act—to punish Boston, compensate the East India Company, protect the customs officers, prevent smuggling, and preserve British trade—but no one was misled. The main intention was to assert parliamentary supremacy over the colonies.[4] "Is this then the best measure in the present case?" he asked, answering that it was. "It is to tell America, that you [the House of Commons] are in earnest, if we do not mean totally to give up the matter in question. We must assert our right at this time, while . . . it is in our power."[5] North wanted the members of the Commons to ask themselves, "whether or not we have any authority there," meaning Boston, adding that "it is very clear we have none, if we suffer the property of our subjects to be destroyed. . . . We must *punish, controul,* or *yield* to them." The sovereignty of Parliament, the secretary of state would later instruct the governor of Massachusetts, "requires a full and absolute submission."[6]

On the whole, the British felt the Boston Port Act mild punishment—appropriately tough and prudent, perhaps, but certainly not severe.[7] The administration thought the legislation so reasonable it would be self-executing. "The good of this act," Lord North assured the Commons, "is, that four or five frigates will do the business without any military force."[8] Boston would have no choice but to pay the East India Company and the crown would have no difficulty reopening the harbor.

A second general assumption was that the other American governments would not care what Parliament did to Boston or to Massachusetts Bay, that, in North's words, "[t]he rest of the colonies will not take fire at the proper punishment inflicted on those who have disobeyed your authority; . . . if we exert ourselves now with firmness and intrepidity, it is the more likely they will submit to our authority."[9]

Again, as always, Lord North depreciated the constitutional aspects of a dispute he hoped was merely political, and, again, he discounted the extent to which principle determined American reaction. The Boston Port Act stunned colonists almost as much as the Boston Tea Party had stunned London. The merchants and citizens of rival ports from New York to South Carolina resolved that the Act "is, in the highest degree arbitrary in its principles, oppressive in its operation, unparalleled in its rigour, indefinite in its exactions, and subversive of every idea of *British* liberty."[10] Future loyalists as much as future rebels were shocked. One, a future chief justice of Quebec, expressed fear that "we shall lose all that Attachm[en]t we once had to so great a Degree for the Parent Country," and another, a Philadelphia merchant, concluded that "all this extensive Continent considers the port Bill of Boston as striking Essentially at the Liberties of all North America."[11]

It was the continental reaction that caused the greatest surprise in London. Had the ministry understood American attachment to the old constitution of customary restraints, it might have anticipated the support Boston would receive from the remainder of North America. Colonial whigs, weighing the Boston Port Act from the vantage point of the two eighteenth-century constitutions, especially the potential of the constitution of legislative sovereignty, concluded that "its principle extends to every inch of English America."[12] "We had been sitting in Assembly near three weeks," Richard Henry Lee wrote from Virginia to a brother in Great Britain, "when a quick arrival from London brought us the Tyrannic Boston Port Bill, no shock of Electricity could more suddenly and universally move—Astonishment, indignation, and concern seized on all. The shallow Ministerial device was seen thro instantly, and every one declared . . . that it demanded a firm and determined union of all the Colonies to repel the common danger."[13]

The expression that best summarized American whig reaction to the Boston Port Act was not "common danger" but "in the common cause." Even imperialists used it. "The general temper of the people as well here as in other parts of America is very warm," the deputy governor of Pennsylvania warned the colonial secretary. "They look upon the chastisement of Boston to be purposely rigorous and held up by way of intimidation to all America, and in short that Boston is suffering in the common cause."[14] Looking back less than a year after passage of the Port Bill, Edmund Burke correctly told the Commons, "it was the very first thing that united all the colonies against us, from Nova Scotia to Georgia."[15] The Boston Port Act was supposed to legislate parliamentary supremacy. In the colonies it had the opposite effect. For the first time, American whigs were forced to think of legislative supremacy, the unchecked commands of a arbitrary sovereign, acting on individuals and on their property—in this case, ordinary Bostonians and the owners of Boston's ships and wharves—without the question being glazed over by taxation and all that the right to be taxed only by consent had meant in English constitutional law. Moreover, the Boston Port Act was less amiable to "avoidance" than were the Declaratory Act, the Mutiny Act, or the New York Suspension Act. As the crown had to certify Boston's compliance with the law, the town would not have been allowed to pay for the tea while pretending the money was for another purpose, the way some colonies skirted compliance with the Mutiny Act by voting funds in amounts slightly different from what Parliament mandated or by deleting one or two items from the list of specified necessities authorized to be purchased. Generally speaking, like the Tea Act itself, payment for the destroyed tea had to be opposed or the doctrine of parliamentary supremacy over the internal governance of the colonies would have gained a leading precedent.

It would be premature to detail the American constitutional case against the Boston Port Act. It was the same as against the other four Coercive Acts, and they may all be treated together in the next chapter. For the moment consider the point made in the last paragraph, that the Boston Port Act, coupled as it was with the Massachusetts Government Act, forced the issue of parliamentary sovereignty and parliamentary supremacy to the forefront of the constitutional controversy, and that American whigs could no longer avoid the question. Like the House of Burgesses, Connecticut's House of Representatives had been in session when news of the Act reached that colony. Connecticut legislators knew that they were taking a stand from which they might have to back down—if not, Parliament would have to back down, or else there could be civil war—when they voted: "That any Harbour or Port duly opened and constituted cannot be shut up and discharged but by an act of the legislature of the Province or Colony in which such port or harbour is situated without subverting the rights and liberties and destroying the property of his Majesty's subjects." Four months later, after the first Continental Congress had been in session for almost seven weeks, the delegates explained the American grievance to "the people of Great-Britain." The Boston Port Act, they claimed, reduced the citizens of that town "to the necessity of gaining subsistence from charity, till they should submit to become slaves, by confessing the omnipotence of Parliament, and acquiescing in whatever disposition they [the ministry] might think proper to make of their lives and property." [16]

The issue of parliamentary supremacy had been joined before, but never had American whigs so definitely delineated the two grounds in conflict: the colonial claim to exclusive legislative autonomy, asserted by the Connecticut House of Representatives, and the Parliament's claim to legislative omnipotency, rejected by the Continental Congress.

THE MASSACHUSETTS ACTS

At the time that the Boston Port Bill was being debated in the House of Commons, rumors were flying about London that it would be followed by other punitive measures, that the charter of Massachusetts Bay would be revoked and the colony would be converted to "a King's Government." [17] Lord North had nothing so drastic in mind, but he did plan a thorough overhauling of the distribution of power in the Bay colony. The Boston

Tea Party had only been the last straw in a long history convincing the ministry that imperial laws could not be enforced in Massachusetts. "The Americans," North explained, meaning the people of the Bay colony, "have tarred and feathered your subjects, plundered your merchants, burnt your ships, denied all obedience to your laws and authority; yet to [sic] clement and so long forbearing has our conduct been, that it is incumbent on us now to take a different course. *Whatever may be the consequence, we must risk something; if we do not, all is over.*"[18]

The conditions of local Massachusetts law, hampering the execution of imperial authority in that colony, have been discussed elsewhere and need not be reexamined here. It is enough to note that with whigs in control of the grand juries no one could be indicted for violating Parliament's statutes of supremacy; with whigs in control of the petit juries British officials were fearful of either civil damages or criminal conviction if they enforced laws the whigs believed were unconstitutional; with whigs dominant in the lists of justices of the peace no riot was ever proclaimed when the people took to the streets to avoid enforcement of imperial taxation; with whigs in control of the executive council the royal governor could not obtain the advice and consent constitutionally required before he could order the assistance of British troops; and, with the whigs a clear majority of the voting population, resolutions of town meetings could give color of law to riots and legitimacy to crowds that used intimidation and threatened violence against crown officials enforcing imperial edicts.[19] The imperial predicament, North told the Commons, was that "no prosecution in that country [Massachusetts], according to its present form of government, will be effectual," that "the military alone, ought not to act, and cannot do so legally," and that

> [t]he force of the civil power consists in the *Posse comitatus:* but the Posse are the very people who commit the riots. . . . If the democratic part [of Massachusetts government] shew a contempt of the laws, how is the governor to enforce them? Magistrates he cannot appoint: he cannot give an order without seven of the council assenting: And let the military be never so numerous and active, they cannot move in support of the civil magistracy, when no civil magistrate will call upon them for support.[20]

"America, at this instant," Richard Rigby argued, also meaning Massachusetts and not all the colonies, "is a downright anarchy, let us give it a government." That was the purpose of the Massachusetts Government Bill introduced by Lord North shortly after passage of the Boston Port Act. It was not just to reform the government of Massachusetts Bay, but to provide it with an imperial component making it what the ministry and other friends of parliamentary sovereignty called a "government."[21]

Only the urgency was new, not the problem. For better than a decade, imperialists—among them Charles Townshend, Governor Francis Bernard, and Governor Thomas Hutchinson—had been calling for reform.[22] As early as February 1769, Lord Hillsborough proposed making the members of the Massachusetts council appointive from London by the crown rather than elected locally by the House of Representatives.[23] Although this reform would have brought Massachusetts governance into line with other royal colonies and although he suspected that Massachusetts' conduct might eventually make reform "necessary," George III objected on the constitutional grounds that "altering Charters is at all time an odious measure."[24] There was subsequent talk of reform, even a bill drafted and approved by the ministry, only to be laid aside due to opposition,[25] until the Tea Party altered the political climate in Parliament. After news was received of what had happened at Boston, any proposal, no matter how drastic, would have had some support.

Constitutional theory and constitutional balance were askew in Massachusetts Bay. Accepted political science then taught that to maintain stability in government the anarchy of democracy had to be balanced by the restraint of monarchy. It was a matter, J. L. De Lolme explained in his treatise on constitutional law, of taming "the irresistible violence" of "the people" by limiting their role in government. "[A]s the power of the people . . . is at all times really formidable, the constitution has set a counterpoise to it; and the royal authority is this counterpoise." Both poise and counterpoise were out of whack in the Bay colony. Most colonial councils were appointed by the crown. The Massachusetts Council was elected by the House of Representatives, giving the democratic lower house control of the upper house, leaving only the governor and his veto as a monarchical check on democracy. "We know by experience," Governor Hutchinson wrote Lord Hillsborough, "that the present form of Government in this Province gives too great a share both of legislative and executive power to the people, to consist with the interest to the parent state, or the welfare of the Colony itself."[26] The experience to which he referred was that the Council would never advise and consent when the governor wished to call for British troops to enforce imperial law and, even when soldiers were on hand, they could not be used to police civilians because the magistrates, appointed by the Council, would not proclaim riots. Even had the governor found some constitutional way to use the military, the "democratic" side of the government in the form of the grand and petit juries would not only refuse to indict and to convict whigs opposing imperial law, they quite likely would indict and convict imperial officers for enforcing "unconstitutional" law.[27] In the political language of the day, the Tea Party had "in part proceeded from the peculiarly democratic form of their constitution, and the consequent weakness of their powers of government;" "for the constitution being formed chiefly on democratic principles, it would always have been subject to the anarchy of popular governments."[28]

The solution, it seemed to London, was "to reform their [Massachusetts] constitution, after the model of the imperial state," putting two opposing theories of what that model should be on a collision course. The colonial model was local legislative autonomy restrained by a crown independent of Parliament. "[S]hould the People of this Province be left to the free and full Exercise of all the Liberties and Immunities granted to them by Charter," the Massachusetts House of Representatives contended, "there would be no Danger of an Independence on the Crown. Our Charters reserve great Power to the Crown in its Representative [i.e., the governor], fully sufficient to balance, analogous to the English Constitution, all the Liberties and Privileges granted to the People."[29]

The trouble was that model was no longer analogous to the British constitution. The Massachusetts model was both too monarchical and not monarchical enough for London. It was too monarchical as it was too independent of parliamentary control. It was not monarchical enough because it contemplated a crown with only the authority to veto and to appoint, not the authority to govern. The British ministry wanted to put a drastically different crown in control of Massachusetts Bay: the crown that then reigned in London, in constitutional theory the first part of the tripartite Parliament, but in constitutional fact beholden to the two houses. "I want to know how *Parliament* is ever to maintain its authority in America but by strengthening the executive power of this country," Lord North told the Commons. "We know well Parliament can control the executive power of this country, and we know there can't be a different interest between the King and his people." There could, however, be a "[d]ifferent interest with regard to America. In this instance if it operates at all [it] must operate, not to the authority of the King, but of Parliament." For that purpose, the administration offered a bill to remedy the defects in the government of Massachusetts. If there was reform it had to be initiated by Parliament. Constitutionalists, jealous of British liberty, could not entrust reform to the Privy Council or any other institution of crown authority. "By what means is authority to be maintained, but by establishing the authority from parliament?"[30] Put more precisely, the ministry not only had to repudiate the dangerous American whig doctrine that the colonies' sole constitutional connection to Great Britain was through the crown, it also needed a reforming bill that would do more than merely new model the government of Massachusetts Bay. The bill had to be another try at legislating parliamentary supremacy.

There is no need to consider the details of the bill Lord North offered. They belong more properly in a constitutional history of the authority to govern than in a discussion of Parliament's claim to supremacy. On that issue mere passage of the bill was more significant than its provisions. The bill's object was to "purge that [Massachusetts] constitution of all its crudities, and give strength and spirit to the civil magistracy, and to the executive power;" to remedy, as Lord Hillsborough had said when drafting an earlier version of the bill, "that defective part of the constitution, which made the Council of Boston creatures of the Assembly, the Justices creatures of the Council," the juries creatures of the town meetings, and the town meetings creatures of the whig crowd. The legislative intent, as reported by the *Annual Register*, was "to take the whole executive power out of the hands of the democratic part, and to vest the nomination of counsellors, judges, and magistrates of all kinds, including sheriffs, in the crown, and in some cases in the King's governor, and all to be removable at the pleasure of the crown."[31]

"I shall propose," Lord North announced, "to take the executive power out of the democratical part of the constitution and put [it] into the hands of the civil Governor appointed by the Crown, who as well as the judges . . . should be justices." He meant that the governor would be vested with the power of a justice of the peace, allowing him to proclaim a riot and to call for military assistance on his own authority, something Hutchinson claimed he had not been able to do during the Tea Party. "I would have the judges, etc., named by the Governor," and removable at the governor's pleasure, except for the chief justice and the judges of the superior court who would serve at the king's discretion. "In tumults I would have the Governor act alone if necessary. In other cases I would have [the] Council consulted." And to make effective whatever action these officials took, both grand and petit jurors would no longer be selected by town meetings. They would be chosen, instead, as in England, by the sheriff, who in turn was appointed by the governor, serving at his pleasure. "The Lieutenant Governor and Secretary I would have in the Council," North went on. "It's a great inconvenience that Government have no one in their Council."[32] What he meant was that there had been no *ex officio* members of the Massachusetts Council, unlike some other colonial councils, where imperial officeholders such as the surveyor general or the superintendent of Indian affairs were appointed.

The most drastic reform concerned selection of the Council. "The measure now proposed," North said, "is nothing more than taking the election of Counsellors out of the hands of those people [the House of Representatives], who are continually acting in defiance and resistance of your laws."[33] Appointment and removal would be at the pleasure of the king, that is, the discretion of the governor in Massachusetts and the ministry in London. The "democratical" influence was eliminated, leading some members of Parliament to wonder what remained. "Does Lord North mean to leave an Assembly or not?" the Speaker of the Commons, Sir Fletcher Norton, queried. "This does not touch the legislative power or choice of Assembly and Council," North replied. "It relates only to the Executive."[34] He was correct that the legislative authority of the General Court was not diminished. What Norton had probably meant, however, was whether the Council's legislative autonomy would be affected, whether by making the Council independent of the people the bill was also making it dependent on the crown. That objection was raised by members of both houses opposing the bill, including the dissentient lords who protested that North's reform would not restore "the Equilibrium" of the Massachusetts constitution. "The Power given to the Crown of occasionally increasing or lessening the Number of the Council on the Report of Governors, and at the Pleasure of Ministers, must make these Governors and Ministers Masters of every Question in that Assembly; and by destroying its Freedom of Deliberation, will wholly annihilate its Use."[35]

For Lord North, the Massachusetts Government Act was the culmination of the administration's program for exerting the legislative sovereignty of Great Britain over the North American colonies. In one masterstroke it both legislated parliamentary supremacy and undermined colonial legislative autonomy. "I am sure that this [act] is adopted as the best method at present," North told the Commons. "I do not say it will succeed, but . . . if the Massachuset[t]s Bay is to be governed by management, this is the only remedy." Other members of Parliament thought the price too high. "[W]e see in this bill," dissentient lords protested, "the same scheme of strengthening the authority of the officers and ministers of state, *at the expence of the rights and liberties of the subject*, which was indicated by the inauspicious act for shutting up the harbour of Boston."[36]

The second of the Massachusetts acts, the third coercive act, was the Administration of Justice Act. Its provisions might have been incorporated into the Massachusetts Government Act had they not been temporary legislation. Like the Massachusetts Government Act, the Administration of Justice Act was concerned with the governance of Massachusetts Bay and even more clearly was an instance of legislating parliamentary supremacy. The preamble mentioned neither the need to preserve British sovereignty in New England nor the need of strengthening colonial allegiance to the crown. The stated purpose, rather, was to support the authority of Parliament: that "in his Majesty's province of Massachusetts Bay, in New

England, an attempt has lately been made to throw off the authority of the Parliament of Great Britain over the said province, and an actual and avowed resistance, by open force, to the execution of certain acts of parliament, has been suffered to take place, uncontrolled and unpunished, in defiance of his Majesty's authority, and to the utter subversion of all lawful government."[37]

The problem that the statute sought to remedy was "discouragement." Massachusetts people in general, not just imperial officials, the preamble said, were discouraged from enforcing parliamentary statutes when provincial grand and petit juries might punish them for violating local "whig" law:

> that neither the magistrates acting in support of the laws, nor any of his Majesty's subjects aiding and assisting them therein, or in the suppression of riots and tumults, raised in opposition to the execution of the laws and statutes of this realm [i.e., acts of Parliament], should be discouraged from the proper discharge of their duty, by an apprehension, that in case of their being questioned for any acts done therein, they may be liable to be brought to trial for the same before persons who do not acknowledge the validity of the laws, in the execution thereof, or the authority of the magistrate in the support of whom such acts had been done.[38]

The ostensible purpose of the Administration of Justice Act was to end this discouragement. Knowing that if they attempted to enforce imperial law they might find themselves being criminally or civilly tried by what Governor Hutchinson described as "a biassed and pre-determined Jury" discouraged crown officials from doing their duty. The practical purpose was the reverse, encouragement: to encourage law enforcement, especially law enforcement by British military officers.[39] To that end the Act provided:

> that if any inquisition or indictment shall be found, or if any appeal shall be sued or preferred against any person, for murder, or other capital offence, in the province of Massachusetts Bay, and it shall appear, by information given upon oath to the governor . . . that the fact was committed by the person against whom such inquisition or indictment shall be found, or against whom such appeal shall be sued or preferred as aforesaid, either in the execution of his duty as a magistrate, for the suppression of riots, or in the support of the laws of revenue, or in acting in his duty as an officer of revenue, or in acting under the direction and order of any magistrate, for the suppression of riots, or for the carrying into effect the laws of revenue, or in aiding

and assisting in any of the cases aforesaid; and if it shall also appear, to the satisfaction of the said governor . . . that an indifferent trial cannot be had within the said province, in that case, it shall and may be lawful for the governor . . . to direct, with the advice and consent of the council, that the inquisition, indictment, or appeal, shall be tried in some other of his Majesty's colonies, or in *Great Britain*.[40]

It was the Act of 35 Henry VIII and the Dockyards Act all over again, and for the same constitutional purpose, enforcement of parliamentary supremacy.[41] The Administration of Justice Act, however, worked on a different set of people. Its function was to protect imperial law enforcers rather than to prosecute imperial crime.

Possibly no other British statute, certainly no other act legislating parliamentary supremacy, was so misrepresented by American whigs and their British supporters,[42] or so misrepresented by scholars of later generations.[43] The Administration of Justice Act did not provide blanket immunity nor did it empower "the Governor, if any magistrate, revenue officer, or military man was indicted for murder, to send him to England for trial in King's Bench."[44] The purview of the statute was narrow. It would not, for example, as is sometimes claimed, have protected Captain Thomas Preston and his soldiers in the Boston Massacre. Preston had not been acting under the direction of a magistrate. In fact, no magistrate had been present and no riot had been proclaimed. Preston had acted on his own authority, as an army officer, not as "an officer of revenue," and, had the Administration of Justice Act been in operation at the time, he could not have moved for trial beyond the venue, even if he had been acting lawfully, which he had not been.[45]

Arguments that had been made against 35 Henry VIII and the Dockyards Act were generally repeated in the debates on the Administration of Justice Bill: that Americans would be denied the constitutional right of trial by peers if the bill was enacted, that trial in England meant trial in a jurisdiction "where they are obnoxious," and, as *ex parte* trials, "nothing but a mockery of justice."[46] There were additional objections raised to this particular bill. One was to the authority the statute vested in the governor "to compel the transportation from America to Great-Britain, of any number of witnesses, at the pleasure of the parties prosecuting and prosecuted." It was said that the law was arbitrary, too harsh on individuals, making no exceptions for "age, sex, health, circumstances, business, and duties." Anyone ordered to England to give evidence was compelled to go. It was an extraordinary grant of power for the eighteenth century, "so extravagant in its principles, and so impracticable in its execution," dissentient lords protested, "as to confirm us further in our opinion of the spirit which animates the whole system of the present American regulations."[47] There was even a suspicion that Parliament may have underhandedly been legislating criminal immunity. "Whenever murder is committed, it must inevitably go off with impunity," George Dempster, Scots advocate and member for Perth, explained. "[F]or whenever any person present shall find he is to go over the Atlantic as an evidence, to the detriment of his family and his fortune, there is no doubt but that he will evade the necessity of his appearance as an evidence." The consequence, Dempster charged, was that the Administration of Justice Act "will be a means of subjecting the people of that country to assassination, in the room of legal trial."[48]

There were other suppositions even more extreme. It was possible, some commentators said, that the ministry was abusing the legislative process by using this Act, an ordinary exercise of legislation, to disguise a drastic change in constitutional law. After all, if soldiers were to be tried in England rather than Massachusetts for crimes committed while acting officially in Massachusetts, what would become of the principle of civilian control of the military? If the Administration of Justice Act "impowers the Governor to withdraw Offenders from Justice in the said Province," petitioners warned the House of Commons, "[w]hat must be the consequence of sending Troops, not really under the Controul of the Civil Power, and unamenable to the Law, among a People whom they have been industriously taught, by incendiary Arts of wicked Men, to regard as deserving every Species of Insult and Abuse; the Insults and Injuries of a lawless Soldiery are such as no free People can long endure." Of course, the petitioners were clutching for any argument they could think of, but the likelihood we might not be persuaded by their arguments should not lead us to forget that fear of military recklessness and irresponsibility was inherent to eighteenth-century constitutional thought. Just a few weeks earlier Colonel Issac Barré, who had commanded British troops at Quebec and was member for Chipping Wycombe, had reminded his colleagues in the lower house that even professional soldiers had constitutional misgivings about mixing troops among civilians. "A soldier feels himself so much above the rest of mankind, that the strict hand of the civil power is necessary to controul the haughtiness of disposition which such superiority inspires," Barré told the Commons. "You know, Sir, what constant care is taken in this country to remind the military that they are under the restraint of the civil power. In America their superiority is felt still greater. Remove the check of the law, as this bill intends, and what insolence, what outrage may you not expect?" It would be worthwhile to consider the implications of what Barré said. From his perspective, it was a political argument why Parliament should reject the Administration of Justice Act. For the American whig, however, the shock was that a "law" could be so easily, so swiftly enacted, proving by action the constitutionalist's argument not only against parliamentary supremacy, but also against legislative sovereignty in general. For what the Administration of Justice Act meant in terms of classic constitutionalism was the authority of legislation over the principle of the rule of law.[49]

A third objection against the Administration of Justice Act is less of interest for itself than for the arguments used by the ministry to answer it. They indicate that fear of military recklessness was not limited to the opposition. The ministry, including Lord North, had similar constitutional concerns. Some members of the House of Commons had asked why it was necessary to transport defendants and witnesses to London when the governor of Massachusetts could pardon them on the spot. Why, Philip Jennings wondered, "send them here to be pardoned" when it could be done in Boston. North admitted that the authority to pardon had just been conferred on the governor by the Massachusetts Government Act. "At the same time," he replied, "it does appear to me, I confess, that it will be right [not to have] a general pardon of all persons indicted." Better to have a trial in England where the facts can be examined and "impartial justice can be expected." Another member, Constantine Phipps, persisted: "I dont mean the general order to pardon all persons indicted, but I mean a power in the Governor to pardon a particular [man] where he sees the impropriety of letting that man even suffer imprisonment for having done his duty there." The solicitor general replied that the inconvenience and hardship of transportation to England was better public policy than allowing members of the military serving in Massachusetts to think "that they carried pardons in their pockets." They should be confident that they would receive justice but not think "that their pardon be assured." The Administration of Justice Act was for the protection of those lawfully doing their duty, not "to encourage men to [break the law]. It breeds no kind of confidence in their mind, than that justice they ought to have will be exactly similar to the same kind of Acts in the statute books, as is now the standing law of this country."[50]

There is a point as well as an irony to be noted. The point is more than that fear of military power was not just American paranoia or propaganda. It is not even that the fear was widely shared in Great Britain. The point to be noted is the extent that constitutional principles were the same across the British political spectrum. The administration, generally considered "conservative" or "mainstream," defended its legislation by appealing to principles with which the "radicals" could not quarrel. The authority to pardon should not be extended because power had to give way to the rule of law. That, too, was the irony. The solicitor general appealed to the rule of law to justify an exercise of legislative power that American whigs thought both promulgated a lessening of the rule of law and, simply by being in existence, threatened an end to the rule of law.

The Administration of Justice Bill easily passed both houses of Parliament as did the fourth of the so-called "Coercive Acts," the Quartering Act, which was intended to provide billets for the troops being sent to Massachusetts Bay, but was applicable to all the colonies. There is no need to consider the Quartering Act or the debate preceding its passage. They mainly concerned issues about the proper governance of North America, not the authority of Parliament to legislate. The Act was primarily intended to remove some of the checks that local American magistrates and juries used to restrain officers seeking quarters for their men.[51] It did not give the governor authority to requisition quarters in private houses, as is sometimes said,[52] but only in "uninhabited houses, out-houses, barns, or other buildings."[53] As very little was changed except adjective process, the Quartering Act is not an instance of supremacy legislation like the Boston Port Act or the Massachusetts Government Act.[54]

It may be that the debate in Parliament over the Massachusetts Acts is a measure for gauging how far American constitutional thought had separated from British constitutional thought by 1774. As will be discussed below, the sovereignty of Parliament had become the American grievance. That had not been the grievance for those members of Parliament who had opposed passage of the Administration of Justice Bill. They said the legislation was unconstitutional, not that enactment of the legislation, the exercise of legislative supremacy, was unconstitutional. The Administration of Justice Bill, Stephen Fox protested, "has a most wanton and wicked purpose; we are either to treat the Americans as subjects or as rebels. If we treat them as subjects, the bill goes too far; if as rebels, it does not go far enough."[55] Supremacy was not Fox's concern. His concern was constitutional government and the rule of law. John Sawbridge, by contrast, was thinking of the older, American meaning of constitutional rule when warning that the Administration of Justice Bill "is meant to enslave America; and the same Minister who means to enslave them, would if he had an opportunity, enslave England."[56] Sawbridge was using the word "enslave" in its eighteenth-century constitutional sense. He was not saying that the ministry wished to change in any manner the civil status or rights of people, but that it wished to rule the nation by representative legislative command rather than by customary right.[57] Sawbridge was voicing the old whig fear of abuse of power, but it is not clear that many in Parliament continued to hold to the old whig tenet that power which can be abused is unconstitutional power. Still it was a matter of gradation, of how much one retained of the old constitutionalism and how much one had rejected. When Lord North replied, "I have no such intention," "to enslave America," his use of "enslave" had fewer legal and constitutional connotations than did Sawbridge's.[58]

THE QUEBEC ACT

There was yet a fifth statute of 1774 that was grouped by contemporaries with the Boston Port Act and the three Massachusetts Acts under the name of the "Coercive Acts" or the "Intolerable Acts." It was the Quebec Act, granting a permanent government to the province recently conquered from France. The grant, however, had been made by parliamentary statute rather than by royal charter which had been the customary instrument of establishing governments in the English-speaking colonies. There were several aspects of the Quebec Act making it "intolerable" to American whigs and British opposition. These were: (1) extension of Quebec's boundaries over western Canada and the region of the Ohio River, including backcountry conquered from France and claimed by New York, Pennsylvania, and Virginia; (2) reinstatement of French civil law; (3) exclusion of juries in noncriminal cases; (4) denial of habeas corpus; (5) toleration of Roman Catholicism, perhaps even "establishing" it by sanctioning traditional privileges of the clergy, including tithes; and (6) the creation of arbitrary government.[59]

The main supremacy issue of the Quebec Act was whether Parliament had introduced arbitrary government as defined in English and British constitutional law, and whether Parliament, if it did create arbitrary government, exceeded its constitutional competency. Asserting that it was "at present inexpedient to call an Assembly," the Quebec Act conferred all legislative authority, except the power of taxation which was retained by Parliament, on the appointed governor and the appointed Council, empowering them to make laws "for the Peace, Welfare, and Good Government, of the Province."[60] As with most other colonies, the bills had to be submitted to London for the crown's approbation, but otherwise the Council, with the governor a member, was the sole legislature. This scheme was arbitrary government by the definition of eighteenth-century constitutionalism if it meant government by one official, as both the opposition and American whigs thought it did. "[T]he governor had not only the power of appointing [the council], but of suspending and dismissing," John Dunning warned, "and therefore would have the council under his command." And as the governor served at the pleasure of the crown, meaning the prime minister or the secretary of state for the colonies, all Quebec officials were, in Alexander Hamilton's words, "creatures" of the crown, "and the property and civil rights of the Canadians are made altogether dependent upon" the will of the king or the ministry.[61]

The Quebec Act was the constitutional opposite of the Massachusetts Government Act. With the Massachusetts Government Act, Parliament had sought to reestablish the constitutional balance between two of the three branches of the legislature, by restoring the function that monarchy performed for the British government in which monarchy balanced democracy. The Quebec Act legislated that balance out of the Quebec government, giving no role to democracy and all power to monarchy.

"[C]an a better legislature be given than a Governor, and Council?" Lord North asked, defending the Quebec Bill. It was a question that could have disturbed colonial whigs more than any other asked in 1774, the year before the war for American independence began. "The Assembly can't be granted," North explained, "because the legislature must be composed of Canadian Roman Catholic subjects, or it will be oppressive to that country." He meant that under the British constitution Quebec could not constitutionally be granted a legislature. Catholics could not be allowed to be members as the constitution did not permit them to hold public office. Yet a Protestant legislature would not be constitutional either because it would not be representative. An elected assembly would mean Quebec was governed by a handful of British Protestant electors, perhaps no more than four hundred, who, Thomas Bernard thought, could "erect themselves into a constitutional *aristocracy*, and tyrannize over and oppress above a hundred thousand peaceable and dutiful subjects, who first settled the country."[62]

The Catholic issue gave the opposition trouble. All British Protestants knew the cultural and constitutional reasons why French Catholics could not be given the vote.[63] Yet, following experience with British freedom even Roman Catholics might change, but the Quebec Act was to be permanent. That fact provided the opposition with their constitutional line of attack. To solve what might be a temporary problem, the ministry was setting up not just an arbitrary government in Quebec, but a permanent arbitrary government, a government that the lord mayor, aldermen, and commons of London asserted was "totally inconsistent with the liberty and principles of the *English* Constitution." Was there, the earl of Abingdon wondered, "any Degree of *Despotism* greater and higher than that, where the *legislative*, the *executive*, and the *judiciary* Powers meet and unite in one and the same Person."[64]

The matter of liberty provided opponents of the Quebec Bill with a second main constitutional criticism, allowing them to question Parliament's sovereignty by asking whether it had authority to create an "unfree" constitution. Stripped clean of mistrust of Catholics and of parliamentary weariness with colonial assemblies, the debate over the Quebec Bill pitted the fundamental principle of eighteenth-century constitutionalism, rule by constitutional restraint, against the bane of eighteenth-century constitutionalism, arbitrary government. The *London Magazine* described the debate as "that struggle between constitutional freedom and arbitrary power," and American whigs were told by Alexander Hamilton that "the principle of arbitrary power . . . is the soul of the act."[65]

The government created by the Quebec Act was only part of the "arbitrary" grievance. The Act itself was arbitrary. Its provisions provided a striking lesson to the eighteenth-century legal mind of how easily the current Parliament could be persuaded to depart from the old constitution of customary and contractual rights. "[T]his bill, if passed into a law," the mayor, aldermen, and commons of London had warned the king, "will be contrary not only to the compact entered into with the numerous settlers of the reformed religion, who were invited into the said province under the sacred promise of enjoying the benefit to the laws of your realm of England, but likewise repugnant to your royal proclamation to the 7 of October, 1763, for the speedy settling of the said new government."[66] They were referring not just to the original colonial contract, but to a special version of the original contract, a proclamation contract, that had been upheld and enforced by King's Bench just eight years earlier in *Campbell* v. *Hall*.[67] The proclamation of 1763, issued by George III, invited Britons to settle in the territories recently conquered from France, promising—Lord Camden said "they were solemnly promised"—that they would be governed by English law and that elected assemblies would be established as soon as feasible.[68]

Constantine Phipps thought he was explaining a theory of contractual enforceability when he told the House of Commons, "I look upon that Proclamation as a compact of the Crown with the subjects of that country, as an inducement to those who shall settle as merchants to purchase land, and mix with the inhabitants." The Commons even heard evidence that British subjects had migrated to Quebec "on the faith of the King's Proclamation."[69] Half a century earlier this combined argument of law and facts would have had relevance both for proving constitutional law and as constitutional law. Passage of the Quebec Act would provide American whigs with new proof of a quite different sort: that under the current constitution, rights they believed had been secured by the original contract and its two offshoots, the second original contract and the migration purchase,[70] now existed at the will and pleasure of Parliament. Lord Mansfield, who, as chief justice of King's Bench, had held that the Proclamation of 1763 was a contract enforceable against the crown, as a member of the House of Lords supported the Quebec Bill. His vote for the Bill indicated that although the Proclamation was a contract binding the king, under the constitution he was expounding no contractarian right, or any other right for that matter, had weight against parliamentary sovereignty.[71] By legislative fiat the Quebec Act took "from a large number of the King's subjects that constitution, which was given to them" by the Proclamation of 1763, a former solicitor general, John Dunning, protested. "The King upon that occasion gave encouragement to future settlers. . . . The King would be thought to act an unbecoming part, if in consequence of his promise, if he in violation of that promise, was to take from them that constitution and give them a different one. But it is proper enough for Parliament."[72]

Another provision of the Quebec Act—extending Quebec's boundaries to the Ohio and Illinois countries—may seem relatively innocuous today, but it confirmed the worst fears American whigs had of arbitrary power. Here was another demonstration of the new constitutionalism, another indication that there was no check on legislative sovereignty. More was jeopardized than mere jurisdictional borders. By shrinking the backcountry of Pennsylvania and other charter colonies, Dunning pointed out, the Quebec Act took away, "by one stroke, the charter properties confirmed by act of Parliament of those Colonies, you violently seize their rights." He meant that British subjects, settling over the mountains need only cross an imaginary line to "find themselves gone from the freedom of the *British* constitution, and meet with all the powers of despotism." Without even knowing it, they would be "deprived of the dearest rights and privileges of *English* subjects." Not only was that "a most tyrannical and inhuman conduct. It is sporting with property in a manner that cannot be defended."[73]

The constitutionalist case against the Quebec Act was most concisely summarized by a writer of 1782. "Instead of giving Liberty and Freedom to the Canadians, and thereby a Taste of the Blessings of English government; we have not only enslaved them, but reduced many Thousand English now living within the Bounds of that Province, to the same Condition." Seen from that perspective, South Carolina's William Henry Drayton would have been correct when he said of the Quebec Act, "Such powers cannot legally exist in Britain," had he added that he meant such powers were illegal under the old contractarian constitution of customary, prescriptive rights. He was not thinking of the constitution of parliamentary sovereignty as it existed in Westminster Hall in 1774.[74]

CHAPTER TWO

THE COERCIVE GRIEVANCE

There was a dynamic to the eighteenth-century British constitution propelling events to a degree that is not often appreciated. It may be thought that the process was due to the nature of the constitution: that because it was prescriptive, customary, or unwritten, it forced Parliament ever to be watchful lest the crown regain authority or the Irish establish rights. More likely, the impetus was due to the doctrine of precedent, with the need to create a precedent or the need to avoid precedent determining a policy and even sometimes promoting principles that would not otherwise be adopted or even desired. Law could be as determinative of politics as politics was of law.

"You keep the Duty on Tea to preserve your right of laying it," Edmund Burke told the House of Commons. The same reasoning, the people of Pennsylvania were informed, "operated on both sides, though in a different manner. If Parliament was so tenacious of the precedent to keep up the claim on the Colonies, it was equally incumbent on them to refuse their submission; for on this the virtue of the precedent depended." The chain did not stop with action and reaction. Lord North had to counter the colonial reaction. As the tax on tea "was as much an anticommercial tax as any of those which were repealed on that principle," Governor George Johnstone later recalled, North would have preferred to repeal all four

Townshend duties, "but the authority of Parliament being disputed, he could not repeal all till that [the tea tax] was fully acknowledged." The cycle went on, from the tea tax, to the Tea Act of 1773, to the Boston Tea Party, to the Coercive Acts.[1]

We must not allow the details to obscure the substance. More was going on than legal one-upmanship or the attempt of either side to control the premises of the political debate. Behind the maneuvers of precedent creation and precedent avoidance, of constitutional action and constitutional reaction, was the struggle to promulgate legal doctrine. "There is indeed a great business in agitation," Horace Walpole wrote, at the time the Massachusetts Government Bill was receiving its third reading in the House of Commons. "Its Parliamentary name is Regulations for Boston. Its essence, the question of sovereignty over America."[2] It is that principle, the doctrine in contention—sovereignty or parliamentary supremacy—which explains both the tenacity of precedent avoidance and the harshness of the final legislating of supremacy by precedent creation.

Even in a constitutional history there are risks to saying that the Coercive Acts were harsh. Contemporaries as well as historians have disagreed about whether Parliament overreacted to the Tea Party. Imperialists thought the Acts quite lenient, perhaps because the provocation had been so politically and constitutionally daring that punitive measures were necessary or all authority could be lost.[3] "But surely this Bill does not destroy any of their civil rights?" Lord North said of one of the Coercive Acts. "All that these Acts profess to do, is to restore some order to the Province."[4] The shock waves sent across the colonies tell us that the Acts did much more than merely deal with peace and order. It may have been an exaggeration to say, as an English pamphlet said, that the Coercive Acts "annulled" the "government" of Massachusetts Bay,[5] but it was a reasonable exaggeration in the context of eighteenth-century constitutionalism. The whigs of Worcester County, Massachusetts, were thinking constitutionally when they resolved as early as August 1774, "[t]hat an attempt to vacate said charter, by either party, without the consent of the other, has a tendency to dissolve the union between Great Britain and this province, to destroy the allegiance we owe to the king, and to set aside the sacred obligations he is under to his subjects here." Two months later, instructing the representative whom they had just elected to the House of Representatives, the voters of the town of Worcester drew the same legal conclusion. Assuming the charter in fact and in law destroyed by the Coercive Acts, they instructed him "to consider the people of this province as absolved, on their part from the obligation therein contained, and to all intents and purposes reduced to a state of nature."[6]

Today we think of the Worcester resolves more as political proselytism than constitutional theory, forgetting that the constitution argued by American whigs was the constitution of contractarian and prescriptive right, not the constitution of sovereign command. The charter that was at least altered and at most abrogated by the Massachusetts Government Act had not been a grant under the old constitution as it would be under the new. Under the constitution of customary, contractarian law, the Massachusetts charter had been a "solemn stipulation and compact."[7] It was that compact that was indissoluble, not the charter. Although lawyers and probably a majority of colonial whigs understood that charters were revocable, at least for cause, there was an extreme theory invoking rules of inherent rights such as that "Charters being Compacts between two Parties, the King and the People, no Alteration could be made in them even for the better, but by Consent of the Parties."[8] What the voters of the town of Worcester seem to have meant was that the Massachusetts Government Act, by altering the provincial charter, destroyed the second original contract of which the charter had been the principal evidence. Destruction of the contract meant destruction of the constitution, dissevering the bonds of allegiance and returning the people of the colony, if not all American colonists, to their precontractual status, the state of nature.

The state of nature was a drastic argument, indicative that many colonists, not just people in Worcester, realized that they had reached the constitutional exigency of their epoch. From the constitutional perspective of American whigs, and perhaps even from the constitutional perspective of some people in Great Britain, the Coercive Acts, especially the Massachusetts Government Act and the Quebec Act, more than any other expression of parliamentary supremacy over the colonies, marked the ending of the old constitutionalism of custom, prescription, and contract, and the coming of the new constitutionalism of sovereign command. It is not certain but entirely possible, that seen from the vantage point of eighteenth-century constitutional theory, the Acts were less jarring for what they attempted to do to the colonial constitution than for what they purported for the imperial constitution. For if the Acts meant anything in terms of the old constitutionalism, it was the ascendancy of what that constitutionalism had taught the English, British, and Americans to fear most—arbitrary power—and the demise of what that constitutionalism had taught them most to cherish—liberty founded on restraints to power and protected by the rule of law.

THE ARBITRARY GRIEVANCE

It is no longer possible to think of constitutionalism in the way that the eighteenth century did. Although we may not value the right to property as it once was valued, we can understand the distress that members of

Parliament felt on learning of the Boston Tea Party and the wanton, open destruction of chests of valuable tea. Knowing that they were the spokesmen for a constituency of property owners, we appreciate what they meant when calling the Tea Party "lawless." Perhaps we also can comprehend the shock of Americans on hearing of the Boston Port Act and the Massachusetts Government Act, but we cannot think as they thought when they called the Coercive Acts "lawless."

As this was the eighteenth century, not just American whigs had such thoughts. There were eighteenth-century Britons, including members of Parliament, who said the Coercive Acts were not law. "I look upon this measure," Charles James Fox told the Commons of the Massachusetts Government Bill, "to be in effect taking away their charter; if their charter is to be taken away, for God's sake let it be taken away by law, and not by a legislative coercion." That is not our language—to say that an act of Parliament is not "law"—but Fox was not using words loosely. No less a lawyer than Lord Camden, former attorney general of England, former chief justice of the Court of Common Pleas, and former lord chancellor of England, not only understood Fox but used the word "law" in much the same way. "It sounds well, indeed, to say it is a Bill to mend in an amicable way, the faults of the constitution of the Province," he told the Lords, also discussing the Massachusetts Government Bill. "But it should be well considered, how far it may be justifiable by law, to wrest a[nd] tear from a people, a charter once solemnly given them. I look upon such a step as tyran[n]ical. I think resistance in such a case is lawful."[9]

Camden was making a statement of law that no common lawyer, not even an American, would make a hundred years later, perhaps not even by 1850. It was precisely because he was discussing eighteenth-century law that his words and his arguments are important. They reveal some of the tension between the old constitution of customary, prescriptive rights, and the constitution of sovereign command. Camden was defending the old constitution against Parliament's execution of the new. He was speaking at a moment of constitutional history when the tension was most acute. Just the year before Parliament had taught constitutionalists of the old tradition a disturbing lesson about legislative power when it reformed the charter of the East India Company by mere legislation. Like Camden, Edmund Burke was speaking from contractarian constitutionalism when he protested that for Parliament to negotiate with the company, to accept "part of the company's proposals, reject the rest, and ingraft new proposals of its own upon those offered by the company, was to . . . assume an unconstitutional right over the company; it was, in short, to all intents and purposes, to destroy the charter rights of the company."[10] The next year Georgia whigs protested violation of the same constitution when they told Virginia whigs, "[t]hat the Act for abolishing the Charter of Massachusetts Bay tends to the subversion of *American* rights; for besides those general liberties, the original settlers brought over with them as their birthright, particular immunities granted by such charter, as an inducement and means of settling the Province: and we apprehend the said Charter cannot be dissolved but by a voluntary surrender of the people, representatively declared."[11]

The constitutional theory was that the government, by granting a charter, vested in a company, colony, or individuals certain inviolable privileges and securities of property that, if not immutable, were answerable only at common law, not to legislative whim and caprice. The government could regulate the grantees according to established law and the specific terms of the grant, but it could not summarily abrogate the privileges and immunities that had vested, not even by legislation. No fact may be more revealing of the still incomplete understanding of parliamentary sovereignty, as it would mean in the nineteenth century, than the opening part of the argument made by counsel for the East India Company before the House of Commons. Appealing to the constitution of secured, prescriptive right, they "contended that the principle and object of the [East India] Bill were unconstitutional; that it did not state any delinquency in the Company, though it invaded their chartered rights, the right of managing their own affairs within the bounds of law and their charter; that it was the happiness of this country to be governed by fixed and known laws, not by *ex post facto* acts passed upon the spur of a particular occasion." The lawyer who concluded the defense "entered into several definitions of arbitrary power." Parliament, he insisted,

> though supreme in every instance in which the public good was concerned, were nevertheless bound by the permanent and established rules of equity and legislation. The India company, said he, as well as all other chartered companies, the Bank, South-sea House, &c. have undoubtedly a right to order and manage their affairs as seems most expedient to them, and which this House can have no right to restrain, so long as those companies do not go beyond the bounds allowed by their charter.[12]

We are limited to the words that are recorded, and we can never be certain if the report is complete. Still, it is worth noting that the lawyer did not say that the Commons should not enact the Bill because it was good policy for it not to restrain or interfere with the East India Company. He said it had "no right" as long as the Company adhered to the law.

Once again the probative concept is "arbitrary power." Arbitrariness is what links the Coercive Acts to the question whether Parliament had authority to overrule the management of a stock company. Parliament had cited the concept back in 1690 when restoring London's charter because it had been seized arbitrarily by the crown. The judgment by King's Bench vacating the charter during the reign of Charles II, Parliament stated in a statute, had been "illegal and arbitrary." The concept of "arbitrary" had legal meaning in the 1690s, for at that time the old constitution of restrained authority was, as yet, unchallenged.[13] Although we, today, think it had already been supplemented by the constitution of arbitrary power in 1772 when the East India Bill was enacted into law, dissentient lords did not not seem to know it. They may, however, have realized they were fighting a hopeless rearguard action. Their protest should be read not just for their critique of arbitrary power, but also for their sense of resignation. Unhappy though they may have been, they must have known that constitutional law had changed. The rights of the East India Company, these lords contended, were "taken away by a mere act of arbitrary power, the precedent of which leaves no sort of security to the subject for his liberties." Even if a person exercised his civil rights "in the strictest conformity to all the rules of law, as well as to those of general equity and moral conduct," there was no protection under the new constitution "to prevent parliament from interposing its sovereign powers to divest him of these rights, by means of which insecurity the honourable distinction between the British and other forms of government is in a great measure lost." It was a constitutional loss made worse, the dissentient lords lamented, by the growing tendency of Parliament "on every petty occasion" to enact statutes "without any consideration of their conformity to the general principles of our law and constitution."[14]

Students of the American Revolution should pay more attention to matters such as the East India Bill. They provide evidence of the origins, the meaning, and the lingering respectability among the rulers of Great Britain, of the constitutional theory of American whigs. That constitutional theory, after all, was the constitutional theory of the dissentient lords. Understanding the lords' protest helps us to understand the shock colonial whigs experienced at passage of the Coercive Acts. Maybe the provisions of the Acts upset them more. Today we would say so, but the earl of Chatham belonged to the eighteenth century and he thought legislative arbitrary power devastating enough. Americans had experienced it before with the Stamp Act[15] and even the Hat Act,[16] but now it was a power they could not avoid or could not excuse as regulation of trade. They had come to a point, Chatham said, at which they had to draw a constitutional line. "Three millions of people refused to be bound by your arbitrary edicts," he told the House of Lords. Unchecked legislative power—that is, arbitrary legislative power—could not govern eighteenth-century Americans. "You condemned a whole province without hearing, without even demanding satisfaction for the injury sustained. . . . [Y]ou deprived them, my Lords, of their most valuable privileges of the unalienable birth right of an Englishman, the trial by Jury; the trial of the vicinage, of Judges acquainted with the parts, the offence, the provocation, and the measure of punishment." Chatham was speaking constitutionally. In eighteenth-century legal jargon he was saying that the Coercive Acts were acts of power, not acts of right. Just a few decades earlier that fact, that legislation was not an act of right, would have meant it was unconstitutional, possibly not even "law." But by 1774 other notions about "law" had taken hold, and power was legitimate to repair law when law was not functioning as power expected. If one of the most fundamental British rights of the eighteenth century was the right to lawful government,[17] then a related right was the right to orderly government, or so John St. John, a barrister, seemed to suggest when expounding the constitution of legislative sovereignty during debate on the Massachusetts Government Bill. "Parliament has saved America from the jaws of tyranny, by amending their constitution," the member for Newport asserted,

> and to say that we have no right to alter their government for such purpose, appears to me the highest absurdity; we are perpetually altering and ameliorating our own constitution, upon emergencies; is there then no emergency at this present instant, when . . . the Magistrates refuse to execute their authority, to keep the peace; when your ships are plundered, and your trade obstructed . . . ? Not to correct these deficiencies in their constitution, but to give up the points which they contend for, would be a base surrender of the rights of posterity.[18]

We can recognize that St. John said nothing new and still think it important that he said what he did. That is because of the legal theorists whom he was criticizing. St. John was addressing more than American whigs. That he was arguing against their law tells us that there were in London people he thought important who were saying that Parliament had "no right" to save "America from the jaws of tyranny," and he was telling them that parliamentary power should not be their only concern. Parliament, St. John expounded, could change not only constitutional law but fundamental law as well. We may wonder, however, if the lesson was necessary. American whigs always knew that constitutional theories of unlimited sovereign command enjoyed some respect in Great Britain. It is not clear, however, that before the Coercive Acts they so well understood what St. John was telling them: that along with the new definition of law, there were new definitions of "rights," "immunities," "vested," and "un-alienable," a constitutionalism that earlier in the eighteenth century would not have been "constitutional."

After two hundred years of law by Parliament's discretionary command, it may be impossible for us to imagine the awakening Americans experienced in 1774. Passage of the Massachusetts Government Act by legislative fiat, without trial, defense, or renegotiation of the original contract was "totally unconstitutional," petitioners told the House of Commons, "and sets an Example which renders every Charter in *Great Britain* and *America* utterly insecure." The essence of the "arbitrary" grievance was that the insecurity was so absolute there was no check on legislative whim except legislative conscience or legislative pleasure. "Let me ask again," Colonel Isaac Barré had said during the Massachusetts Government debate, "what security the rest of the colonies will have, that upon the least pretence of disobedience, you will not take away the assembly from the next of them that is refractory." By the premises of what American whigs had once understood as law and constitutionalism, there was no security, and a few of them had been warning that there was none even before the shock of the Coercive Acts. "It is hard to say," Charles Turner had told Massachusetts legislators the year before the Acts were passed, "whether this country ever has seen, or ever will see, a more important time than the present, when it *seems* as if the question, whether this people and all they enjoy shall be at the *absolute* disposal of a distant Legislature, is soon to be determined."[19]

The reality of the Coercive Acts was more arbitrary than Turner foretold. He had warned of an absolute, distant legislature, but Parliament, with the Quebec Act, did more than exercise arbitrary power, it established arbitrary government in North America. From the perspective of the "arbitrary" grievance, the Quebec Act was the predictable extension of the Massachusetts Government Act. Together they could establish "a constitutional right to exercise *Despotism* over America."[20] "The *Quebec* act makes the king of *Great Britain* a despot over all that country," Richard Price explained. "In the Province of *Massachuset's Bay* the same thing has been attempted and begun."[21]

The Quebec Act, the first Continental Congress asserted, made the people of that province "the subjects of an arbitrary government," an appraisal widely echoed in the mother country. Hugh Baillie, a Scots advocate and formerly admiralty judge in Ireland, explained what was meant when he wrote that Quebec's government "is entirely arbitrary, and has not the look of a government established by the king of a free people: for the king names what council he pleases—turns them out when he pleases; and this is called the legislative power."[22]

It is important to ask what is being said and whether the arguments made were political exaggeration or had substance at law. What we are seeing is one of the constitutional theories discussed in an earlier book of this series applied to one legal issue, the constitutionality of the Coercive Acts. In recent years, it has become acceptable for scholars to discount the validity of the constitutional theory and, therefore, to cast doubt on the sincerity of any eighteenth-century lawyer, representative, or whig who argued it. Consider the assertion made by the first Continental Congress that "the legislature of Great Britain is not authorised by the constitution to . . . erect an *arbitrary form of government* in any quarter of the globe."[23] Referring to the Quebec Act, the Congress was addressing the British people, trying to persuade them that the American constitutional grievance was based on substantial principles. In that context, Congress had no reason to draft an argument of law so fallacious in theory it would damage the colonial whig case. Yet a history of the American Revolution published in 1985 has suggested that, although American whigs might complain of certain provisions in the Quebec Act, such as the extensive boundaries or the acceptance of Catholicism, "they would have little ground to attack the principle that Parliament could pass such an act if it chose." The author does not explain what he means, but his judgment may be based more on twentieth-century than eighteenth-century law. No one in the 1970s could have doubted Parliament's power to revoke the charter of Northern Ireland, but innumerable Britons in the 1770s questioned Parliament's authority to reform the charter of Massachusetts Bay. Just as innumerable were people in Great Britain who raised doubts not only about the policy of the Quebec Act but about Parliament's authority to legislate such policy. "The constitution of Quebec is given up, unconditionally by parliament, into the hands of the crown," was how David Hartley, member for Kingston-on-Hull, put it, and an Irish magazine, reprinting an item from a London newspaper, said the Quebec Act was "nothing less than *high treason against the constitution of this kingdom.* The parliament hath no more a rightful power to pass such a bill into law, than it hath to send the soldiery to murder us all." The legal theory supporting this argument, of course, came from the constitutionalism of customary right and could be either that Parliament's authority was in trust, by contract, or delegated. "The power of Parliament," it was argued against the Quebec Act,

> is a power delegated by the people, to be always employed for their use and benefit, never to their disservice and injury. It is a power limited to, and bounded by the good and service of the people; and whenever such power shall be perverted to their hurt and detriment, the trust is broken, and becomes null and void. . . . The free con-

stitution of England abhors all ideas of slavery, and does not admit that the people inhabiting any part of its dominions should be under arbitrary power.[24]

No matter if this theory of law is not persuasive today and was not compelling then. It is evidence that in the eighteenth century a legally plausible argument could be made against the right of Parliament to do as "it chose" with Quebec.

There was one more ingredient to the "arbitrary" grievance deserving mention. Besides being arbitrary legislation creating arbitrary government, it was said, the Quebec Act might be the first step of an arbitrary program by an arbitrary ministry. One observer of the contemporary scene, paraphrasing arguments by the parliamentary opposition, imputed the Quebec Act "to the utter dislike which the ministry bore" to elected representative assemblies, "as well as to all the rights of the people at large. The measure was called an experiment for setting up an arbitrary government in one colony . . . in order to extend by degrees that mode of ruling to all the others." The London newspaper editor, Robert Macfarlane, charged that "[w]ithout a necessity pleaded, or even suggested, an arbitrary influence is extended by act of parliament to this province [Quebec], furnishing a dangerous precedent, and an additional instance of the aversion which ministry bear to the rights of the people."[25] There is no need to quote the conclusion that American whigs drew from this argument.[26] The conclusion drawn by members of Parliament will do as well. In the House of Lords, Earl Camden contended that the "enlargement" of Quebec's boundaries down to western Virginia "could only be intended to extend the shackles of arbitrary power and of Popery over all the future settlements and colonies of America." And in the House of Commons, former solicitor general John Dunning charged that the Quebec Act was intended "to operate two ways, first, for establishing arbitrary power in that vast extent of country; and second, to employ that power, thus modified and rendered obedient to the will of the possessors, in assisting to overthrow the liberties of America."[27]

The warning was farfetched, made more to illustrate the potentials of arbitrary power than to sound a serious alarm. There was, however, one fear that a remarkable number of people said had real substance: the Quebec government was a model for the future goverance of North America. In 1763, when it was first suggested that Canada be governed without an elected assembly, the duke of Newcastle had demurred. A constitutional innovation so extreme, he objected, would "shake the very Foundation of our Colonies, who could with entire Justice, expect that it would be their fate very soon."[28] Moreover, even if the ministry had no designs "to overthrow the liberties of America," Quebecers subject to arbitrary rule quite likely would not side with American whigs in the struggle for the old constitutionalism, but would serve Britain's interests if there were a civil war. That possibility was considered likely enough to be included as a grievance in the preamble of South Carolina's first constitution. An "absolute government" was established in Quebec, the preamble contended, "and its limits extended through a vast tract of country, so as to border on the free Protestant English Settlements, with design of using a whole people, differing in religious principles from the neighbouring colonies and subject to arbitrary power, as fit instruments to over awe and subdue the colonies."[29]

THE "LIBERTY" GRIEVANCE

In the language of eighteenth-century constitutional law, the antithesis of arbitrary power was liberty.[30] "Arbitrary" and "liberty" were legal concepts that, despite being opposites, easily came together in the same sentence to convey a single constitutional idea. The method was easy because "arbitrary power," like "slavery" and "licentiousness," defined liberty by being the bane of liberty and the reverse of liberty as well as liberty's antithesis.[31] The Delaware Convention showed how constitutional opposites could be united into a single legal argument when resolving that the Massachusetts Acts were "arbitrary in their principles, unparalleled in their rigour, oppressive in their operation, and subversive to every idea of justice and freedom."[32]

Liberty, along with the rule of law, the security of property, and restraint on government, was the inherent given of eighteenth-century British constitutionalism. Liberty was vital for constitutionalism though not for a constitution. There could be unfree constitutions, but the essence of the British constitution was that it was free. Massachusetts also had a free constitution, although it would be free mainly in its internal operation if the Massachusetts Government Act was enforced. What would it matter to a colony "that it enjoys within itself a free constitution of government, if that constitution is itself liable to be altered, suspended or over-ruled at the discretion of the state which possess the sovereignty over it?"[33] The Quebec constitution, by contrast, was arbitrary and, therefore, not free. For eighteenth-century constitutionalists it was a "monstrous incongruity," for "a British legislature" to create "a form of arbitrary government,"[34] that is, as John Dunning stated the liberty grievance, to have "a most despotic tyrannical system of laws administered by a free government." "[T]he whole Legislative Power of the Province," the corporation of London protested to George III, "is vested in persons to be solely appointed by your Majesty, and removable at your pleasure, which we apprehend to be repugnant to the leading Principles of this free Constitution, by which alone your Majesty now holds, or legally can hold, the Imperial Crown of these Realms."[35]

There was a rhetoric of liberty in the eighteenth century, a shared, learned, articulated way of arguing, of urging action, and of expecting an audience to understand that icons were threatened or that innovations could be dangerous. It was a rhetoric used not only to shape the constitutional programs that the opposition would put forward but also to frame those the administration would defend.[36] Words were often as potent as concepts when used according to the set formulae of constitutional advocacy. "The acts for altering the charter and the administration of justice in the colony," the Massachusetts Congress told Governor Thomas Gage, "are manifestly designed to abridge this people of their rights, and to license murders; and, if carried into execution, will reduce them to a state of slavery."[37] The epiphanous word—what in the eighteenth century was called the constitutional word—was "slavery." When Gage read that Massachusetts whigs feared being reduced "to a state of slavery" he did not think of chattel servitude. For him, as for all Britons, a warning about slavery raised questions about constitutionality. Constitutional slavery was the curse of people lax about liberty, who practiced nonresistance when threatened by arbitrary power, submitted tamely to oppression, and were passively obedient to military rule. Had Massachusetts people not opposed Gage's troops, they would have been unworthy of the liberty bequeathed them by their ancestors, a liberty they had a duty to pass inviolate to generations yet unborn. True, they would not have been in physical servitude to the British army and the material aspects of their lives would not have been changed. But in the constitutional jargon of the eighteenth century, they would have become slaves to power.[38]

The word "slavery" told eighteenth-century constitutionalists more about the meaning of liberty than did any other legalism. A second concept that helped assure them that they had liberty was "consent." American whigs feared that the Coercive Acts, if enforced, would take from Massachusetts voters the right to consent. It was not only that the Acts were promulgated by Parliament and that "they, who have *no* vote in the electing of representatives in parliament, are *not* freemen, but are truly and really slaves to the representatives of those who *have* votes."[39] More immediate were the provisions in the Massachusetts Government Act narrowing the role of consent by making the council appointive and confining town meetings to official business approved by the governor. The loss to Massachusetts of its elective council made American whigs aware of the constitutional implications of crown appointment. Previously, it had not been a constitutional grievance in those colonies where councils were appointed either by the governor or the ministry in London. After passage of the Massachusetts Government Act many whigs saw the practice in a new light. "[T]he exercise of Legislative power in any Colony, by a Council appointed, during pleasure, by the Crown," Georgia's Commons House of Assembly resolved, "may prove dangerous and destructive to the freedom of *American* Legislation." In Massachusetts, loss of town meetings may have been perceived as an even greater threat to liberty, as it affected so many people directly by taking from them their right to comment on the constitutional issues and to vote onto the public record protests against imperial programs. "[T]he Act which prohibits these constitutional meetings," Middlesex County residents resolved, "cuts away the scaffolding of *English* freedom, and reduces us to a most abject state of vassalage and slavery."[40]

Too much should not be made of the elective council and the bludgeoned town meetings. They were details illustrating the larger "liberty" grievance and would not, standing alone, have caused traumatic constitutional anxiety. The Massachusetts Government Act, after all, brought that province into constitutional conformity with other royal colonies and did not introduce startling constitutional innovations. What was alarming was not the reforms but the method of reform, not the exercise of parliamentary sovereignty alone, but the open-ended, unlimited, and unilateral aspects of sovereignty. If the Coercive Acts were constitutional, what was unconstitutional? "The *same authority* upon the *same principle*," James Iredell, the future United States Supreme Court justice, protested, "might have declared the king, by his representative, sole legislative as well as executive power," something that had virtually happened in Quebec. "What was the case of Massachusetts Bay to-day," Iredell warned, "might be that of New York, Pennsylvania, or any of the others to-morrow."[41]

It was less the specific exercise of parliamentary supremacy that shocked colonial whigs, than the principle of an absolute, unlimited sovereignty. That principle, William Gordon warned, "rendered every dwelling, plantation, and right, thro' the continent, precarious, and dependent on the will of the parliament, or rather the junto or individual, that hath the power of managing it." If we are going to understand the American Revolution, we must understand a constitutional mind-set made apprehensive by the most farfetched scenarios of power abused. Like Iredell and Gordon, Ebenezer Baldwin imagined a series of parliamentary oppressive acts, not because they were plausible or even likely, but because, by illustrating what was possible under a constitution of arbitrary power, they alerted his fellow whigs about what to fear.

The principle upon which the parliament proceeded in vacating the Massachusetts charter; will equally warrant them, whenever they shall see fit, to vacate all our grants of lands, i.e., when they shall judge it expedient, or for the good of the nation. If the parliament should once take it into their wise heads, that it is expedient, or for the general good, that all lands in America should revert to the crown, that they may be regranted all upon the same tenure,—upon large *quit-rents* to defray the charges of government; what will hinder their carrying it into execution? And indeed the Boston *port act* doth actually afford us a precedent of the exercise of this power: all their wharves and water-lots round the whole of Boston bay, are really *confiscated* to the king. . . . Now what is this but a vote of parliament to take away our landed property. And that power which hath been once exercised have we not all reason to fear will be exercised again.[42]

Historians who scoff at such alarms as irrational imagings of conspiracies run the risk of imposing the political thought of the twentieth century onto the constitutional thought of the eighteenth century. Baldwin and other whigs were not writings of conspiracies but of power. It was irrelevant to most constitutionalists if Parliament's arbitrary power would not be abused or that established rights would be respected. Their constitutional world was unsafe if customary right was not absolute but existed at the theoretical discretion of arbitrary power. The right Baldwin discussed, it should be noticed, was the right to security. In the pantheon of rights that had to be held absolutely if liberty was to survive, no right was more vital than the right to security. It ranked with the right to property, the right to government, the right to isonomy, and the rule of law, as an indispensable guardian of constitutional liberty.[43]

"The charter of Massachusetts was changed without necessity, without provocation," Hugh Williamson claimed in a tract written for British whigs. "By that single stroke every other province was informed that nothing was sacred or secure." The argument was that if Parliament had power to change both the Massachusetts charter and provincial statutes enacted by the General Court and approved by the crown, there was no theory of constitutional law preventing it from doing what it pleased with the charters and statutes of all the colonies. By eighteenth-century legal premises, if the Boston Port Act and the three Massachusetts Acts were both legal and constitutional, Americans not only were deprived of the right of security, but also could lose another basic right on which the rights of property, liberty, and life depended, the right to government.[44] American whigs and their British supporters intended to make serious statements of law, not spin conspiratorial fantasies, when they bemoaned, for example, that as a consequence of the Coercive Acts, "not even the shadow of liberty to his person, or of security of his property, will be left to any of his Majesty's subjects residing on the American continent."[45]

Before concluding that the colonial argument was overblown or emotional, consider that American whigs were not often criticized on that account by friends of the administration in Great Britain. Language that we today think excessive was not peculiar to the colonies. Inherited from the English, the phraseology of American petitions and resolutions was interchangeable with what was said in Great Britain in the remonstrances of London's Common Council or the protests of dissentient members of the House of Lords. As both British and Americans in the eighteenth century tended to think of government as abusing power and, generally, did not think of government as creating or granting rights, they would be less likely to state the "liberty" grievance against the Coercive Acts as we would state it in the twentieth century: to say that if Parliament had the constitutional authority to promulgate the Coercive Acts American colonists could claim no constitutional, legal, or civil rights but those Parliament saw fit to concede to them.[46] That would, of course, be another way of saying that the power claimed by Parliament was arbitrary, so arbitrary, in fact, that under the old constitution of customary, prescriptive rights, such authority would be mere "power," not "right," or, in other words, it would not be "law."[47] That doctrine was the justification for the proposition, usually stated as a legal principle, that the Coercive Acts did not have to be obeyed.[48] Put another way, the argument, as London's Common Council said, was that "the *Americans* are justified in every constitutional opposition to the said Acts";[49] that the Boston Port Act, at least, could "be legally resisted" by arms.[50] These are theories of law that should not be dismissed just because law in our century no longer tolerates them. They were good law once and deserve the attention of anyone who hopes to understand why American whigs would believe in 1776 they were justified by law to oppose forcefully parliamentary supremacy.

A second legal theory drawn from the old contractarian constitution of customary rights, also making forceful resistance legitimate, was that the Coercive Acts, especially the Massachusetts Government Act, terminated the second original contract. As explained eight years earlier, "the abolition of their [colonial] charters and privileges, annulling their governments and legal securities, abolishes their oaths of allegiance and connection with Great-Britain," leaving Americans free to form new constitutions and civic connections.[51]

A different constitution prevailed in London, even among officials inclined to be lenient toward the Americans. Its tenets were never better applied to the Coercive Acts than by the earl of Dartmouth in a private letter to Joseph Reed, a leading American whig. "The mother country," he wrote, "very unwilling to proceed to extremities passes laws (indisputably within its power) for the punishment of the most flagrant offenders, for the reformation of abuses, and for the prevention of the like enormities for the future. The question then is, whether these laws are to be submitted to: if the people of America say no, they say in effect that they will no longer be a part of the British Empire; they change the whole ground of the controversy; they no longer contend that Parliament has not a right to exact a particular provision, they say that it has no right to consider them at all as within its jurisdiction."[52] The conflict between the two constitutions had been joined on the issue of the Coercive Acts.

CHAPTER THREE

THE SUPREMACY ISSUE

There is no need to examine the statutes Parliament enacted to reassert the claim to sovereignty over the North American mainland after London realized that all thirteen colonies would resist enforcement of the Boston Port Act and the Massachusetts Government Act. Giving colonial whigs another governance grievance, these laws certainly helped push Americans to the decision for independence. They did not, however, add any new assertions of legislative supremacy to those already made by the Coercive Acts and, therefore, did not contribute to the legislative grievance.[1]

Another matter that need not be weighed is the relative extent to which the legislation grievance contributed to the breakdown of the imperial constitution in 1776. It is simply amazing the number of leaders and observers, especially in Great Britain, who, despite all that was said about individual rights and about the authority to legislate and the authority to govern, believed that the sole point in conflict was the authority to tax. People were making that claim as late as 1782.[2] Even after the battle of Lexington, Governor William Franklin told the New Jersey Council and Assembly that as taxation was "the principal source of the present disorders, when that important point is once settled, every other subject of complaint which has grown out of it will, no doubt, of course, be removed."[3] Surely, Franklin knew that there was more to the constitutional conflict, but then so did members of Parliament who were saying the same thing.[4] Later, as the war was drawing to a close, there were many contemporaries who, adopting a perception the reverse of that which would be taken by some twentieth-century historians, claimed that the ministry had tried to change the constitutional argument. Until 1775 or 1776, it was charged, the administration had insisted that "the dispute was not about Revenue, but the Supremacy of Parliament."[5] Then, after fighting commenced and support was needed for the war effort, "they change their principles, and think that the manufacturers and the nation at large shall be entirely satisfied, when they are told that it is not a contest for honour, or the dignity of parliament, but the acquisition of a substantial revenue."[6]

That charge is of interest mainly for showing that almost every argument was made about the causes of the American Revolution. Strictly opposition politics, it cannot be taken seriously. After all, it should not be forgotten that had taxation been the only issue in controversy, the ministry would have ended the conflict by giving American whigs the constitutional security they demanded.[7] The duke of Manchester, a leader of "the lords in Opposition," admitted that fact when he asked the administration lords to explain "the motives" for the American war. He knew it was not taxation as "that has been disclaimed by them in this House, on the first day of the present session; and it has been since frequently and openly avowed, that no revenue is expected." Manchester then "quoted" what he indicated the administration had been telling the House of Lords: "We want America only to acknowledge a constitutional dependency on this country, an acknowledgment of the power of this legislature; and then we wish to give them perfect security and full enjoyment of their subordinate constitutional rights."[8]

Manchester was right. The ministry had said that if Americans first acknowledged the right, Great Britain, most likely, would concede everything colonial whigs asked. This possible solution will be examined in detail below. Manchester, however, was not right if he meant that Lord North, in his February 1775 proposal for ending the controversy, "openly avowed" that Americans would never again be asked to contribute revenue. "When his Majesty's ministers said, that the idea of taxation was abandoned," Lord North had told the other house just a month before, "they never intended by that expression more, than that it was abandonded for the present; that is, to explain it further, that taxation was but a matter of secondary consideration, when the supremacy and legislative authority of this country was at stake."[9]

Many members of Parliament thought North stated a new policy, that the battle of Lexington had brought the supremacy issue into sharper focus and had made other causes of the constitutional conflict appear of lesser importance. That perception may have been misleading. The tax, after all, that had led to the Coercive Acts and to the fighting in Massachusetts was the Tea Act, a tax imposed less for revenue than as a "test" for keeping up "the right." At least, from the moment Parliament voted to keep the tax on tea to support supremacy, taxation had been what Lord North termed "a matter of secondary consideration."

There were not many other issues that participants said were the cause or one of the causes for the revolutionary conflict. Stationing troops in certain colonies without the consent of the local assemblies was mentioned,[10] for example, as were the Trade and Navigation Acts by some members of Parliament,[11] despite the persistent and unqualified American insistence that their only quarrel with the trade laws was that their legislatures, not Parliament, should regulate intracolonial commerce. Still, no matter what other claims were made, it seems that most participants in the dispute, at least in 1775 when fighting broke out in Massachusetts, believed that the bone of contention was parliamentary sovereignty. When London merchants, contending that they were suffering with trade stagnation, petitioned the Commons to be heard on American affairs, Hans Stanley protested that everyone had known that "a stoppage of trade would be occasioned by the American disputes." "[B]ut what of that?" he asked. "Unless the supremacy of parliament and the rights of sovereignty were vigorously asserted by Great Britain, the American traffic could not subsist. To support the sovereignty was therefore to support the trade of Great Britain." In the other house, Earl Camden used the same words as North, "secondary consideration," to say what Stanley had said although speaking on the other side of the controversy. "[I]n this great question, trade is a secondary consideration," he told the Lords. "[T]o maintain a legislative power over America, is the primary, the sole, and the necessary object; for the attainment of which, and for the reduction of the colonies to an unlimited obedience, all considerations of the benefits of trade . . . are to be suspended."[12]

Camden wanted Parliament not to push supremacy. Like every other member of the Lords and Commons anxious to avoid war, he urged legislative restraint, but did not propose a political compromise because there was little middle ground on which to compromise.[13] A New England newspaper, as early as April 1765, reported a member of the Commons saying of the Stamp Act crisis, "That where the Colonies stand on such high Pretensions of Independence on the supreme Legislative Authority of Great-Britain, there is no moderating any Thing." At the first Continental Congress, Joseph Galloway, the most extreme of the "conservative," "moderate," or "reconciliatory" delegates did not differ much from the delegates whom historians call "radicals." "[A]ll the Acts of Parliament made since [the emigration of our Ancestors], are Violations of our Rights," he insisted. Other participants in the revolutionary controversy treated the issue as uncompromisingly pertinacious. "[C]onsider the question in ever so many lights," the Lord Chief Justice told the House of Lords, "every middle way, every attempt to unite the opposite claims of the contending parties, ends, and is ultimating founded on one resolution or the other; either the supremacy of the British legislature must be complete, entire, and unconditional, or, on the other hand, the colonies must be free and independent."[14]

Agreeing with Mansfield that the constitutional controversy could be reduced to a choice between unconditional supremacy or American independence, many imperialists reduced it further, to a simple matter of authority. "Parliament must be obeyed," the earl of Suffolk explained to the Lords, "or it must not; if it be obeyed, then who shall resist its determinations? If it be not, then we may as well at once give up every claim of authority over America."[15] That dichotomy—obedience or no authority— was why Earl Gower insisted that "America, before she had a right to expect any favour or indulgence from the mother country, must first acknowledge her sovereignty, and the supremacy of this legislature,"[16] why Lord George Germain claimed that people who supported the Declaratory Act, no matter if they believed American taxation unconstitutional, "were bound to support the idea of subduing America," and why Isaac Wilkins told the New York General Assembly that because the Boston Tea Party, "absolutely denied her [Parliament's] authority," it had carried colonial opposition too far.[17]

The Tea Party had been an absolute denial because the supremacy issue was so absolute. Responding to a challenge that brooked no compromise, the Tea Party was uncompromising. The whigs of Boston had taken a constitutional stand that left Parliament no alternatives or choices. If the ultimate issue was London's legislative supremacy, Parliament had to obtain obedience or be beaten. "If they deny authority in one instance it goes to all," Lord North warned. "We must control them or submit to them." "To retreat," the earl of Rochford agreed, "was to be vanquished."[18]

Although the Tea Party made imperative London's need to vindicate Parliament's supremacy, the argument that the colonists had to be taught to obey was not new. American whigs had acquired copies of Thomas Hutchinson's letters to British officials, and from them learned that for several years he had "been begging for measures to maintain the supremacy of parliament."[19] "I cannot help thinking that this authority might have been preserved intire, if more attention had been given to the colonies," he had argued in 1770. "They ought to have been used to acts of parliament every session, some to respect the colonies in general, others particular colonies. . . . Perhaps it is not too late to recover what has been lost by going into this practice now; and if at the beginning of every session a committee was appointed for America . . . it would have a good effect."[20] Hutchinson even submitted a list of statutes he thought precedents for legislating parliamentary supremacy and which could be extended, reenacted in stronger form, or analogized into even more effective precedents. "The late act permitting the issuing bills of credit at New York, was extremely well adapted to maintaining the authority of Parliament," he advised the earl of Hillsborough."[21]

Hutchinson's legal theory may be obvious, but, as he thought it important enough to explain to Hillsborough, his own words are available, and they tell us much of imperialist constitutional thought. It is amazing how easy Hutchinson thought it would be to solve the supremacy problem. "Every act of Parliament carried into execution in the Colonies tends to strengthen Government there," he argued. "A firm persuasion that Parliament is determined, at all events, to maintain its supreme authority is all we want. . . . If acts were passed more or less to controul us, every session, we should soon be familiarized to them, and our erroneous opinions would die away, and peace and order would revive."[22]

Hutchinson was speaking with the special knowledge that an American-born imperialist acquired when serving as a high official in a colonial government. He knew the depth of whig opposition to arbitrary sovereign power, yet seems to have been impressed by the authority of precedent and custom, and thought principle could be overcome by the forceful habit of practice. Hutchinson may have been wrong on the last point. Although the British administration did not adopt the sustained, yearly, calculated legislative program he wanted, the Coercive Acts, though quite late, were exactly what he had been calling for. They did not, however teach American whigs to change their "erroneous opinions." What is worth marking down is Governor Hutchinson's certainty that the issue of parliamentary supremacy was the cause of the controversy tearing apart the constitutional world in which he lived. "Every thing," he claimed, "depends upon the settlement of this grand point."[23]

THE SUPREMACY CAUSE

There is no need for a quantitative study. In a constitutional history it is enough to note that leaders on both sides of the conflict said that parliamentary supremacy was the "cause" in contention. "Is there a man in England (I am confident there is not an officer or soldier in the King's service) who does not think the parliamentary rights of Great Britain a cause to fight for, to bleed and die for?" John Burgoyne announced in the House of Commons. Across the Atlantic, in the very colony to which General Burgoyne would soon be stationed, a clergyman told his congregation that British troops had been "sent here expressly and professedly, to FORCE the Americans to own and acknowledge that the British parliament have a right to make laws binding upon them in ALL CASES WHATSOEVER."[24]

There were even participants on both sides who said that parliamentary supremacy was the sole cause of the controversy. "When the War with America was lighted up by this Country," the earl of Abingdon charged, "the Pretence of it was to force Submission to the Parliamentary Rights of England. It was therefore *a War* of Parliament."[25] Even the members of Parliament who opposed legislation binding the colonies internally, used the supremacy issue to motivate action. When, in December 1775, the administration was talking of sending a peace commission to North America, dissentient lords protested that the commissioners ought to be appointed by Parliament. Peace was constitutionally within the crown's prerogative, but the "powers of parliament being the matter of complaint, the commissioners ought to derive some previous authority [directly from Parliament], in order to give weight and efficacy to their negociations, and to preserve some appearance of dignity in ourselves."[26] Less than a year later, most of the same lords would protest that no ground had "been laid for removing the original cause of these unhappy differences, which took their rise from questions relative to parliamentary proceedings, and can be settled *only* by parliamentary authority."[27]

In the colonies loyalists, like members of Parliament, generally said that parliamentary supremacy caused the war, and many stated their allegiance to the crown by conceding sovereignty to the imperial legislature. At their first session following the battle of Lexington, the representatives of Nova Scotia voted Parliament "to be the supreme legislature of this province, and of all the British dominions."[28] Perhaps no loyalist summed up the importance of the supremacy issue better than Joseph Galloway. Calling it "the great question between the two countries," Galloway told the first Continental Congress that "advocates for the supremacy of Parliament over the Colonies contend, that there must be one Supreme legislative head in every civil society, whose authority must extend to the regulation and final decision of every matter susceptible of human direction; and that every member of the society, whether political, official, or individual, must be subordinate to its supreme will, signified in its laws."[29]

This part of Galloway's speech deserved the close attention of his fellow delegates. He had an unusual, even striking talent for constitutional analysis. Although not original, and, by the standards of the day, certainly not deep, he had an ability for discussing questions of power and right by

blending two constitutional traditions. He took substance, not just frip-
pery, from the constitution of restrained government and vested rights,
always making clear his belief that behind the authority of custom, precedent, and prescription was an overriding authority, the mailed fist of sovereign command. In a sense, Galloway's approach to the constitution of the
1770s was similar to that of Earl Camden and the earl of Chatham. Galloway, in his speech to the Constitutional Congress, attempted to explain
both sides of the constitutional controversy, and to weigh the comparative strengths. Perhaps he succeeded, for his motion passed by a majority
of one colony. Then again, he may have succeeded too well, at least in
the words just quoted, at outlining the constitutional reality of sovereign
command. On reflection some delegates changed their votes and Galloway's proposal was expunged from the record. The era was swiftly fading
when people could believe that the constitution of customary rights could
coexist with the constitution of parliamentary sovereignty.

It is risky to be too dogmatic. No one should assume that the supremacy
grievance was against the claim rather than the exercise. A good deal of
time was spent by the Continental Congress, by local colonial congresses,
and by members of Parliament listing offensive parliamentary statutes and
suggesting that the constitutional controversy could be adjusted if they
were repealed.[30] As late as December 1777, the member for Bristol, New
York born Henry Cruger, assured the Commons "that independency is
not yet the great object of the majority of the [American] people; but a
rooted and unconquerable aversion to those impolitic Acts prevail in every
mind."[31] The argument sometimes was that the supremacy grievance was
caused by specific legislation not by Parliament's claim of right. "The exercise was the thing complained of, not the right itself," Charles James Fox
had said of the right to tax in May 1775. "When the Declaratory Act was
passed, asserting the right in the fullest extent, there were no tumults in
America . . . ; but when the right came to be exercised, in the manner we
have seen, the whole country was alarmed, and there was an unanimous
determination to oppose it. The right, simply, is not regarded; it is the
exercise of it that is the object of opposition."[32]

We will never know what Fox meant. Perhaps he was exaggerating for
effect. Close observers of the American Revolution were more likely to
argue the other extreme, though that too was an exaggeration. "It was,"
Baron Rivers recalled in 1784, "evidently *the power*, and not the unjust
use of it, against which the Americans have rebelled." The claim to right,
not the exercise, was the grievance.[33] The concern was new to English constitutional history only in that it related to Parliament and not to the king.
"Whoever will attentively consider the *English* History," Blackstone had
pointed out, "may observe, that the flagrant Abuse of any Power, by the

Crown or its Ministers, has always been productive of a Struggle; which either discovers the Exercise of that Power to be contrary to Law, or if legal restrains it for the future."[34] It would never have occurred to Blackstone that the American whigs might be engaged in the same struggle, but it did to another British official, General Thomas Gage. "The Question," Gage wrote the colonial secretary back in October 1765 when the controversy had just begun, "is not of the inexpediency of the Stamp Act, or of the inability of the Colonys to pay the Tax, but that it is unconstitutional, and contrary to their Rights, Supporting the Independency of the Provinces, and not Subject to the Legislative Power of Great Britain."[35]

Earl Gower, lord president of the council and former lord privy seal, was another imperialist who had no sympathy with the American whig constitutional cause, yet twelve years later he restated Gage's observation even more strongly. "A paltry tax upon tea," he told the House of Lords, "a particular insult, a single act of violence or sedition, was not the true ground of the present dispute. It was not this tax, nor that Act, nor a redress of a particular grievance; the great question in issue is, the supremacy of this country, and the subordinate dependence of America. It is not a single act of legislation the people of that country dispute with this; it is our claiming to bind them in any case whatever."[36]

Gower's words should be compared to those of a colonial whig, William Gordon, pastor of a church in Roxbury, Massachusetts. "It may be objected," Gordon noted in a footnote to a sermon he preached on a thanksgiving day appointed by the whig provincial congress,

> that the points in dispute are too trifling to justify the hazard of such severe trials. It will be answered, that the *principles* are what the continent is opposing, and to prevent the establishment of precedents. The real dispute is, whether the long enjoyed constitution of these American colonies, they not consenting to it, shall be liable to every alteration, that a legislature, three thousand miles off, shall think convenient and profitable to themselves.[37]

We should not be misled. Gower and Gordon seem to be saying the same thing, but they were not. They agreed on the cause of the constitutional conflict but not on the constitution. Gower thought the American whigs were acting illegally. Gordon thought it was the British Parliament that was breaking the law.

The Revolution, a second colonial clergyman said a year later, preaching on a day appointed by the Continental Congress, had been "forced, by a wanton exercise of arbitrary power." The Continental Congress agreed that the cause was arbitrary power, but complained as much of Parliament's claim to the right as to its exercise. "[T]he Parliament assert, that they have a right to bind us in all cases without exception," the Congress told the British people, "that they may take and use our property when and in what manner they please; that we are pensioners on their bounty for all we possess, and can hold it no longer than they vouchsafe to permit. Such declarations we consider as heresies in English politics."[38]

The issue could now be stated in general principles as easily as in specific grievances, and what the Continental Congress said was not much different than was said by a Philadelphian for whom the central issue was "opposition to the omnipotence of Parliament"[39] or by Sir William Meredith when complaining to the House of Commons in December 1777 that there could have been peace "if the government of this country would have refrained from their idle speculations and definitions of supremacy, which had brought on this fatal war."[40] The controversy was being summed up by words—"arbitrary," "mother country," "supremacy"—showing how easily in eighteenth-century constitutionalism, with no final judge, no tribunal of dernier review, the concept of power could become separated from its application. Even the cause of war could be transformed from a specific grievance to an abstraction summarized by a single concept such as "the right," "legislative sovereignty," or "parliamentary omnipotence." "[I]s there any thing so fit to solve this dispute," Governor George Johnstone asked the House of Commons, "as the unity of the British empire,— the supremacy of the legislative authority of G. Britain,—the omnipotence of parliament? Is there any man so ignorant, after having heard those sounding words, as not clearly to comprehend the whole of the controversy?"[41]

CHAPTER FOUR

THE GLORIOUS
REVOLUTION ISSUE

Contemporaries did not much heed the arguments of Governor George Johnstone, but we should. He had a knack for explaining the issues separating Great Britain and the American colonies more clearly than his more influential and better remembered colleagues. For one thing, he knew where to look for the source of colonial whig constitutional doctrines. "It is now clear," he told the House of Commons in a widely printed speech of December 1774, "that the people of America, actuated with the same firm and resolute spirit, and tinctured with the same enthusiasm which enabled our ancestors to withstand the unjust claims of the crown, in the days of Charles the 1st, are determined to resist the high doctrines of parliamentary supremacy, held forth by this country, which must, in its consequences, reduce their liberties to a level with the colonies of France and Spain."[1]

Johnstone's theme was not original. American whigs were often depicted as the heirs of old English and even British[2] constitutional struggles. Addressing the Massachusetts Superior Court in the Writ of Assistance case, which John Adams later called the opening event of the revolutionary controversy, James Otis described himself as arguing "in favour of British liberty" and "in opposition to a kind of power, the exercise of which in former periods of English history, cost one King of England his head and another his throne."[3] On 10 April 1775, just nine days before New England minutemen met British troops on the town green of Lexington, the lord mayor, aldermen, and livery of London warned King George III that legislative grievances had "driven" Americans to despair, and "compelled them to have recourse to that resistance which is justified by the great principles of the Constitution, actuated by which, at the glorious period of the Revolution, our ancestors transferred the Imperial Crown of these Realms from the Popish and tyrannical race of the *Stuarts,* to the illustrious and Protestant House of *Brunswick.*"[4]

The political argument was that the British should support not oppose American resistance to parliamentary supremacy because the Americans were doing what the English and Scots had done in 1688. Colonial whig mobs, it was said, were no different from the mobs that "more than once preserved the *British* Constitution from absolute ruin; such a *mob* as rose in *England,* in the reign of *James* the Second. . . . The difference is, they opposed an arbitrary Monarch, while we are only defending ourselves against the unconstitutional, despotick power of our fellow-subjects—the Lords and Commons of *Great Britain.*"[5] The constitutional theory was that American resistance to Parliament was sanctioned by English and Scottish precedents. Colonial whigs, a British observer wrote, objected to the Coercive Acts and other parliamentary legislation as acts of oppression, "and if they are right in this, we have no reason to call them *Rebels,* because, in this State of the Case, their Opposition and Resistance is founded on the same Principles on which the Resistance and Opposition made to *King James* II. was founded."[6]

The two main precedents American whigs cited for providing legitimacy to their opposition to parliamentary sovereignty were the English Civil War against Charles I and the Glorious Revolution against James II. Colonial whigs and their British supporters confidently drew analogies between the 1640s and the 1770s, between Charles I's effort to extend the customary tax of ship money and Parliament's Stamp Act,[7] and between the royalist claim that allegiance was due to King Charles rather than the laws and the imperialist claim that allegiance was due to the king in Parliament rather than the ancient constitution. The issues even seemed to be the same, in part because the constitutional language was so much the same. "[T]he declared grounds of War betwixt the late King and the ever Renowned *Parliament,*" the *Remonstrance of the Cities* asserted in 1659, "was . . . the Kings illegal imposing Taxes upon the People, without their consent in *Parliament,* contrary to the known Laws of the Land, his subverting the *Fundamental Lawes* of the Nation, His neglecting and refusing to bring Delinquents to Tryal, that had been Instruments in obstructing Justice, promoting Monopolies, and other grievances to the great

Oppr[e]ssion of the People."[8] Although eighteenth-century constitutionalists looked back to the Saxons and to the Gothic constitution for the
authority of law as an autonomous force, they looked to the Civil War
against Charles I as the struggle of rule by law against rule by the will and
pleasure of arbitrary command.

The parallels between the Glorious Revolution of 1688 and the American Revolution seemed even more obvious. James II threatened to subvert
what seventeenth-century Englishmen considered the established constitution just as Parliament threatened to subvert what Americans whigs
thought the lawful constitution. The language was also the same. Parliament accused James II of "breaking the original contract between king and
people" and of "having violated the fundamental laws" much as colonial
whigs accused George III in the Declaration of Independence.[9] In 1776
the whig chief justice of rebellious South Carolina justified the American
Revolution by the Glorious Revolution saying, "we need no better authority than that illustrious precedent," and Edmund Burke later recalled
that he considered the Americans as standing at that time, and in that controversy, "in the same relation to England as England did to King James
the Second in 1688."[10]

The Glorious Revolution, of course, was the event that established Parliament's supremacy over the crown, and the coronation oath was modified
so the king swore to maintain the "statutes in Parliament agreed upon" instead of the laws and customs upheld by earlier monarchs.[11] By the second
half of the eighteenth century that change in wording no longer seemed
important in Great Britain. Had anyone thought about it in 1776, however,
it could have been quoted to summarize why Americans had gone to war.

There was another similarity that American whigs thought linked the
issue of 1776 to the issue of 1688. It was that the constitution appeared
to be the same. The parliamentarians of the 1640s and the English whigs
of 1688 had opposed arbitrary power, and the colonials saw history being
repeated. It was immaterial that the lawmaker was Parliament and not the
king. "Notwithstanding all the Terrors which your Excellency has pictured
to us as the Effects of a total Independence," the Massachusetts House of
Representatives told Governor Thomas Hutchinson, "there is more Reason to dread the Consequences of absolute uncontrouled Supreme Power,
whether of a Nation or a Monarch, than those of a total Independence."[12]
Legislative sovereignty was no more constitutional than monarchical sovereignty, parliamentary arbitrary power was no less unconstitutional than
crown arbitrary power. The Coercive Acts, people of a New England
county pointed out, were "a great and high-handed claim of arbitrary
power."[13] For American whigs, Parliament was now Charles I and James II.
Parliament was king.

Many issues would arise out of the Glorious Revolution's constitutional legacy, and none was more important than the preservation of liberty. The concept of liberty was not vague, ambiguous, or difficult for people to understand, but it did have a many-sided definition. Above all, it was freedom from arbitrary power and governance by the rule of law.[14] For the British of the 1770s, arbitrary government still meant the Stuart monarchs, Charles I and James II, a manner of governance they had rejected and left behind with the Glorious Revolution. Parliament had saved them from the arbitrariness of rule by one man, by decreeing it was supreme over all men. Time had brought change as always. The English concept of liberty that had been institutionalized in Parliament's supremacy over the crown in 1688, had, as discussed in the earlier volumes of this series, by the 1770s, for some people, been transformed from the principle of parliamentary supremacy over the crown, into parliamentary sovereignty. Not, however, for Americans, whether whigs or tories. In the colonies liberty was still what it had been in seventeenth-century England: freedom from arbitrary power. Sometime between 1765 and 1774, Americans realized that parliamentary government, at least for them, was arbitrary government. The discovery could be called the kingship of Parliament, the kingliness of Parliament, or, looking back to the Glorious Revolution, the Stuartness of Parliament.

THE KINGLINESS OF PARLIAMENT

American whigs had discovered something about Parliament that British whigs and tories only vaguely understood and were reluctant to admit. They found the lesson in the seventeenth-century past as much as in Parliament's legislation between 1765 and 1774. The indictment of high treason exhibited against Charles I had charged that he had been "trusted with a limited Power to govern by, and according to the Laws of the Land, and not otherwise," and that he had violated that trust.[15] In the 1770s, American whigs, still clinging to the constitution of restraint, said Parliament had been trusted with a limited power to govern by and according to the constitution, and not otherwise, and that it was violating that trust.

That parliamentary power might be as arbitrary as crown power had been noticed before in English history, even if most eighteenth-century British seem to have forgotten that fact. As early as 1642, John Spelman had warned that Parliament could be as "arbitrary" as a king.[16] After the execution of Charles I many in England found that the Puritan Parliament "bore a striking resemblance to [the] old King," that is to Charles.[17] In 1649, with the crown and the House of Lords abolished and the Commons controlled by the military, a tract asked whether government had changed. "[W]e were ruled before by king, lords, and commons, now by a general, a court-martial, and a house of commons: and we pray you what is the difference?"[18] By 1774, Americans might well wonder what the difference was between a Parliament that could enact the Coercive Acts and a Charles I or James II. It was, however, more common to draw the analogy to the arbitrary governments of contemporary Europe, to ask if "we are reduced from free men to a level with the subjects of France and Spain; . . . for the parliament of Great Britain is that to us, which their princes are to them." "To an American Colonist," Benjamin Franklin argued, "our Parliament is . . . the same as the Parliament of Paris."[19]

The American constitutional predicament was that the Glorious Revolution had turned full circle. "Our ancestors," the Massachusetts House of Representatives lamented to the secretary of state for the colonies, at a time that taxation was the main American grievance, "when oppressed in the unfortunate reign of James the Second, found relief by the interposition of the Parliament. But it is the misfortune of the colonies at present, that by the intervention of that power they are taxed; and they can appeal for relief from their final decision to no power on earth, for there is no power on earth above them."[20]

We should recall a point that has been extensively discussed. It is that in Great Britain during the age of the American Revolution there were still constitutionalists unaware that the constitution was subject to Parliament's command. There is no need to rehash the evidence. What should be done is to put it into the context of the Glorious Revolution issue. Like Americans, the British of the eighteenth century had not needed Locke to tell them that Parliament could be as arbitrary as kings. As noted, the warning had been sounded before Locke[21] and was repeated often in the eighteenth century.[22] In the constitutional language of the day, the fear was that the very Parliament that had saved the people from becoming slaves to kings might make them slaves to their representatives.[23] Again, it must be understood that not all students of constitutional limitations on Parliament were saying that Parliament could not change the constitution or that there was fundamental law beyond Parliament's reach. The principle for many was that constitutional change should not be legislated without the consent of those whose rights were affected. In other words, Parliament should not alter rights arbitrarily and Parliament was able to act arbitrarily only when its power was unchecked by constitutional law. According to the conventional wisdom of the eighteenth century, Parliament's authority would become arbitrary should the crown, which was responsible to Parliament's supremacy, became dependent on Parliament. "If," the London Journal, Sir Robert Walpole's newspaper, explained in 1733, "the English

Government was changed in such a manner, that the People not only chose their Representatives, but the Representatives chose a certain Number of Persons every Year to execute the Laws, who should be *accountable* to them; the Consequence would be, that, in a Course of Years, the *Parliament*, having all Power *unchecked* and *uncontrouled*, would become as *arbitrary* as the most *absolute Monarchy*."[24] That would happen, of course, when cabinet government evolved with the ministry responsible to the Parliament and not to the king. Worry that would come about was why so much of the political literature of the day urged George III to name his own ministers and not be obsequious to a majority of either house of Parliament. If, an antiadministration newspaper argued in 1775, "instead of removing the Causes of our Sufferings, and fixing our Rights and Liberties [as a result of the Glorious Revolution], we then gave to a House of Commons, an unlimited Power to dispose of the last [our rights and liberties] according to their Inclination; it was only changing the Possessors of Arbitrary Power, by granting to a PROSTITUTED set of Representatives what was denied the King. . . . In what Manner can a Nation be more settled in its Freedom, by transferring ARBITRARY POWER from one Part of the Constitution to another."[25]

Some of the strongest arguments made in eighteenth-century Britain against the constitution of sovereign command were made in the context of the Glorious Revolution puzzle. If Parliament was absolute and could render decisions at pleasure, it was asked, "then, what did King James do more than this by his Prerogative? and of what Advantage has the Revolution proved to us, if Subverting the Constitution be legally placed in the Hands of the Representatives?"[26]

Parliament encountered the Glorious Revolution predicament several times during the era of the American controversy, as for example when lawyers for the East India Company, appearing before the House of Commons against the bill reforming the Company, argued "that it matter little what was the name of this wanton violator of the fundamental maxims of the constitution; that the thing was the same whether done by the *Grand Monarque* or by a parliament."[27] Perhaps the most revealing instance was when the Commons ordered the arrests of London's lord mayor and an alderman for contempt of Parliament.[28] To preserve their Glorious Revolution victory over the crown, the two houses of Parliament during the eighteenth century were uncompromisingly jealous of their privileges. Those privileges, after all, originally protected Parliament from the supremacy of the pre–Glorious Revolution executive. A different constitution prevailed, of course, when London's elected officials, claiming the privileges of London, the liberties of the subject, and freedom of the press, interfered with agents dispatched by the House of Commons to arrest printers accused of breaching parliamentary privilege by publishing its debates. The House ordered the lord mayor and an alderman confined in the Tower for contempt, and, although the controversy was clouded by Wilkite politics and claims of local autonomy, many people used the arrests to warn of Parliament's contempt for constitutional law.[29]

"We look," the inhabitants of the ward of Broad-Street told the lord mayor, "with the greatest Horror upon Power assumed over the Laws of the Land, which we think more to be dreaded under the Name of Privilege than Prerogative; (as many Tyrants are worse than one;) and that such Power, invested in any Set of Men, would reduce us to a State of the most abject Slavery, which God forbid." Answering a similar address from the inhabitants of Aldgate Ward, the alderman who was arrested with the lord mayor also appealed to constitutionalism by the rule of law, warning "that the House of Commons . . . has assumed a Power superior to those Laws by which Magistrates and Englishmen can only be bound, the Danger of suffering such an established Power in that House to supersede them, would be equally or more alarming, than Submission to the Tyranny of an unlimited Prerogative in one Person."[30]

The hold that the Glorious Revolution had on the constitutional values of the day is as inconsistent as it is striking. Many people thought of the Revolution as parliamentary supremacy and defined British liberty as the institution of an independent, autonomous, supreme representation.[31] There were others, a minority but an articulate minority, who defined liberty as the rule of law rather than representative government. For them the Glorious Revolution was as much a precedent for resisting an arbitrary House of Commons as it was authority for parliamentary supremacy. Another London alderman, one who had not been arrested, told his colleagues in the House of Commons that not everyone in Britain equated law with Parliament's command. "The sovereign formerly claimed the power of suspending the laws and of issuing proclamations suspendent to statutes, and even to Magna Charta," he reminded the House. The Glorious Revolution established that the king did not possess such authority. "You now claim the same power of suspending the laws, and of passing votes paramount in authority to the most sacred and fundamental constitutions of the realm. You swallow up everything in the gulph of your privileges. How can you imagine that the people should not resist? They resisted on the same principle in the reign of Charles the Second; they resisted on the same principle in the reign of Queen Anne."[32]

Arguments of this strain, made as part of the constitutional controversies occurring between the Seven Years War and the end of the century— the Middlesex elections, the cider excise crisis, the arrest of London's officials, the corn embargo, the Jew Bill, the East India Company Act, the

American Revolution controversies—were less defenses of the constitution of customary, prescribed vested rights than the last stand for a declining constitutionalism as the tradition of rule of law gave way to the practice of responsible government. The theory, however, was the same restrained constitutionalism that the seventeenth century had associated with Sir Edward Coke and the Parliament of 1628, and which had been brought to denouement in 1688. It is important to us for highlighting otherwise hidden roots of American constitutional principles. It was a theory of restraint that utilized the related concepts of delegated and reserved authority. "[A]rbitrary power," Earl Camden tried to explain to the House of Lords, "was unlawful," and could not be claimed even by Parliament. "[T]his was no novel doctrine, but as old as the constitution, . . . that therefore acts of the state were not always infallible doctrines, but were, and ought to be, in particular cases, subject to the rights and freedoms of the people at large, who had the original right vested in them, of delegating their power and authority."[33] The other way to say the same thing was that the people had reserved powers even against Parliament. "If an endeavour to subvert the Constitution shall impower the people to supersede one branch of the Legislature," the earl of Caryfort asked, recalling the Glorious Revolution, "why not another? If the people may resume the power of the Crown, because it is delegated by them, why not also the power of the House of Commons, or the whole Legislature, which is equally delegated?"[34]

A main prop of the eighteenth-century doctrine of delegated power was the original contract. In American whig constitutional theory the contract controlled Parliament as in 1688 it had controlled the king. In fact, it may have been strengthened by the Glorious Revolution. At least, that was what a barrister of Lincoln's Inn wrote sometime around the beginning of the nineteenth century. True, he admitted, the Declaration of Rights said nothing of a contract between Parliament and the people "and the reason is, that the Parliament not having been oppressors of the People, the words of the Declaration were confined to the point in question—the *words*, I say, were so confined; but the *spirit* of this Declaration went evidently to say, that there existed a contract between the governors and governed, between the people and those to whom they had delegated their sovereign power." The idea, of course, was not that the Glorious Revolution completed the development and perfection of the English constitution as Sir William Blackstone and others were saying. It was, rather, that there was continuity and that Parliament was restrained by the same constitution that had given legality to the Civil War against Charles I and legitimacy to the Glorious Revolution against James II.[35]

It might be helpful to think of that barrister of Lincoln's Inn as saying something that was more American than British. Carry that approach one step further and think of the Americans as English and not as British. They were constitutionalists of the English constitution, in the spirit of Sir Edward Coke, John Selden, and Algernon Sidney, sharing an English faith that government could be balanced and power could be restrained. They were not constitutionalists of the British constitution like Sir William Blackstone, Lord North, and Lord Chief Justice Mansfield, who had been taught by the Glorious Revolution that power alone, subject to constitutional restraints, did not endanger liberty. If we ask what it was that they feared we will discover one of the differences between English and British constitutionalists. American whigs, like the seventeenth-century English, feared power. British constitutionalists in the late eighteenth century feared power in the wrong hands.

THE ENGLISHNESS OF AMERICANS

In Great Britain there were three theories current concerning the Glorious Revolution and the American constitutional controversy. One was that Parliament's authority to legislate for the colonies was restrained by the same constitution that had restrained Charles I and James II. The second also held that parliament was restrained by constitutional law but that the principles of the constitution that had overthrown the two Stuarts were irrelevant to the American question. And, third, there were those who believed that the supremacy Parliament obtained at the Glorious Revolution had made Parliament supreme over the colonies, that by establishing supremacy over the crown, Parliament also established supremacy over the charters, privileges, and contracts granted the original settlers by James I, Charles I, and Charles II.

Most British observers who commented could not see how Charles I's ship money was a precedent for the American controversy. "The ship-money was demanded by the king *alone*," the Reverend John William Fletcher pointed out, adding that "a money-bill passed by the king *alone*" was "no law at all according to the British constitution." "What difference does it make," Richard Price wanted to know, "that in the time of *Charles the First* the attempt . . . was made by *one man:* but that, in the case of *America*, it is made by a body of men?" The answer most frequently given was historically anachronistic but legally sound. "[T]he difference between the whole legislature, and a third part only!" James Stewart insisted. Was not Charles I "[a] single branch attempting to annihilate the other two, consequently to overturn the constitution? does this make no difference?" "The king by levying ship-money, &c. of his own authority," John Roebuck added, "is in reality constituting himself sole legislator: The parliament by taxing the colonies acquires no new authority; she is already their supreme legislature." Addressing the House of Commons, Attorney General Edward Thurlow summed up the answer. "Our ancestors," he said, "opposed the encroachments of one branch of the Legislature upon the constitutional rights of the other two. The Americans rise in arms against the legal acts of the whole Legislature, King, Lords, and Commons, in their full plentitude of incontroulable authority."[36]

It was not much of a debate. Supporters of parliamentary supremacy, seeing no substance to the analogy American whigs drew between the arbitrariness of the Stuarts and the arbitrariness of Parliament in the reign of George III, thought there was nothing of substance about which to argue. Moreover, for any student of English constitutional history the concept of arbitrary just could not be tagged on Parliament. "*Arbitrary* power is That which is exercised by *kings*, in despotic governments," the author of the British *Common Sense* argued in 1775, "it is the *will* of the *despotic* sovereign." John Dickinson might be right to say that arbitrary power provided misery, a critic observed. "But I affirm, *That misery is not so likely to flow from* MANY *as from* ONE; *and therefore freedom has greater security under the rule of* MANY *than of* ONE."[37]

Supporters of Parliament's supremacy over the colonies thought the Glorious Revolution not relevant to the American controversy, but if it was, they said, it should have made the colonists grateful to Parliament, not grateful to those Stuart monarchs who had granted colonial charters. American whigs were reminded that those kings got in trouble because they tried to govern without Parliament. "Had parliaments been abolished in Great Britain by those kings who wished to rule without them, is it to be supposed that *General Assemblies* or *General Courts* would have long subsisted in America?" John Gray asked. "How absurd then is it to found the independency of any British colony upon the principles and actions of kings, subversive of the general liberty of the subject." It was even more absurd to liken parliamentary supremacy to arbitrary government when it was Parliament's supremacy at the Glorious Revolution that rescued the colonies from arbitrary government. "Would America," John St. John asked the House of Commons, "return to its original dependence on the Crown, and adopt the language of the Secretary of James I, who told the Parliament they had no right to interfere, that America was the King's own private property? For God's sake let her reflect on the alternative. Government has been asked whether they are prepared to await the consequences of their measures [meaning, the Coercive Acts]. I ask America, is she prepared to await the consequences of such doctrine? That whatever grievances she may endure, whatever be her condition, Parliament can not be applied to to better it, but she must fly for refuge and redress to the grace of the Crown alone."[38]

American whigs would reflect on the consequences, and their answer would shock members of Parliament. Before being pushed to that position, however, they argued that it did not make a bit of difference constitutionally whether power was exercised by one individual or five hundred members of Parliament.[39] Parliament's claim to the right of internal legislation, John Dickinson pointed out, did more than place it in the same constitutional position vis-à-vis the colonies that Charles I and James II had been vis-à-vis the seventeenth-century English and Scots. Even more striking, it put the Americans in the same constitutional position as the Independents who had opposed Charles and the whigs who had opposed James. "Such a right vested in parliament, would place us exactly in the same situation, the people of *Great Britain* would have been reduced to, had *James* the First and his family succeeded in their scheme of arbitrary power," Dickinson explained. "Changing the word *Stuarts* for *parliament* and *Britons* for *Americans*, the arguments of the illustrious patriots of those times . . . apply with inexpressible force and appositeness, in maintenance of our cause."[40]

Perhaps because taxation was such an important aspect of the American controversy, analogies were more frequently drawn to Charles I and the ship money precedent than to James II and the Glorious Revolution. Whoever condemned ship money must also condemn the Tea Act, Richard Pennant insisted in the House of Commons, "[i]ts principle is the same as the ship money in Charles."[41] In a widely reprinted argument, Arthur Lee explained how the seventeenth-century English perception of Charles was similar to the eighteenth-century American perception of Parliament. "[T]he King was independent of them, unconnected with them, save in a political relation, not participant in the burden, but profited by the exorbitancy of taxes. The same reasons precisely govern the *Americans*, in not acquiescing under the having their property given and granted by a *British* House of Commons."[42]

It would not be useful to think the argument ahistorical, to assume it must be bad history to claim that the American constitutional arguments of 1775 were the "same" as arguments made against Charles I 130 years before.[43] We should remember that they were talking law not history. What they were saying was that Charles had posed the same threat to the seventeenth-century English that Parliament posed to the eighteenth-century colonists. Both were perceived as threatening arbitrary government as both claimed authority to impose laws arbitrarily.[44] "To introduce the legality of Ship-scot," Henry Parker had argued in 1640, "such a prerogative hath been maintained as destroys all Law, . . . and such Art has been use to deny, traverse, avoid or frustrate the true force or meaning of all our Laws and Charters, that if wee grant Shipmoney, on these grounds, with Ship money wee grant all besides." American whigs said they would grant "all" if they were bound in all cases whatsoever. "Having no share in constituting any part of this power, all its actions are unconnected with and independent of our will," it was explained in 1776. "[I]t is immaterial to us whether we suffer by the imperious will of one man, or whether the wills of five hundred are the cause to our ruin."[45]

The concept of arbitrary power was what made eighteenth-century Americans think of Parliament as the seventeenth-century English had thought of Charles I. Parliament was now the king, not because Parliament exercised power that once constitutionally belonged to the king, but because Parliament was asserting authority constitutionally denied the king. In fact, the Americans were theoretically worse off than they would have been had Charles I established arbitrary government and had he and his heirs ruled all the British dominions without calling parliaments or assemblies. "An absolute prince," it was pointed out in 1776 by a Scots theologian, "is under no temptation to purchase the favour of one part of his dominions at the expense of another; for it is his interest to treat them all upon the same footing: But lords and commons have a private and separate interest to pursue, and must be wonderfully disinterested, if they would make us bear every disproportional part of the public burdens, to avoid them as much as possible themselves."[46]

There was much irony here. Parliament's role in the seventeenth century had been to check arbitrary government. That role had begun to change commencing with the Glorious Revolution. Parliament was slowly being transformed from the instrument restraining power to an authority that, for Americans at least, appeared to be unbounded by constitutional restraint.[47]

REVOLUTION PRINCIPLES

In the political and constitutional language of the eighteenth century, for people to claim that they adhered to "revolution principles"—meaning principles of the Glorious Revolution—was a shorthand way of saying they supported the principle of parliamentary supremacy over the crown. "The Rights and Liberties of every member of the British Constitution," Jonathan Watson explained, was "settled by the glorious Revolution, which has raised this kingdom to a state of happiness and prosperity unknown to former ages."[48] People of the right[49] as well as the left[50] thought the sovereignty of Parliament as established at the Glorious Revolution was the final institutional triumph of English and British liberty, as well as English and British constitutionalism. "What then was the Revolution, as it affected the Constitution?" the staunch tory John Brand would ask 108 years after the event. "A successful resistance against an attempt to overthrow the system of Government established by the Laws," he answered. "And what is it now to act upon Revolution principles? To resist all attempts, whether popular, aristocratical, or regal, to subvert such Government."[51] The most fundamental revolution principle was that the subversion of lawful government was best prevented by preserving pure and undiluted the sovereignty of Parliament.

We must be careful of the word sovereignty. It can obscure our view of the American Revolution. "In the final analysis," H. T. Dickinson has observed, "the most serious point at issue between the mother country and her colonies rested on a fundamental disagreement over the nature and location of sovereignty."[52] That statement is true if it is understood that disagreement over the nature of sovereignty included the question whether sovereignty had to be arbitrary power, and that disagreement over its location included the question whether sovereignty had to be indivisible.[53] Looked at from the perspective of the Glorious Revolution settlement, the fundamental issue surrounding sovereignty in the eighteenth century was not its location but whether preservation of British liberty permitted any diminution of the Glorious Revolution principle of Parliament's supremacy over the crown. Was British liberty so rooted in the Glorious Revolution settlement that it could be lost if the two houses of Parliament did not exercise absolute, arbitrary sovereignty? It is necessary to consider again why imperialists over and over insisted that "either the Americans *are* dependent upon us, or they *are* not. Either they *are* subject to the legislative Authority of this Kingdom, or they *are* not." The reason was not a blind eighteenth-century dogmatism that sovereignty had to be absolute and could not be divided. The reason was that American constitutional theory threatened revolution principles, especially the fundamental Glorious Revolution principle of parliamentary supremacy over the crown.[54]

The twentieth century has forgotten how much the eighteenth century was attached to revolution principles. To illustrate how tenaciously they were held, consider one of the most gravid revolution principles, the unmitigated independence of the two houses of Parliament. "[T]he dependence of Parliament, in *every degree* is an infringement of British liberty," Viscount Bolingbroke was quoted in 1780 as having said.[55] And he meant "in *every degree*." A free Parliament, a constitutional Parliament was one that maintained its privileges inviolate. The two houses not only had to be "the sole Judges of their own Rights and Privileges," they could not allow any challenge to their independence, not even by a subject vindicating private rights at common law. Viscount Barrington implied it was a revolution principle that a person aggrieved by the crown could seek redress at common law, but could not if aggrieved by Parliament.[56] To preserve the people's liberty Parliament had to be independent not only of the crown, but also of the courts and of the people, even if it meant abusing the rights and the liberty of individuals. "I pay no regard whatever to the voice of the people," Charles James Fox, member for Midhurst, told the Commons in 1771. "[T]heir business is to chuse us; it is our business to act constitutionally, and to maintain the independency of parliament: whether it is attacked by the people or by the crown, is a matter of little consequence; it is the attack, not the quarter it proceeds from, which we are to punish. . . . I stand up for the constitution, not for the people; if the people attempt to invade the constitution, they are enemies to the nation."[57]

Fox's speech must be seen in its context. He spoke very strong words in defense of an action that today would have no constitutional justification. He was defending the order that sent the lord mayor and an alderman of London to the Tower for interfering with the arrest of printers ordered by the House of Commons. They claimed the privileges of London, the rights of Magna Carta, and the liberty of British subjects, but were imprisoned without trial—on vote of a majority of the House—for breach of parliamentary privilege. It was a confrontation of the liberty of the ancient constitution against the liberty of the Glorious Revolution. "Whenever the commons assumed this monstrous power, there was an end of liberty, and the constitution," Sergeant John Glynn argued in behalf of the city of London. "Put the case, that the king had taken the same violent step, when his proclamation was set at nought. Is there a man of sense in England, who would not have been alarmed for his liberty?"[58] Glynn was right, but his example was unpersuasive. The king could never again order an arbitrary arrest as long as the houses of Parliament maintained their independence. They remained independent by safeguarding their privileges. When London's officials, in the name of liberty or what they called liberty, undertook to question the exercise of one privilege, they had to be punished in the name of the Glorious Revolution.

A revolution principle invoked during the American controversy was the honor of Parliament. In May, 1775, Edmund Burke presented New York's long-awaited remonstrance to the House of Commons. It should be recalled that following the Coercive Acts this was the only colony assembly officially to communicate with Parliament, that all the others spoke to the mother country through the Continental Congress. Not only was the document drafted in what Fox, with much tongue in cheek, would describe as "the most affectionate and respectful terms that could be, considering the state of the contest,"[59] but Lord North was eager to accommodate New York, hoping to separate it from the other colonies.[60] In the Commons, North "spoke greatly in favour of New-York, and said, that he would gladly do every thing in his power to shew his regard to the good behaviour of that Colony." But the remonstrance could not be received by the House as "the honour of Parliament required, that no paper should be presented to that House, which tended to call in question the unlimited rights of Parliament."[61] In the document, the New York General Assembly had claimed "an exemption from internal taxation, and exclusive right of providing for the support of our own civil government, and the administration of justice in this colony."[62] That claim, as well as the refusal of New York to acknowledge Parliament's authority by submitting a "representation" or a "remonstrance" rather than a "petition," tarnished the document. It was, Charles Wolfran Cornwall reminded the House, "contrary to every idea of the supremacy of Parliament to receive a paper in which the Legislative rights of Parliament were denied."[63]

What appeared to be an opportunity to reestablish contact with a legitimate American whig institution, a way of getting around the problem of recognizing the Continental Congress, had been lost, the earl of Dartmouth lamented to the governor of New York. He had presented one of New York's companion messages—this one called a "petition"—to the king "who was pleased to receive it with the most gracious expressions of regard and attention to the humble requests of his faithful subjects in New York, who have on this occasion manifested a duty to his majesty and regard for the authority of the parent state." Even Dartmouth agreed, however, that the petition to the king had to be rejected after finding that "in the memorial to the House of Lords and in the representation to the House of Commons"[64] there were "expressions containing claims which made it impossible for Parliament consistent with its justice and dignity to receive them." Too bad, the earl added, for otherwise the petition to George III "might have laid the foundation of that concilation we have so long and so ardently wished for."[65] The "revolution doctrine" of the supremacy of Parliament over the crown, which had been evolving since 1688, was too sacrosanct to be tinkered with in 1775—at least, it could not be relaxed enough to try and find a new revolutionary settlement to the current constitutional controversy by answering New York's General Assembly.

The Glorious Revolution of 1688 was the constitutional lodestar for American whigs just as much as it was for British whigs and British tories. It was for them as much as for their fellow subjects in the mother country both the definition and the guarantee of their liberty. It was, however, a beacon guiding them to separate constitutional paths because the American definition and the American guarantee of liberty, following Glorious Revolution principles, were different than the definition and guarantee of British liberty. For Americans, the Glorious Revolution had been the triumph of the constitution. The Revolution had not changed the law, it had preserved the law by rescuing the old constitution of vested rights and limited government from the threat of arbitrary royal power. Liberty for the Americans remained what it had been before 1688, the liberty of the constitution protected by the rule of law. For the British the Glorious Revolution had also been the triumph of liberty, but of a liberty that had been institutionalized in Parliament's supremacy over the crown. By the 1770s in Great Britain, the legacy of the Glorious Revolution had made American liberty the direct institutional opposite of British liberty. The concept of arbitrary government had acquired the limited meaning of royal government and the concept of liberty had acquired the institutional meaning of parliamentary supremacy. It was because they were defending *British liberty*, not because they were careless about *American liberty*, that the rulers in London found it so difficult to offer the colonists the accommodation both sides so much desired.

What the Glorious Revolution issue meant to the coming of the American Revolution is addressed in the remainder of this book. It was a problem very much on the minds of those who participated in the controversy, frequently discussed if never solved. It has not, however, been considered worthy of attention by most historians, and as many students of the American Revolution may not be aware of the Glorious Revolution predicament, it should not be premature to state what it was even before it is developed as a historical topic. The predicament was summed up by Alexander Elmsly, a lawyer writing about the Coercive Acts to the man who would become North Carolina's first United States senator. He reported that British public opinion was not favorable toward the Americans. Although most Britons thought the colonists ought not to be taxed without their consent, "they think it also dangerous to allow the sovereign to have more parliaments than one, at least independent of that one, and think as I always did, and said, that the king of England, as King, can have no subjects that are not under the control of the Parliament of Great Britain."[66]

That was the Glorious Revolution issue, the king and his relationship to two peoples. If the Americans were constitutionally blinded by their fear of arbitrary power exercised by a sovereign Parliament, the British were constitutionally blinded by their confidence that constitutional liberty was secure only with a sovereign Parliament. That certainly was the difficulty of one British observer in 1774 who was astonished that American whigs argued "that the colonies are the king's domain, and not annexed to the realm." His warning that the Americans risked losing their best chance for liberty, was almost a caricature of contemporary British constitutional thought.

Such a position was the most unfavourable to their cause as could possibly be advanced, as it throws the government of them entirely upon the crown, and takes from them the liberty they now enjoy, the jurisdiction of parliament. If they are not annexed to the realm, the interference of the legislature must be allowed an indulgence from the crown, and a most valuable liberty to the colonists; as by that they enjoy every particular freedom of Englishmen, the government of the supreme legislature in every degree as British subjects.[67]

The argument was ridiculous, of course, so contrary to American constitutional interests that today it would be dismissed as black humor. But from the perspective of British constitutional law, how else could Americans be free?

CHAPTER FIVE

THE LIBERTY ISSUE

A few historians have doubted the significance of the Glorious Revolution predicament in part—and it must be stressed *only in part*—because of a commonality of ideology uniting the trans-Atlantic political culture. "Indeed," Colin Bonwick noted in the 1970s, "the consonance between colonial thought and contemporaneous English radical thought was so close that they can be legitimately described as two branches of a single tradition."[1] The idea is not new. Participants in the American revolutionary controversy often commented on the common constitutional values and common constitutional danger shared by citizens of the empire. "People of *England*" should listen to the colonists, the people of Great Britain were told by *Junius Americanus*, for Americans "are pursuing the same sacred cause of freedom, with the same virtuous determination to succeed, or to perish in the attempt. The cause is common, let us be united in its support, the liberties of both countries are embarked on the same bottom; the same storm that sinks the one will overwhelm the other." That argument was repeated frequently in Great Britain. "[T]he cause of liberty in England and America is one common cause," London's *Political Register* had said the year before. "The attacks on both have been made and carried on by the same set of men, with the same views, and with the same illegal violence."[2]

69

It has been noted before that there was also a unity of constitutional ideology among British leaders. Administration and opposition, conservatives
and so-called radicals, tories and whigs, all boasted of their "liberty-
preserving" constitution. "The crucial distinction between them," Jack P.
Greene has said, was that "mainstream thinkers" "spoke mainly with pride
of the constitutional and political achievements of Georgian England,"
while "opposition thinkers" viewed contemporary Britain with alarm,
"stressed the dangers to England's ancient heritage and the loss of pristine
virtue, studied the process of decay, and dwelt endlessly on the evidences
of corruption they saw about them and the dark future these malignant
signs portended."[3]

When studying eighteenth-century constitutional history it is important
to draw eighteenth-century distinctions. It is not enough to note that both
British opposition and American whigs were unhappy with the Parliament
led by Lord North. As the distinctions drawn by Professor Greene indicate, it would also be wrong to say that "British reformers refused obedience to parliament because the House of Commons was not freely elected
and did not adequately represent the British people. Colonial leaders on
the other hand, opposed parliament for the simple reason that it was not
American." Those two statements are incorrect. First, no matter what
we call them—radicals, reformers, commonwealthmen, opposition—the
people unhappy with Parliament in Great Britain during the 1770s wanted
many more reforms than merely free elections and a more representative
House of Commons. Second, colonial whigs had much more substantial
grievances than that Parliament was British and not American. Parliament had been no more American before 1765 than after, yet it was not
until Parliament began enacting unprecedented legislation in 1765 that
the colonists questioned its authority to legislate. There is a consideration
to which scholars of the British-American connection should give more
attention. It is that although just about every American whig who is on
record reacted against Parliament's arbitrary power, there were members
of the British opposition or other people whom historians identify as radical who did not see the same problem. "The omnipotence of Parliament,
its power to alter the very Constitution of England through its changing
laws," Claude H. Van Tyne pointed out, "was a fact not fully grasped even
by Englishmen. However, there were some forward-looking Englishmen
who did see it, and who were demanding reform."[4] The reform they demanded was different than reforms Americans sought. Here was another
difference dividing British constitutionalists from their American counter-
parts; another reason for saying that the Glorious Revolution legacy more
than any other constitutional cause was pushing them apart.

"Parliaments originally were the great bulwarks of our Freedom," Sheriff Frederick Bull told the livery of London in 1772, "they are now the Destroyers of it." Taught by the same constitutional tradition, British and Americans employed the same language when speaking constitutionally: "freedom," "slavery," "custom," "contract." When expressing uneasiness with Parliament, however, they tended to use a different vocabulary, with Americans likely to employ old English constitutional terms such as "power," "arbitrary," "innovation," and "right," and British likely to use words more clearly associated with eighteenth-century politics such as "corrupt," "place," "influence," and "pensioners." Consider the "engagement"signed by the "radicals" John Wilkes and John Glynn when nominated to stand for Parliament in the election of 1774. They pledged that if elected the representatives of Middlesex, they would endeavour, "to promote acts of the legislature for shortening the duration of parliaments, for excluding placemen and pensioners from the House of Commons"; to "force more fair and equal representation of the people," and to draft "an act for the repeal of the four late acts respecting America; . . . being fully persuaded, that the passing of such acts will be of the utmost importance for the security of our excellent constitution, and the restoration of the rights and liberties of our fellow-subjects in America." The concerns were the same as American concerns, and so were some of the words—"rights," "liberties," "security." But the purpose was "to restore and defend" the form of government "established at the Revolution." The grievances against Parliament were septennial elections and the corruption of pensioners, not supremacy or arbitrary power.[5]

The legislative program of British reformers during the first three years of the 1770s, included shortening the duration of Parliament's sessions, excluding placemen and pensioners from the House of Commons, establishing a more free and equal representation of "the people," and supporting the rights of the Americans against the administration of Lord North.[6] These matters went hand in hand, after all, for if the crown or the ministry succeeded in taxing and remodeling the governments of the North American colonies, it would obtain more revenue and many more places with which to complete the corruption of Parliament through influence. It was with this danger to liberty that the interests of American whigs and British parliamentary reformers both coincided and diverged. The colonists defended American liberty by denying Parliament's sovereign authority to legislate. British reformers defended British liberty by protesting expansion of the national government through the exercise of Parliament's undoubted sovereignty over the colonies. For the sake of colonial liberty, American whigs wanted Parliament to return to the constitutional theory of the Restoration, where the constitution was sovereign and the law, not power, supposedly guided practice. The British radicals wanted a supreme, sovereign Parliament, independent of the crown, mistrustful of the ministry, representative of the people, and, above all else, practicing and guarding Glorious Revolution principles.

It is surprising—perhaps it is even a mystery—how some American whigs failed to give sufficient weight to the Glorious Revolution predicament when they encountered it. Delegates to the first Continental Congress such as Pennsylvania's John Dickinson and Maryland's Thomas Johnson, seemed to think that American liberty could still flourish under the British constitution. "The first political Wish of my Soul," Dickinson claimed, "is for the Liberty of America. The next is for a constitutional Reconciliation with G[reat] B[ritain]." "You and I and America in general," Johnson told Horatio Gates, "may almost universally wish in the first place to establish our Liberties; our second wish is a reunion with Britain; so may we preserve the Empire intire and the Constitutional Liberty founded in whiggish principles, handed down to us by our Ancestors." For Americans, unlike the British, whiggish principles were not limited to revolution principles and liberty was not limited to the liberty of the Glorious Revolution.[7]

The concept of liberty, then, both united and divided American and British students of constitutional government. They thought liberty a unifying possession held in joint tenancy, a blessing that they alone shared, a stroke of good fortune, making them unique among all the peoples of the world. They did share and they did cherish it, colonists and Briton, whig and tory, alike, but once Americans began open defiance of parliamentary sovereignty following passage of the Coercive Acts, Glorious Revolution principles intruded upon that unity and the concept of liberty came to divide the two parts of the empire. It is, necessary, therefore, to look again at the concept of liberty, this time largely from the American perspective, for passage of the Coercive Acts was the final expression of parliamentary policy to drive Americans back in theory to seek their liberty in the prerogatives of the crown and away from the new eighteenth-century British definition of liberty, the legacy of the Glorious Revolution, the supremacy of Parliament.

THE SECURITY ISSUE

We have looked at the concept of liberty several times in this series of books,[8] including chapter 2 of this volume where infringement of liberty was discussed as one of the main American grievances against the Coercive Acts. Here we are concerned with how the constitutional principle that liberty constrained sovereign power was argued by colonial whigs when formulating their legal case against parliamentary supremacy. The principle might be called "the constitutional constraint of liberty," and the problem, as John Lind observed in 1775, was to "strike out some method of reconciling British superiority with American 'liberty.'"[9]

There is an aspect of the liberty issue so special to English and British constitutionalism that it must be given separate treatment. It is the doctrine of consent, perhaps the best-known constitutional principle in all of English history. It will be covered in the next chapter, and all that need be noted here is that American whigs frequently stated the doctrine of consent in terms of freedom. An example is the preamble of South Carolina's first constitution which began with the proposition that the British Parliament's claim to "a right to bind the North-American Colonies by law, in all cases whatsoever . . . was altogether unconstitutional, and, if admitted, would at once reduce them from the rank of Freemen to a state of the most abject Slavery."[10]

Stripped of elements of consent and representation, the liberty issue provided a straightforward, rigidly dogmatic defense for colonial whigs. "The question is," Virginia's Richard Bland told the first Continental Congress, "whether the rights and liberties of America shall be contended for, or given up to arbitrary power."[11] Stated from the British perspective, although also from the same side of the controversy, "the question . . . should be, Whether we have a general right of making slaves, or not?"[12] "What can," Georgia's John Joachim Zubly asked, "an emperor of Morocco pretend more of his slaves than to bind them in all cases whatsoever?" Other words and expressions, synonyms for slavery and defining liberty were "tyranny" and "despotism." As with most eighteenth-century political language the vocabulary was a trans-Atlantic vocabulary, the same expressions appearing in British arguments as in American arguments.[13] When generalities were made about liberty, and about what political conditions were dangerous to liberty, the two sides understood each other. Where communication broke down was when the Americans said Parliament had taken away their liberty. The British could not comprehend how the institution that made British liberty secure could be the institution endangering American liberty. American whigs did understand. "[S]hould the authority now claimed by Parliament, be fully supported by power, or submitted to by the colonies," the Massachusetts House of Representatives warned Rhode Island's House, "it appears to this House, that *there* will be an end to liberty in America, and that the colonies will *then* change the name of freemen, for that of *slaves*."[14] Of course, if the British did not understand, the Irish did for they had the same grievance against the same Parliament. "Our slavery is complete," an Irishman argued in 1780, "as long as we are subject to regulations made by a legislature, in the election of which we had no voice, and over whose members we have not the least controul. If any thing could add to a slavery in its nature so perfect, it would be, that we are under the government of a power, whose views may be distinct, and whose interests may be [the] opposite of ours."[15] The authority of Parliament to bind the colonies by statutes, future loyalists argued on behalf of the Connecticut legislature early in the controversy, was "an Exception from the general Rule by which British Subjects (according to the constitution) are governed," and, therefore, could not be exercised to deprive Americans "of those Privileges which are essential to their Liberty and Freedom."[16] That rule, of course, had once been basic constitutional doctrine in England, that liberty was the gauge for restraining power.

Liberty, in fact, was everything in the eighteenth century. If it provided some students of constitutional government with a test for restraining authority, it told others what could be lost if power was unchecked. Once the Americans, like the British, had feared the power of the crown, but after the Coercive Acts the threat to their liberty came from only one source. About a month and a half before the battle of Lexington took place in New England, the General Committee of Charleston, South Carolina, warned the New York Committee that the crisis of liberty was at hand for unless Parliament's authority to legislate was checked constitutionally America would have no constitution and, therefore, no liberty. All the clichés, all the anxieties of eighteenth-century constitutionalism were summed up by these South Carolinians.

> The present struggle seems to us most glorious and critical. We seem to ourselves to stand upon the very division line, between all the blessings of freedom, and the most abject vassalage. The very idea of an earthy power which shall bind the present and future millions of *America* in all cases whatsoever—in the direction of which we are to have no more voice than our oxen, and over which we can have no constitutional control, fills us with horrour;—to hold not only our *liberty* and *property* at will, but our lives also, as well as the lives of all our posterity!—to be absolutely dependant for the air in which we breathe, and the water which we drink, upon a set of men at the distance of three thousand miles from us—who, even when they abuse that power, are out of reach of our vengeance, is a proposal which this Colony hears with indignation, and can only submit to when there is no possible remedy.[17]

American arguments against the authority of Parliament to legislate their internal governance tended to run in and out of one another. They were generally made in single paragraphs. Just as protests about the loss of liberty were apt to be the reverse side of protests against the imposition of arbitrary government, so claims for liberty were often a way of expressing concern about equality breached or security threatened. It was not even necessary to consider the Coercive Acts. The Delaware Convention, for example, made a listing of Parliament's commands about American trade, taxation, admiralty jurisdiction, and trials beyond the venue, and asked if they did not amount to "unwarrantable assumptions of power; unconstitutional, and destructive of British liberty." Another question asked by converting the liberty issue into an equality issue, was whether Parliament would have treated Britons living in England, Wales, and perhaps even Scotland in a comparable way. Ireland did not count. Looking back over the same statutes that the Delaware Convention thought "destructive of British liberty," John Winthrop, the Hollis professor in Harvard, concluded that "they appear to be trifles when compared with the acts passed in the last session of Parliament which, I believe, are not to be paralleled in the British annals." He was saying that Parliament would not have imposed the Coercive Acts on the people of England and Scotland. It was an assumption that Americans thought so obvious they ignored contrary evidence such as the punishment of Edinburgh in the Porteus case or the many instances where Britons were denied trial at the vicinage. "Regardless of every principle of justice and policy," an *Anti-Despot* told New Yorkers in a typical instance of the conclusion, "the British Parliament are trying against our liberty experiments which, if hazarded against the people under their immediate legislative authority, would infallibly involve *Great Britain* in a civil war, and might produce another revolution there."[18]

In the twentieth century equality may be the most significant element in the definition of liberty. In eighteenth-century constitutional theory, the right to security was more important to liberty than was equality. When the prerevolutionary controversy commenced with passage of the Stamp Act, Charles Carroll of Carrollton immediately realized that American constitutional security was at risk if the British Parliament could exercise legislative supremacy. "The preamble of ye Stamp Act is as alarming as ye Act itself," he pointed out to a British friend. "[A]llowing this unbounded power in a set of men at so great a distance, so little acquainted with our circumstances, and not immediately affected with ye taxes laid upon us, what security remains for our property? What fence against arbitrary enactions?"[19] A decade later, the right to security seemed to be in such jeopardy that American whigs were defending it in some unexpected places. "[I]f the parliament of Great Britain takes from us our property, and our lands, without our consent," the Massachusetts Provincial Congress told the Stockbridge Indians, "they will do the same by you; your property, your lands will be insecure; in short, we shall not any of us have anything we can call our own." [20]

Today the right to security has changed so much that the eighteenth-century right is no longer an element of constitutional liberty. In Great Britain it exists at legislative pleasure, and in the United States it is at best marginal, generally sneered at by civil libertarians. It may be that we can no longer understand what security meant to eighteenth-century liberty, a fact explaining why historians have generally discounted it as a factor in the American grievance against parliamentary supremacy. Also, because security was the main element in the definition of liberty, may be why some scholars have not given credence to colonial despair over the liberty issue. The eighteenth century was a different era than today, and American whigs and British imperialists in the age of the American Revolution shared a felt need for security that has long since been lost. Still, even if we cannot appreciate what was being said, we can realize that there were members of Parliament who understood what *Cassandra* meant when telling readers of the *Maryland Gazette* they could not remain in the empire under the insecurity of parliamentary supremacy. "On an impartial inquiry into the *present* state of the British constitution," he wrote less than a month after the battle of Lexington, "it appears to me that it is out of the power of the British legislature to give us *security* for the future enjoyment of our *rights* and *liberties,* and on this general ground I have opposed a re-union." [21]

THE SUBJECTS-OF-SUBJECTS ISSUE

In May 1770 the duke of Richmond offered resolutions in the House of Lords questioning the administration's colonial policy. He was criticizing instructions that the secretary of state, the earl of Hillsborough, had sent to governors of the North American colonies. "If, indeed," Lord Hillsborough answered, "it is repugnant to the principles of the British constitution to execute the laws of Great Britain, I am a culprit of the first magnitude." But he would not apologize for ordering assemblies dissolved nor would he tolerate American insolence. "The colonies are our subjects," Hillsborough reminded his colleagues, "as such they are bound by our laws; and I trust we shall never use the language of supplication, to beg that our subjects will condescendingly yield obedience to our inherent pre-eminence." [22]

Hillsborough said explicitly what Parliament's claim of legislative supremacy said implicitly, that the American colonists were not only the subjects of George III. They also were the subjects of Parliament, if not the subjects of the British people. In 1768, *Philo Britania,* writing in London's *Public Ledger* and hoping to "cut the debate short," proposed that the ministry "state matters fairly between us and the colonists" by putting a series of questions to the Americans as to whether they "are subjects of Great Britain." His fourth and last question was: "Whether they consider themselves as subjects or vassals of the King of Great Britain only, independent of the parliament, in the same manner, as Hanover, or any other foreign dominion?" This was the question that American whigs would eventually have to answer, confronting them with the predicament of the Glorious Revolution issue, but first they sought to avoid it by asking the exact opposite constitutional question. It was, in fact, asked as early of 1765, at the beginning of the revolutionary controversy. "[C]an it possibly be shown," Governor Stephen Hopkins of Rhode Island had wondered, "that the people in Britain have a sovereign authority over their fellow subjects in America?"[23]

The issue was posed as much by the authority to tax as the authority to legislate. Parliamentary taxation, *Caius Memmius* wrote in the *Boston Gazette,* made Americans "the *subjects* of *subjects.*" Before taxation was attempted British colonists had been constitutionally more secure than the colonists of other European powers, a New York pamphlet published in 1768 contended. They were no longer better off. Other colonists "are upon a par with their fellow subjects in Europe; we are become the absolute slaves of ours, their legislature being independent of the people, ours so far as it relates to taxation, entirely directed by them; thus are we the only people in the world, that are the subjects of subjects." The same argument could be made about the authority to legislate in general. In 1774 a number of colonial newspapers published a letter they supposed had been written by Edmund Burke. It told Lord North that "should the people of *England,* by their Delegates, continue to exercise the powers of legislation and taxation upon the Colonies . . . they must exalt themselves to the sovereignty of *America,* and render the inhabitants of that country the *subjects* of *subjects.*"[24]

Participants in the American debate treated the subjects-of-subjects issue as part of the larger liberty issue. "[A] great people," *Americus* told the editor of the *London Magazine,* "whose property is in all cases, and without reserve, at the disposal of another people at an immense distance, can never be persuaded that they live in the enjoyment of freedom."[25] Just the exercise of supremacy, such as the New York Suspending Act, *Brutus* argued in an address to Virginians, should be sufficient "to convince us that the British parliament have not viewed us with an eye of brotherly love and affection, but with a determination to make us subservient to our fellow subjects in *Britain,* in all cases whatever, and our condition as wretched as that of slaves."[26]

Slavery was an eighteenth-century word describing the status of subjects of subjects. For Parliament to make law for the unrepresented Americans, it was said, was "for one half of a kingdom, to hold the other half in chains." Richard Price thought it a common species of slavery. "[T]he slavery most prevalent in the world has been internal slavery," he explained. "Internal slavery . . . takes place whenever a whole community is governed by a *part*."[27] As usual, familiar, taught, synonymous words were used, such as "masters," "vassals," "villienage," and "tenants at will." The Boston Port Act made "the inhabitants of the *English* Colonies . . . vassals to the *British* House of Commons," the whigs of Rye, New York, voted. "You are the real proprietors," James Iredell told the people of Great Britain, "we [are] only the tenants at will."[28]

The subjects-of-subjects perspective was utilized by American whigs to raise just about every eighteenth-century constitutional doctrine. An obvious one was the right to security. What parliamentary sovereignty over the colonies meant, New York County told the Corporation of London, was "a despotism consisting in power assumed by the Representatives of a part of His Majesty's subjects, at their sovereign will and pleasure to strip the rest of their property." Even more obvious was the constitutional right to equality. If the colonists were the subjects of their fellow subjects in Parliament, David Griffith told the Virginia Convention on the last day of 1775, "their situation is truly slavish . . . they contend that their fellow subjects in Britain are but their equals. . . . They say the claim of the commons is an innovation; that it is unnatural, unjust and oppressive; and destructive of that equal justice and liberty which, by the constitution, was meant to be secured by all."[29]

The strongest constitutional arguments against the authority of Parliament to treat the colonists as the subjects of subjects emerged out of the doctrines of the constitution of prescription, customary restraint. One example, the doctrine of Parliament as a trust, should illustrate the argument. "The Members of the British Parliament can only be consider'd as Trustees for the Care and Direction of the Liberty and Property of their Constituents," a New Yorker wrote during the Stamp Act crisis. "[W]ith what Appearance of Reason, do They claim the Disposal of Property with which They were never entrusted, or arrogate to Themselves a Power to determine upon that Liberty which was never committed to their Care?" Related constitutional doctrines could be used the same way, the doctrine of consent's restraint on the exercise of government and the doctrine of the original contract, to cite two discussed elsewhere.[30]

The subjects-of-subjects issue was probably best analyzed by Thomas Jefferson in the working paper he wrote for the House of Burgesses, published as *A Summary View of the Rights of British America*. It is the most effective argument that he made, a fact that may explain why the pamphlet had a greater influence in Virginia than in London where the subjects-of-subjects issue was less well understood than it was in the colonies.

> Not only the principles of common sense, but the common feelings of human nature, must be surrendered up before his majesty's subjects here can be persuaded to believe that they hold their political existence at the will of a British parliament. Shall these governments be dissolved, their property annihilated, and their people reduced to a state of nature, at the imperious breath of a body of men, whom they never saw, in whom they never confided, and over whom they have no powers of punishment or removal, let their crimes against the American public be ever so great? Can any one reason be assigned why 160,000 electors in the island of Great Britain should give law to four millions in the states of America . . . ? Were this to be admitted, instead of being a free people, as we have hitherto supposed . . . we should suddenly be found the slaves not of one but of 160,000 tyrants. . . .[31]

Jefferson's last argument was not *sui generis*. The general notion among eighteenth-century constitutionalists was that rule by a single tyrant was preferable to rule by an absolute assembly, especially if the members of that assembly were the representatives of a free people. An arbitrary king was more likely to treat his peoples equally, even those separated from the seat of power, but a house of elected delegates possessing arbitrary power had reason to fashion laws that relieved their constituents at the expense of colonies.[32] "If we must be reduced to Slavery," a Pennsylvanian reasoned, "let us not have so many hard Masters to lord it over us, for doubtless one will be more than enough, and the latter may probably be much sooner intimidated from Tyranny, than a great Number of powerful combined Oppressors, perpetually inflaming each other against us." It was better to "endure the Rod of an Absolute Monarch . . . than arbitrary Scourgings" of "the British Parliament."[33]

Jefferson differed from most constitutional commentators when saying that the subjects of whom Americans were subjects were the electors of Great Britain. Most observers thought the colonists the subjects of the British people in general. "[T]he word *colony* became nearly synonymous with *subject*," the economist James Anderson noted, and he seems to have been right, at least if he was talking of the English and not his fellow Scots.[34] "The meanest person among us is disposed to look upon himself as having a body of subjects in *America*," Richard Price complained.[35] The attitude was noticed less in the colonies, although at least once it was mentioned as something about which Americans should be concerned.

"It is now an established principle in *Great Britain*, that we are subject to the *people* of that country," Rhode Island whigs were warned at the dedication of Providence's liberty tree. "They expressly call us their subjects. The language of every paultry scribber, even of those who pretend friendship for us in some things, is after this lordly stile, *our colonies— our western dominions—our plantations—our islands—our subjects in America—our authority—our government*—with many more of the like imperious expressions."[36]

The subjects-of-subjects issue was not very important in constitutional law. It was, however, extremely important to the revolutionary controversy for it provided a very special perspective for comprehending parliamentary sovereignty, giving both Americans and British a dramatic vista for considering the problem of legislative supremacy, simplistic perhaps, yet striking. Just to think of Americans as subjects of fellow subjects made vulnerable Parliament's claim of authority to legislate. "But from what source does this mighty, this uncontrolled authority of the house of commons flow?" James Wilson asked. "From the collective body of the commons of Great Britain," he answered, meaning that the House of Commons' authority was delegated by the people. If so, he wondered, "By what title do they claim to be our masters? What act of ours has rendered us subject to those, to whom we were formerly equal?"[37]

The subjects-of-subjects perspective provided not just a different way of seeing the issue of parliamentary supremacy but different ways of analyzing it. Parliament's claim of sovereignty was an attempt at "reducing the Americans beneath the rank of British subjects," David Williams explained. The host of Benjamin Franklin during the political storm of 1774 and a leading voice in Britain for religious tolerance, Williams accused the British of going to war with the colonies "not only for your *pecuniary* relief; but for your immediate *glory;* it was to give *you* subjects."[38]

Opponents of parliamentary sovereignty over the colonies could turn the subjects-of-subjects issue backward and forward, approaching it not just from the anomaly of Americans being subjects of Britons, but the constitutional abhorrency of any British subjects being the subjects of their fellow subjects. "The people of *America* are no more the subjects of the people of *Britain*, than the people of *Yorkshire* are the subjects of the people of *Middlesex*," Richard Price argued.[39] Solomon Southwick, a Rhode Island printer, wondered about the British as subjects of the colonists. "[T]he people of America," he concluded, "have as good a right to *legislate* for, & *tax*, the people of Great-Britain, as they [British] have to legislate for, and tax, the Americans."[40] Another Rhode Islander, a lawyer, looked at the issue from American analogies. "The claim of the commons to a sovereignty over us," Silas Downer told a Providence audience, "is founded by

them on their being the *Mother Country* . . . . Would it not be thought
strange if the commonalty of the *Massachusetts-Bay* should require our
obedience, because this colony was first settled from that dominion?"[41]

To start with the premise that they were the subjects of subjects allowed
American whigs to state the constitutional grievance in very strong terms.
The town meeting of Leicester, Massachusetts, for example, kept the com-
plaint simple: "we are oppressed by our fellow subjects the Commons of
Great Britain." Americans could also highlight their objections to being
governed by a Parliament corrupted with royal patronage and influence,
by saying that parliamentary sovereignty over the colonies not only put
American property "into the power of their fellow-subjects in *England*"
but "at the pleasure of any Minister who is knave enough to bribe an
English Parliament." In fact, corruption employed to bribe Parliament in
the future quite likely could be financed by American revenue. If thought
of in terms of a constitutional liberty, William Hicks pointed out, the colonists as subjects of the House of Commons were in greater danger than
were the people in the mother country. The British had to be on constant
guard to preserve their liberty "lest a designing minister should extend
the prerogative of the crown." Americans had to be even more alert. "They
have not only to guard their liberties against the encroachments of the
royal prerogative, but even to protect their property against the invasions
of their more powerful brethren."[42]

It is possible—although it is by no means certain—that the subjects-
of-subjects issue helped Americans to see more clearly the constitutional
solution toward which the doctrine of parliamentary sovereignty was driv-
ing them. The very fact that the colonists were subjects persuaded many
British constitutional theorists that they had to be under Parliament's authority to legislate. "The Americans," the argument went, "surely will not
deny they are subjects of Great Britain . . . and their being subjects, im-
plies subjection to the supreme authority; which in this country is vested
in King, Lords, and Commons. What are Americans subject to, if not to
the Legislature?"[43]

Americans agreed they were subjects, but not of the legislature. There
was another sovereign commanding their allegiance. "It is not easy to conceive," a New Yorker said of the members of Parliament, "how they, who
are but British subjects, came to be invested with a sovereign power over
the other subjects, as free as themselves, and under the same constitution
and common sovereign."[44] The assumption must not be made that Americans arrived at this conclusion late, any more than it should be understood
that the subjects-of-subjects issue developed late in the revolutionary controversy. Both perceptions were part of the American constitutional understanding before the controversy began with the Stamp Act. "I confess that

we have the same King with the good people of England," a correspondent told the *Providence Gazette* in August 1764, "but that the people of New England especially are dependent on the people of Britain, any more than the people of Britain are dependent on them, I utterly deny."[45] "I could wish," the same newspaper said less than a year later, "that some *civilian* would settle how for the *people* of *America* are dependent on the *people* of *Britain*: I know of no *dependence* or relation, only that we are all the common subjects of the same king."[46]

We will return to the constitutional logic of the American conclusion. It was not derived from the subjects-of-subjects issue. For the moment we are concerned only with the conclusion. It was never stated more clearly in relation to the subjects-of-subjects issue than by *Phocion* in a 1774 letter to the *Virginia Gazette*. "[T]o *you* we look for protection," he told George III, addressing the king directly, "*you* are the sovereign and ruler, and not our fellow subjects in parliament."[47] It was a matter of constitutional law, as an item printed in the *Virginia Gazette* less than four months earlier had explained. "*Allegiance* and *subjection* are due from a people to their sovereign; but the allegiance of subjects to subjects, is an absurdity unknown to the laws of this kingdom." It was also a matter of liberty. "The freedom of Britons consists in this, that they participate [in] the power of making those laws by which they are governed; and wherever this freedom is enjoyed, the legislative power must necessarily be confined to those who partake of it, either in person or delegation."[48] It was a matter of constitutional law, of liberty, and of representation.

CHAPTER SIX

THE REPRESENTATION ISSUE

In eighteenth-century British constitutional theory, representation was more than an element of liberty. It was the institutionalization of liberty in the House of Commons, the guardian created for liberty by the Glorious Revolution. The Continental Congress knew it was defying revolution principles, but believed it was expounding good constitutional law when, in its first address to the inhabitants of North America, it asserted that "the subjugating these Colonies, that are not, and, from local circumstances cannot be represented in the House of Commons, to the uncontrollable and unlimited power of Parliament," was "in violation of their undoubted rights and liberties."[1] This was the representation issue. It had been part of the controversy since the Stamp Act crisis and now was declared a continental grievance.

We know too little about constitutional law in the eighteenth century for anyone to make a definitive assertion, but it seems safe to suggest that with no other doctrine of constitutional law had American constitutional theory separated so much from English constitutional doctrine than with the concept of representation. American representation was not universal suffrage, but it was actual and direct, with all white males eligible to participate if they met statutory requirements. In England and Wales representation was vicarious and virtual, with custom, constitution, charter, and inheritance determining the electors and constitutional theory designating those electors as "the nation" on whose behalf the elected representative gave consent.[2] With the coming of the American Revolution, theory would begin to change in Great Britain and the impetus for change was the liberty imperative. When John Cartwright in his "Declaration of Rights," contended that "they, who have *no* vote in the electing of representatives in parliament, are *not* freemen, but are truly and really slaves to the representation of those who *have* votes," he was doing more than urging reform of British constitutional law. He was proposing that British constitutional law adopt American constitutional theory.[3]

Britons did not have to adopt the doctrine of actual representation to realize that there was contradiction between parliamentary supremacy over the colonies and American liberty. A student of the British constitution could believe that virtual representation protected the liberty for all citizens living in Great Britain yet admit that it did not protect Americans because they were not "represented." A "subject of Great Britain, *and there resident,* is the freest member of a civil society in the known world," a London publication suggested in 1776. It did not matter if the subject was a woman who, because of her sex, could not vote, or a man who did not qualify to be an elector and who also could not vote. Both had representation in the House of Commons, and it was that representation that made them free. "But if the Americans are not represented in that parliament which enacts their laws; and that parliament enacts separate laws for the Americans . . . surely their situation in point of liberty and freedom is just the reverse of that of British subjects resident in Great Britain."[4]

More than liberty was at stake. Obedience to government was as well. The legitimacy of public authority was anchored in representation. Late in the war, when the British army occupied sufficient territory for London to consider restoring royal rule, imperial agents would report that civilian control could not be reestablished over Americans without representation. Earlier, a month before the battle of Lexington, one of General Thomas Gage's spies reported why the people of Massachusetts were then giving their obedience not to Gage as governor but to the extralegal provincial Congress. There was, the spy wrote, "a natural fondness for old customs and a jealousy of sinister designs on the part of administration. Stripped of the means of exerting their popular influence in the usual channel the people have had recourse to Provincial Congress to which they would willingly annex the full powers of a regular representation."[5] It is possible that at that time, only consent through representation made power legitimate in American constitutional thought.

Although Sir William Blackstone claimed in a speech to the House of Commons that the authority to legislate was derived from sovereignty, not representation, he was not denying that representation, together with custom, was the basis of legitimate government in British constitutional theory. What he meant was that Parliament was sovereign because it was the constitutional representative of the British people and, for that reason, he also insisted that the Americans were constitutionally represented in the House of Commons. The right of representation was too well entrenched in constitutional thinking to have been denied in the eighteenth century. Representation and consent, with the rule of law and balanced government, were the four main elements of eighteenth-century British constitutionalism, with representation an element of the rule of law and a third part of the tripartite balance. The concept of representation was so essential to constitutionalism that they were linked in the political speech of the day. The Americans, John Cartwright would recall in 1796, "timely resisted the unconstitutional pretensions of an unconstitutional House of Commons over themselves." The House of Commons was unconstitutional because it was unrepresentative. Defending parliamentary supremacy over the colonies in a speech to the Continental Congress, Galloway admitted, "I am free to confess that the exercise of that authority is not perfectly constitutional in respect to the Colonies." He meant that it was based on virtual and not direct representation.[6]

Every important loyalist like Galloway had to grapple with the issue of representation. This is not the place to outline the difficulties they encountered. It will be enough to consider Galloway's jurisprudence when it is discussed in chapter 8. We should keep in mind, however, that he may have had more trouble than most other loyalists as he believed that representation was the only constitutional solution to the controversy over Parliament's authority to legislate for the colonies in all cases whatsoever. Despite what would become his militant loyalism after fighting began, Galloway thought that on the constitutional merits the American whig claims were stronger than those of Parliament. "The matters in dispute between the two countries lie in a very narrow compass," Galloway explained. "They may be all reduced to one great object, viz. *The right of the supreme authority of the State over the Colonies.*" On one hand, the British imperialist "contends, and justly contends, *for the necessity of a supreme authority over every part and member of the empire.*" On the other hand, "the Americans assert, that by the constitution of the English Government, settled and confirmed by the great Charter of Rights, it is essential to the freedom of America, that its landed interest or freeholders should be *represented* in the great Councils, which make the laws by which *their properties, their liberties, and their lives are to be* affected; and that without this the British Government is certainly *despotic* over them."[7]

The right to representation was called "the first established principle of the constitution," by the Assembly of Jamaica. Summarized, that principle was that "the people of England [meaning, Great Britain] have a right to partake, and do partake, of the legislation of their country, and that no laws can affect them but such as receive their assent, given by themselves or their representatives." The primary constitutional function of representation was to maintain the balance of balanced government by providing, as Viscount Barrington pointed out in his study of revolution principles, the third of the three "Bodies, which are a check to one another, to prevent any thing passing in a Law, that may be prejudicial to the Publick."[8]

Under one version of the eighteenth-century doctrine of attenuated, virtual representation, the American colonists certainly were represented in the British Parliament. For people to be represented it was not necessary for them to be empowered to vote for members of the House of Commons. Women, children, and nonelecting males were as much represented in Parliament as were the few electors resident in Great Britain, the men who actually cast votes in elections. These electors were, in theory, persons of means, forming an element in the population wealthy enough to remain independent of the crown's influence and not to be overawed by the aristocracy in the upper house, that is, to be counted upon to elect independent representatives who, by constituting the third house of the legislature, guaranteed it also would be independent, a true constitutional check. In this constitutional sense of the word "representation," Americans, along with other peoples throughout the empire, were "represented" in Parliament. This theory broke down when Americans applied to themselves the various safeguards that supposedly made the representatives in Parliament representative of the nonelectors resident in Great Britain.

One constitutional safeguard was the doctrine of local interests and local knowledge. Although existing more as theory than practice in eighteenth-century Britain, this doctrine supposed that representatives represented the interests, conditions, and circumstances of the constituency sending them to the House of Commons. This constituency was as often said to be property or the whole nation as the people of an electoral district. By any criterion, the doctrine was not applicable to the North American colonies. No imperial Parliament, Charles James Fox observed, "can legislate with justice and propriety, where the contingencies of locality and interests of individuality cannot be ascertained. Indeed, the greatest principle of legislation, in this instance is lost. —The representatives themselves having no local attachment for their constituents."[9]

A second safeguard for virtual representation was the doctrine of shared interests. In Parliament there was always some member who shared the interest of every nonelector and, therefore, represented the interests of that nonelector. It might be the shared interest of locality, profession, land ownership, trade, financial investment, or craft. When making decisions, legislators had these interests in mind and truly represented all persons with whom they shared those interests. In addition, there was the shared interest of the nation's welfare. "The members of parliament, their families, their friends, their posterity must be subject, as well as others, to the laws," the future United States Supreme Court justice, James Wilson, pointed out. "Their interest, and that of their families, friends, and posterity, cannot be different from the interest of the rest of the nation. A regard to the former will, therefore, direct to such measures as must promote the latter. But is this the case with respect to America?" It was a question that loyalists were apt to answer one way and whigs in quite a different way.[10]

The most important constitutional safeguard making members of Parliament representative of the unenfranchised was the doctrine of shared burdens. The nonelectors of Great Britain were protected and, therefore, represented by the representatives for whom they could not vote because those representatives could not impose on them burdens without imposing the same burdens on themselves and on the electors who had voted when they were elected. If Parliament authorized a land tax, for example, everyone in Great Britain, except members of the royal family, was liable to pay that tax, members of Parliament and electors just as much as nonelectors. It was with this doctrine—that legislators shared the burdens they imposed—that the justification of virtual representation most completely broke down when applied to Americans. In Great Britain, Richard Price explained, "it is impossible that the represented part should subject the unrepresented part to arbitrary power, without including themselves. But in the Colonies it is *not* impossible. We know that it *has* been done." More than that, there was strong incentive for Parliament to do it, especially with taxes. Taxes laid on Americans for purposes of a British revenue not only relieved the burdens on the constituents of members of the House of Commons, it relieved the burdens on the members themselves. "We have experienced," Wilson complained, "what an easy matter it is for a minister with an ordinary share of art, to persuade the parliament and the people, that taxes laid on the colonies will ease the burdens of the mother country." With the doctrine of shared burdens American whigs had an argument based in accepted constitutional theory for opposing the arbitrary authority of Parliament to legislate for the colonies. Can anything, a "Freeholder" of Worcester asked, "be more terrible than to yield up our lives, and property, to be solely at the arbitrary will of a parliament, which is under no restraint in our favor either of interest or affection; but whose interest and affection are against us."[11]

The failure of the doctrines of local interests, local knowledge, shared interests, and shared burdens was of greater importance to eighteenth-century Americans than historians have credited. At least that was the opinion of Joseph Galloway. In 1780 he attempted to explain the constitutional theories of loyalists who, like himself, were caught between the understanding that Parliament possessed supreme authority to legislate for the colonies in all cases whatsoever, and the realization that because the doctrines of local knowledge and shared interests did not operate for them, the Americans were unrepresented in Parliament. "They also saw," Galloway wrote, "that a Parliament in which they were not represented, in which no person and no property in America was represented; a parliament which had no constitutional means of knowing their wants, necessities, and circumstances, in order to regulate their conduct or to relieve their wants, was not so competent in reason, however it might be in law, to bind them."[12]

The legal premises that troubled these loyalists were changing in Great Britain. Before the American Revolution ended the British ministry admitted that in constitutional law as well as fact Americans were not represented in Parliament and made that admission motivation for policy. In his speech of July 1782, announcing that Great Britain's war effort would cease, Lord North's successor as leader of the administration, the earl of Shelburne, told the House of Commons that he "was a man who acted upon Revolution principles, and was a friend to the constitution and to the liberties of the people." He was also, Shelburne said, a great "enemy" of the American war, and "had always contended, that it was unjust in its principle, because it militated against that great maxim of our constitution, which declares, that English subjects, in whatsoever quarter of the globe, had right to the benefit of the British constitution, the most boasted and peculiar franchise of which was, to be governed by those laws only which they themselves had enacted, either in person or by their Representatives." He gave no other motivations for ending the conflict except to mention misfortunes, probably the battle of Yorktown, and to note that the British people had turned against the war. The only constitutional reason that Shelburne gave for ending the war, therefore, was the principle of representation. In the context of 1782 when the fighting ended, the earl was applying an emerging British principle of representation. In the context of 1775 when the fighting started the principle that Shelburne stated was American, not British.[13]

The Autonomy Issue

There was yet another doctrine eighteenth-century constitutionalists used to define representative government, the doctrine of consent. It has been extensively discussed in relation to Parliament's authority to tax,[14] and the doctrine of consent to legislation is close enough to the doctrine of consent to taxation that it does not require separate treatment. The constitutional theory was that just as taxes could not be imposed on citizens without their consent or the consent of their representatives, no laws binding them could be made or abrogated without their consent or the consent of their representatives.[15] One of the most basic principles of English constitutionalism, the doctrine of consent was not only part and parcel with the authority to tax,[16] but also part and parcel with the liberty issue[17] and the right of representation.[18]

Consent should not be mistaken for a fiction. It was a rule of constitutional law, more vicarious than actual in application, and more often implied from facts, circumstances, and institutions than conferred by direct participation. That people interpreted facts in contrary ways and drew different implications from the same historical events, did not weaken the legal reality of consent but rather is evidence of the importance given to it by eighteenth-century students of constitutional government. The same historical event could imply a different meaning of consent to each side of the revolutionary conflict. From the fact that their ancestors had freely migrated to the New World, for example, American whigs implied that the first settlers had intended to carry with them, and by agreement with the English sovereign had taken with them, all their common-law and constitutional rights, including the right to consent to legislation either in person or through a representation, a right that they surely intended would be exercised in a colonial assembly where they would have representation, not in Parliament where they would be without direct representation.[19] Some American imperialists thought the whigs' theory important enough to answer with a counter implication drawn from the same migration. "[C]onsidered in a legal and constitutional view," *Phileirene* wrote in the *Boston News-Letter* a few days before the war started at Lexington,

> our very existence as Colonies, renders us dependent upon the parent state, and subject to it's laws; with an implied consent to this, our ancestors emigrated hither, and received charters and laws expressly declaring it; with such consent, we continue the inhabitants of the Colonies, and consequently by the acts [of Parliament] here complain'd of, *our property is not taken from us without our consent.* [20]

It was the migration by the same ancestors, but a different consent and a diametrically different theory of the authority to legislate.

A fact worth evaluating is that few American loyalists based their case for parliamentary supremacy on the doctrine of sovereignty alone. They usually treated the doctrine of consent just as seriously as did colonial whigs. Perhaps they had no choice. Consent was too much part of British constitutionalism to be disregarded, even by sovereignty. There were, of course, differences. American imperialists established the consent which they gave to Parliament's supremacy in the same virtual or constructive way that the consent of British nonelectors was found: by the acquiesence implied by their birth, their ancestors' prior consent, and their continued citizenship in the nation. American whigs by contrast, although they might also imply the consent of nonelectors, stressed the representation as much as those represented. Consent was constitutional when the representation possessed local knowledge, levied equal assessments, and shared both the interests of the constituency and the burdens imposed. It was this concept of consent, as much as actual participation, that the Continental Congress meant when it defined the right to constitutional representation. "It is a fundamental Principle of the *British* Constitution," the Congress told the inhabitants of Great Britain one year before the Declaration of Independence, "that every Man should have at least a Representative Share in the Formation of those Laws by which he is bound."

In that sentence, Congress summarized the right of representation. In the next it summarized the representation grievance. "Were it otherwise," Congress said, referring to the right of every person to "at least a Representative Share," "the Regulation of our internal Police by a *British* Parliament, who are and ever will be unacquainted with our local Circumstances, must be always inconvenient, and frequently oppressive, working our wrong, without yielding any possible Advantage to You."[21]

The representation grievance could also be stated in terms of consent, as the Massachusetts General Court stated it when charging that the ministry was attempting "to establish a sovereignty in America, not founded in the consent of the people, but in the mere will of persons a thousand leagues from us, whom we know not, and have endeavoured to establish this sovereignty over us, against our consent, in all cases whatsoever."[22]

In addition to local knowledge and consent, there was a third way to state the grievance: to say that there was a right to legislative autonomy. That was the right Lord North found so offensive in the famous Remonstrance from the New York General Assembly that he persuaded the House of Commons not to receive because "the said Assembly claim to themselves rights derogatory to, and inconsistent with, the Legislative authority of Parliament." It is likely that the Commons took even greater offense at the way the autonomy right was stated by the General Assembly in its companion memorial to the House of Lords. There the issue was stated in terms of representation, consent, security, equality, and the royal prerogative. Moreover, the origins of the right to autonomy were traced to the authority of migration.

> [T]he Colonists carried with them all the rights they were entitled to in the country from which they emigrated; but as from their local circumstances they were precluded from sharing in the representation in that Legislature in which they *had been* represented, they of right claimed and enjoyed a Legislature of their own, always acknowledging the King, or his representative, as one branch thereof. This right they have pointedly, repeatedly, and zealously asserted, as what only could afford them that security which their fellow subjects in *Great Britain* enjoy . . . ; because no money can be raised upon the subject in *Great Britain*, nor any law made that is binding on him, without the concurrence of those who have been elected by the PEOPLE to represent them.[23]

Thomas Hutchinson had a talent defining eighteenth-century constitutional concepts. No other imperial official more strenuously opposed the autonomy right, yet no one stated it more accurately than he. "[E]very colony," the governor explained, "has a legislature within itself, the acts and doings of which are not to be controuled by parliament, and that no legislative power ought to be exercised over the colonies, except by their respective legislatures."[24] Although Hutchinson, as the historian of Massachusetts Bay, appreciated that this constitutional theory had been prevalent in New England in the seventeenth century,[25] it probably was not known in London until it was expounded by the various Stamp Act resolutions of 1765 with respect to the authority to tax. Patrick Henry later recalled that his famous Virginia Resolves had asserted "that the General Assembly of this Colony have the *only and sole exclusive* Right and Power to lay Taxes and Impositions upon the Inhabitants of this Colony." The Maryland Stamp Act Resolves claimed "that the Representatives of the Freemen of this Province in their Legislative Capacity together with the other part of the Legislature have the Sole Right to lay Taxes and Impositions on the Inhabitants of this Province or their Property and effects."[26] These constitutional principles were restated throughout the prerevolutionary controversy, with little change in wording from assembly to assembly.[27] Toward the end of the period, the North Carolina Provincial Congress recast the taxation autonomy principle into a general constitutional right belonging to all the colonies. "[O]ur Provincial Assemblies," it voted, "the King by his governors constituting one branch thereof, solely and exclusively possess that right."[28]

Earlier, at the time that taxation was the area of parliamentary legislation in controversy, when colonial assemblies were successfully avoiding the question of general legislative autonomy,[29] knowledgeable imperial officials were reporting to London that American constitutional theory claimed exclusive legislative authority in all internal matters, not just taxation for purposes of raising revenue.[30] Although some of the lesser units of colonial government, such as town meetings, asserted that the assemblies possessed legislative authority exclusive "of all other powers of legislators in the world,"[31] the lower houses of assembly in North America seem to have been able to avoid the question until Governor Thomas Hutchinson forced the Massachusetts General Court to state a position. Hutchinson was reacting to resolutions adopted by a number of towns in the colony that he thought amounted to declarations of independence from all British authority except the crown. Believing that "the wound may be skinned over but can never be healed until it be laid open to the bone," Hutchinson decided he had to explain correct constitutional principles to Americans and blundered into the most serious mistake made by any imperial official in the colonies prior to 1775. He commenced a constitutional debate with both houses of the General Court.[32]

The problem, Hutchinson explained to his superior in London, "is a false opinion, broached at the time of the Stamp Act and ever since cultivated until it is become general, that the people of the colonies are subject to no authority but their own legislatures and that the Acts of the Parliament of Great Britain, which is every day in print termed a foreign state, are not obligatory." Until people learned differently, he saw little hope for enforcing parliamentary statutes in Massachusetts. "I know the cause of the disease but am at a loss for a proper remedy," Hutchinson concluded. Within two months he thought there might be a cure. If he debated constitutional law with whigs in the General Court he could talk over their heads to the people, propagate proper constitutional principles and, it was to be hoped, false doctrines recently voted by town meetings would be repudiated. In his opening message to the first session of the General Court in 1773, the governor, interpreting resolutions passed by the town of Boston, stated the autonomy issue:

It has been urged, that the sole Power of making Laws is granted by Charter to a Legislature established in the Province . . . that it is Part of the Liberties of English Subjects, which has its Foundation in Nature to be governed by Laws made by their Consent in Person or by their Representative—that the Subjects in this Province are not and cannot be Represented in the Parliament of Great Britain and, consequently, the Acts of Parliament cannot be binding upon them.

Hutchinson then carefully and correctly explained the law.

> I do not find, Gentlemen, in the Charter such an Expression as *sole* Power or any Words which import it. The General Court has, by Charter, *full* Power to make such Laws as are not repugnant to the Laws of England. A favourable Construction has been put upon this Clause when it has been allowed to intend such Laws of England only as are expres[s]ly declared to respect us. Surely then this is by Charter a Reserve of Power and Authority to Parliament to bind us by such Laws, at least, as are made expressly to refer to us and, consequently, is a Limitation of the Power given to the General Court.[33]

For the first time a colonial legislative body could not avoid the autonomy issue. Governor Hutchinson had laid down the imperial constitution and challenged the Massachusetts General Court to put some answer on the record. Both the House of Representatives and the Council had to reply. It is believed that John Adams, who was not a member, was recruited to write the answer for the House. For authority he turned to the right of representation and the second original contract which was, of course, the implied compact between Charles I and the original settlers of the Massachusetts Bay colony, for which the charter was evidence. Those settlers had migrated to a dominion not part of the realm of England, freeing them "from the Subjection they were under before their Removal," because the "Power and Authority of Parliament" was "constitutionally confined within the Limits of the Realm and Nation collectively, of which alone it is the Representing and Legislative Assembly."

> Your Excellency further asks, "Will it not rather be said, that by their voluntary Removal, they have relinquished for a Time at least, one of the Rights of an English Subject, which they might if they pleased have continued to enjoy, and may again enjoy, whenever they return to the Place where it can be exercised?" To which we answer; They never did relinquish the Right to be governed by Laws made by Persons in whose Election they had a Voice. The King . . . stipulated with them that they should enjoy and exercise this most essential Right . . . ; and they did and ought still to exercise it, without the Necessity of returning, for the Sake of exercising it, to the Nation or State of England.

We have seen John Adams employ this forensic method before: using anachronistic history to fashion a constitutional argument.[34] The eighteenth-century British right of representation—the right to have two branches of the legislature, the crown and the hereditary aristocracy, checked by a third branch representative of a small independent part of the nation was transformed into the eighteenth-century American right of representation—"the Right to be governed by Laws made by Persons in whose Election they had a Voice." Then Adams took that eighteenth-century American right and made it a stipulation of the seventeenth-century second original contract between Charles I and the settlers of Massachusetts Bay. It was a clever example of forensic history, but did it make good law?[35]

London thought it made new law and reacted strongly. During the debate on the Boston Port Bill, Lord North cited the answer to Hutchinson as reason for punishing Boston. At Boston, he announced, "we are considered as two independent states." The dispute no longer was about taxation but "whether or not we have any authority there." "[We are] now disputing, not I trust with the whole colonies, but with those who have maintained that we have as a Parliament no legislative right over them. That we are two [in]dependent states under the same Prince. That is the opinion that has been held by several of the towns of Massachusetts Bay . . . held, likewise, by the Assembly . . . in answer to the Speech of the Governor."[36]

North soon learned his error. Parliament was disputing with all the colonies. The American theory of representation, direct not virtual, actual not constructive, dictated legislative autonomy. Americans were not represented in Parliament, therefore Parliament could not consent for Americans. The authority to legislate was vested exclusively in the colonial assemblies, "except," of course, "in the instance of regulating Trade," as Joseph Hawley put it.[37] Had war been avoided and a settlement reached, the exception might have been broader, along the lines of a proposal by New York's General Assembly when it told the House of Lords: "we shall always cheerfully submit to the CONSTITUTIONAL exercise of the supreme regulating power lodged in the King, Lords, and Commons of Great Britain, and to all Acts calculated for the general weal of the Empire, and the due regulation of the Trade and Commerce thereof."[38]

That statement reached the constitutional limit. It is doubtful if any American assembly would have gone further. The legislative autonomy issue was the one on which colonial whigs at an early date took a relatively extreme, uncompromising position, as, for example, the North Carolina Provincial Congress which asserted that "the Legislature of this province, have the exclusive power of making laws to regulate our internal Polity subject to his Majesty's disallowance."[39] If there is any aspect of these resolutions to be marked, it is the emphasis given to the prerogative. In 1774 there were many American whigs still royalist enough to put the king first even when asserting the right to autonomy; to say, "That the King at the head of his American Assemblies, constitutes a supreme Legislature in the respective Colonies, and that as Free men we can be bound by no law, but such as we assent to, either by ourselves, or our Representatives."[40] They were admitting that although they had to have legislative autonomy to assure local consent to law, that should all representatives assent, yet the crown veto, there would be no constitutional consent.

There is no need to consider the counterarguments of the loyalists. They were the same as those of the administration in London: that "subordinate Legislative power" could not be autonomous because sovereignty was indivisible, that there could not be two supreme legislatures, and that in the empire there could only be one sovereign legislature.[41] The American whig constitutional theory was much more complicated. Legislative autonomy was grounded, in part, on the apparently self-evident principle that Parliament did not have a right to legislate for the internal governance of the colonies either because, as the Assembly of Jamaica explained, it would make the colonists subjects of subjects,[42] or because time had made the colonists a separate people,[43] who, by custom and prescription, enacted laws for themselves in "Legislatures, duly constituted and appointed with their own consent."[44] This theory, that Parliament simply did not have the authority to legislate and that, therefore, the power of colonial assemblies was autonomous, was summarized by resolutions of Spottsylvania County, Virginia:

> That the Colonies, since their separation from *Great Britain* having no representation in the *British* Parliament, and having Parliaments of their own, under the authority of the same King, adequate to all purposes of legislation, the *British* Parliament can have no power of making laws for the government of the Colonies, but in such cases wherein the authority of the Colony Assembly does not extend.

It followed as a constitutional principle and a political right, "That we owe no obedience to any Act of the British Parliament that is, or shall be made, respecting the internal police of this Colony, and that we will oppose any such Acts with our lives and fortunes."[45]

More commonly, American whigs preferred to state their claims to legislative autonomy on British constitutional principles rather than on the negative proposition that Parliament lacked authority. These were the principles that have been outlined in this chapter. One principle was liberty: liberty would be endangered if "the sole right of making laws for the Government of this his Majesty's ancient Colony and Dominion of *Virginia*" was not "vested in the General Assembly of the said Colony."[46] A second was equality: "we have, within ourselves, the exclusive right of originating each and every law respecting ourselves, and ought to be on equal footing with his majesty's subjects in Great Britain."[47] The primary theory for claiming legislative autonomy combined the British constitutional principle of consent and local knowledge[48] with the American constitutional principle of the right of direct representation. "That it is the inherent right of British subjects," two Virginia counties resolved, "to be governed and taxed by representatives chosen by themselves only, and that every act of the British parliament respecting the internal policy of North America is a dangerous and unconstitutional invasion of our rights and privileges."[49]

The American assemblies gave the Continental Congress the last constitutional word, and very early in its deliberations it endorsed the doctrine of legislative autonomy. In the pivotal Resolution Four, the statement in which the delegates resolved the issue of why Parliament had authority to regulate trade—by acquiesence to which the colonists "cheerfully" consented—the principle of legislative autonomy was located in "English" and natural or general liberty.[50]

> Resolved, 4. That the foundation of English liberty, and of all free government, is a right in the people to participate in their legislative council: and as the English colonists are not represented, and from their local and other circumstances, cannot properly be represented in the British parliament, they are entitled to a free and exclusive power of legislature in their several provincial legislatures, where their right of representation can alone be preserved, in all cases of taxation and internal polity, subject only to the negative of their sovereign, in such manner as has been heretofore used and accustomed.[51]

It was liberty that underlay the right to legislative autonomy, a liberty, however, that was defined by both the American doctrine of participation through representation and the English-British doctrine of consent given by a representative legislature.[52]

CHAPTER SEVEN

REPRESENTATION SOLUTIONS

To consider for the last time the representation grievance it may be helpful to state the issue in words incorporating both the British and American constitutional theories of representation. "We present, as a grievance of the first magnitude, the right claimed by the *British* Parliament to Tax us, and by their Acts to bind us in all cases whatsoever," the grand jury told the judges of Cheraw District, South Carolina, in November 1774. "When we reflect on our other grievances, they all appear trifling in comparison with this; for if we may be taxed, imprisoned, and deprived of life, by the force of edicts to which neither we nor our constitutional Representatives have ever assented, no slavery can be more abject than ours."[1]

By using the words "constitutional Representatives" rather than "actual representatives," the grand jurors were stating the grievance in a way that could have contemplated the current British theory of representation, not what they probably intended, the American theory. In Great Britain, constitutional representation was the legal criterion. A writer in London, calling himself the *Constitutional Advocate* and seeking a solution to the American Revolution, reexamined the doctrine of representation in 1776. "In the *British* Government," he explained, "every free Subject has absolutely in himself, a Part of the Supreme Power: and before he can be bound by it's Decisions, he must have delegated his Share to a Representative of his choosing, who is to act for him in the national Council." That notion of popular sovereignty was mainstream constitutional theory, endorsed by tory as well as whig, and by the British even more than Americans who, due to their emphasis on a constitutional need to restrain legislative power tended to be more monarchical, at least until 1776. The aspect of the theory about which British and Americans had drawn apart was the concept of constitutional representation. The British theory of representation was summarized by a second political observer seeking a solution to the American conflict. "The consent of the whole," he explained in 1775, "must, in the British government, be included in that of a part, because by the constitution, only a part have votes for representatives; and as by the consent of that part, the supreme power is constituted and perfected, so it becomes constitutionally binding upon the whole, and must necessarily be so, until every individual has a voice in the election."[2]

Under British rules of constitutional representation, Americans were not only represented in the House of Commons but in the House of Lords, and if taxed or bound by Parliament's legislation they were taxed and bound by consent. They had consented constitutionally, for, "so long as they approve of that form of government, and continue under it, so long do they consent to whatever is done by those they have entrusted with their rights. This is the *British Constitution*."[3] It was not, however, the American constitution, and although today we may find it hard to understand, most people in Great Britain who commented on the colonial representation grievance in the 1770s did not realize what the Americans were saying. One who thought that he did was the *Constitutional Advocate*. "The Supreme Power then, requisite to bind the Colonists," he explained, "is incomplete, till by delegating their inherent Right, to Representatives of their chusing, they are admitted to their constitutional Participation of it." That statement is correct if read from the perspective of twentieth-century representation. In the eighteenth century, however, the Americans were not thinking of universal manhood suffrage or of citizen participation. American whigs, rather, rejected the British notion, inherited from the Glorious Revolution that the institutional role of the representative branch of the legislature was to be independent, not just representative, because its primary constitutional function was to guard the liberty of the nation, not to legislate the wishes of a constituency.[4]

Americans appreciated the institutional role of the House of Commons. Had they direct representation in the Commons it was conceivable that Parliament would have guarded their liberty. The rights of Great Britain, after all, "are solely divided between the King and the People of it, and as no Bill can pass without the Assent of both Parties; and had we a Negative in the British Legislature, such Laws might constitutionally extend to us also, because they could have no force without our Concurrence."[5] The analogy was flawed because it contemplated the members of the Commons as representatives looking out for the interests of the locality rather than as independent agents providing the third weight of the tripartite balanced government that no longer was balanced. To have the "Negative in the British Legislature" the Americans needed "actual" representatives, or so some observers of the imperial scene claimed. Actual representation, they said, was the solution to the controversy. "This is the Palladium of their cause," Governor Francis Bernard had argued in 1765 referring to colonial whigs, and he never gave up his belief that American representation in the House of Commons would remedy London's imperial problems.[6]

It is interesting that it was primarily imperial officials in the colonies who thought that actual representation could resolve the conflict,[7] governors like Bernard of Massachusetts and William Franklin of New Jersey, and former governor Thomas Pownall.[8] Hardly anyone in London wanted American representation. The most influential exception was George Grenville.[9] There was even less support among American whigs,[10] with James Otis almost alone speaking out for representation,[11] another sign, perhaps, of his eccentricity.

Governor Bernard cannot be blamed for making so much of American representation. From where he sat, it would have been the solution to all issues. First, actual American representation in Parliament would have ended the taxation controversy. "If the parliament cant tax the Americans because they are not represented," he reasoned, "it may allow them representatives, & the Authority is compleat."[12] By the same process the dispute over the authority to legislate in general would have been resolved.[13] "[A]n American Representation," the governor insisted, "will absolutely take away all Pretence of disputing the Ordinances of Parliament."[14] It would also make Parliament better informed on colonial circumstances by giving Americans an opportunity to state their grievances before legislation was enacted.[15] As a result, American representation in the Commons could have united the several parts of the British empire. For "if there is any Danger of its falling to pieces," Bernard argued, "[i]t seems to me that Nothing would so Effectually guard against so fatal an Event, as binding the Colonies to the Mother Country by incorporating Union And giving them a Share in the Sov'reign Legislature." "If they will not be obedient to Parliament without Representatives," he concluded, "In Gods Name let them have them."[16]

THE PROBLEMS OF REPRESENTATION

Although there is slight direct supporting evidence, it has to be suspected that one reason there was so little talk of American representation in Parliament is that once people thought about the mechanics of this arrangement they saw too many problems. When the knowledgeable William Knox suggested a plan, Edmund Burke chided him for not having "troubled his head with the infinite difficulty of settling that representation on a fair balance of wealth and numbers throughout the several provinces of America and the West-Indies, under such an infinite variety of circumstances."[17] By just mentioning the West Indies Burke revealed a problem that most commentators did not even consider. What about the other colonies, the ones not likely to join a rebellion? On the North American continent there were Quebec, Nova Scotia, and the two Floridas. In addition to all the West Indian islands, some of which had recently been conquered and whose voters would have been Roman Catholics, there were the possessions in Asia which could have meant representation for the East India Company.[18] Then, too, there was Ireland. No one discussed problems of equality, as, for example, whether Georgia or Pennsylvania could send members to Parliament and also keep their own assemblies, while Ireland was left with just its subordinate, unrepresentative Parliament.[19]

There were several questions which might never have been answered because there could be no agreement. One was the number of representatives. Governor Bernard felt "30 for the Continent & 15 for the Islands would be sufficient," Attorney General Maseres thought there should be a total of 80, and John Adams, on the assumption that the mainland colonies had half Great Britain's population, said that the 13 colonies were entitled to 250 members.[20] Just to have mentioned parity would have created endless controversy, not only because London would never have accepted it, but even more because it was not a factor in the British theory of representation. Members of Parliament did not represent equal numbers of people or equal geography, they represented property, interests, and "the condition of the country."[21] Benjamin Franklin had been thinking British thoughts, not American thoughts, in the 1750s when he suggested it would be enough if the colonies were given a "reasonable" rather than an equal number of representatives. "It is not that I imagine so many representatives will be allowed the Colonies, as to have any great weight by their numbers," he admitted, "but I think there might be sufficient, to occasion those laws [restricting colonial trade and manufacturing] to be better and more impartially considered, and perhaps to overcome the interest of a petty corporation, or of any particular set of artificers or traders in England, who heretofore seem, in some instances, to have been more regarded than all the Colonies." It is worth noting that once the revolutionary controversy began, Franklin no longer favored American representation.[22]

There was a bit of debate on the mechanical problems of an American representation, especially the process of election and the procedures of contested elections. Governor Pownall thought the only problem was that newly elected American members would be late arriving for a session of Parliament. Edmund Burke replied that the problems of remoteness were so serious they were insurmountable.

> The writs are issued for electing members for America and the West Indies. Some provinces receive them in six weeks, some in ten, some in twenty. A vessel may be lost, and then some provinces may not receive them at all. But let it be, that they all receive them at once, and in the shortest time. A proper space must be given for proclamation and for the election; some weeks at least. But the members are chosen; and, if ships are ready to sail, in about six more they arrive in London. In the mean time the parliament has sat and business far advanced without American representatives. Nay, by this time, it may happen, that the parliament is dissolved; and then the members ship themselves again, to be again elected. The writs may arrive in America, before the poor members of a parliament in which they never sat can arrive at the several provinces.

And what about reelection? Burke wondered. "[I]s the American member the only one who is not to take a place, or the only one to be exempted from the ceremony of re-election?"[23]

There were ideas for getting around the problems. For example, if Americans were elected for set terms there would be no need for the king's writ. Maseres said they should be elected for one year.[24] Another plan was to have elections every seven years,[25] which would have meant that American representatives were always on hand, ready to serve no matter how often and how quickly elections were called, especially if a representative voted out of office was permitted to hold the seat until his replacement arrived in London. If the last solution were used in all cases there would have been no need for set terms or separate colonial elections. Were American representatives elected by writ like British representatives, Governor Pownall suggested, "the old representatives of the Colonies, might by law, be permitted to sit in the new parliament, (if assembled within six months) until they were re-elected, or others sent in their room."[26]

Supposing elections could be held, there was the problem of who could be elected.[27] It seemed obvious that no one should be a representative who would be ineligible in Great Britain either because of religion or because he did not possess estates of independent means.[28] There were residents in every colony who met the requirements of an estate worth £300 a year, but outside of Virginia and the West Indies there were few who could afford the expense of living in London where they would have to reside not only for the sessions but the long recesses of Parliament. "Connecticut and Massachusetts Bay," Burke protested, "have not in each of them two men who can afford, at a distance from their estates, to spend a thousand pounds a year. How can these provinces be represented at Westminster?" One answer was to have the colony pay them, but that would have violated the constitutional principle that members of Parliament were "independent" and would have meant that American representatives were paid while British representatives were not.[29] Moreover, the expense would have been too great: "If . . . each of the colonies be admitted to send four members to parliament (which number will give them no great weight in the house of commons, which consists of 558 members) the charge of supporting them will amount to £4000 . . . which vastly exceeds the current expenses of government in most of them."[30]

To have had the crown pay salaries was unthinkable. It would have made American representatives the worst of all eighteenth-century political bugbears, "pensioners and dependants at court."[31] Yet none of the other suggestions how the colonies could afford representatives were any better. It was, for example, suggested that many men resident in the mother country would have been happy to represent the colonies, even that there were "more Jamaica men alone in England than will be sufficient for all America."[32] Consider the "sorts of persons" living in Great Britain who, some British commentators said, would have made excellent representatives for the colonies: (1) former imperial officials such as governors, chief justices, and army officers who had served in the colonies; (2) merchants who did business with North America and knew "the mercantile interests of the Colonies they trade to, and would be sincerely concerned for their welfare"; and (3) "English gentlemen of independent fortune."[33] What does it tell us that educated, literate observers of political affairs could make such suggestions? Perhaps it is striking evidence of how little people in Great Britain thought of representatives as representing anything except the independent interests of the nation. Then again, it may tell us what they thought of Americans.

REPRESENTATION REJECTED

The topic of American representation would deserve extensive discussion were we concerned with the eighteenth-century meaning of representation or eighteenth-century jurisprudence. In a study of the authority of Parliament to legislate for the American colonies, however, the subject does not merit much attention because it was never a viable constitutional solution to the revolutionary controversy. George Grenville is said to have abandoned all thought of making American representation official administration policy after concluding that "the House of Commons would not endure the proposition."[34] Governor Pownall, however, did not give up on the representation solution until 1774. In the fourth edition of his *Administration of the British Colonies* he continued to argue that "[t]here is no other practicable or rational measure." In the fifth edition, he explained, he had dropped the plan "since America as well as Great Britain will have it so."[35] "We wretched empirics who have entertained the idea," he lamented, "have been treated as Utopians."[36] Pownall was referring to people like Burke who thought American representation in the House of Commons "impossible" and said no minister would "be wild enough even to propose such a representation in parliament."[37] Secretary at War Lord Barrington used that argument to discourage Governor Bernard, telling him that "no Influence could make ten Members of either House of Parliament agree to such a Remedy."[38]

British opposition to American representation in Parliament ranged from the extreme of the sovereignty absolute—that the Americans were subjects of Parliament and it would be "a piece of self-denial" to admit they were not constitutionally represented in the Commons[39]—to the argument that representation would harm the colonists by making them a permanent minority.[40] It was said, of course, that by migrating to North America, the colonists themselves had "voluntarily" created the "impossibility" of representation,[41] and that representation would be of no benefit to them without other constitutional protections such as the rule that "every tax imposed upon America was to be at the same time imposed upon ourselves."[42] Moreover, because the Atlantic Ocean was so wide, it would become "almost as great a mockery as virtual representation"[43] since American representatives would not know the sentiments of their electors or even their current circumstances.[44] They would not, for example, be able to receive instructions from constituents about how to vote on legislation introduced unexpectedly. At that time, instructions were an important element of the American theory of representation, especially in New England.[45]

The main British objections to American representation in Parliament concerned the potential harm it might inflict on the mother country. The House of Commons, already too large,[46] could, with the addition of Americans and West Indians, become "such a numerous, tumultuous, unwieldy, and unmanageable body, as might give an opportunity to a powerful faction, to overset the throne; or, to a bold and able minister, to enslave the people."[47] Then too, where would a line be drawn? If New Hampshire or North Carolina must have representation, "why should not the isles of Guernsey and Jersey be represented as well as the isle of Wight," or for that matter, Leeds or Manchester?[48] Even if American representation did not threaten to undermine the established constitution, it could introduce political chaos, "from the incompatibility of their partial interests with ours, in matters of trade and manufactures."[49] Certain to form an opposition to every tax or regulation proposed for the colonies, the American members would also "be a party, a faction, a flying squadron, always ready, and in most cases capable, (by uniting with opposition to administration, or with commercial factions,) to distress government, and the landed interest of the kingdom."[50]

The most serious objection to American representation voiced by British commentators, the one that appears to have persuaded people in the mother country, was the predicted growth of colonial populations. Even if representation was very unequal, the sheer numbers of Americans eventually would overwhelm Great Britain. "The idea of a representative from that country is dangerous, absurd and impractical," the usually pro-American Isaac Barré warned. "They will grow more numerous than we are, and then how inconvenient and dangerous would it be to have representatives of 7 millions there meet the representatives of 7 millions here."[51] The result was inevitable: an always growing population producing new colonies needing more representation. "The increase of number, and the occupation and cultivation of new lands, would lay a foundation of equal right, for the same claim of representation, at least every twenty-five or thirty years," a London writer observed in 1768, referring to the period of time that, according to generally accepted theory, the American population would double. "This representation of America would, therefore, in a very short time, overbalance the natural representation of Great Britain; the interest of America would preponderate; and that of the mother country would be lost."[52] The outcome was as certain as tomorrow. The colonial interest would become predominant, the capital would be moved to Philadelphia, and "Great-Britain, from being the head of a vast empire, will dwindle away to an American province."[53]

Americans were on record at the highest levels of their government— the colonial assemblies—as opposing representation in the House of Commons even before the Stamp Act crisis.[54] Members of the Massachusetts House of Representatives had a favorite word, "impracticable," to make the point emphatic. Representation in Parliament was "impracticable for the subjects in America," they resolved at the height of the Stamp Act crisis. "[A] representation of your Majesty's subjects of this province in the Parliament, considering their local circumstances, is utterly impracticable," they told George III during the Townshend duties controversy, and then two days later wrote the leader of the administration, the marquis of Rockingham, that American representation was "impracticable."[55] Toward the end of the controversy, in his famous *Novanglus* letters, John Adams was repeating the same word: an American representation in Parliament, he wrote, was "totally impracticable." So too, interestingly enough, wrote the loyalist with whom Adams was debating constitutional law. "Were it possible for the colonies to have an equal representation to parliament, and it were refused upon proper application," Daniel Leonard explained in his *Massachusettensis* letters, "I confess I should think it a grievance; but at present it seems to be allowed, by all parties, to be impracticable, considering the colonies are distant from Great-Britain a thousand transmarine leagues."[56] Leonard was right about "all parties." One constitutional conclusion on which colonial whigs and American loyalists were agreed was that an American representation in Parliament would be "impracticable."

Leonard thought distance alone made representation impractical, and almost every other American who wrote about the question concurred. The distance was just too much to contemplate, especially for whigs. It should be noted that when most colonial whigs thought of government in Great Britain they thought of a corrupt Parliament controlled by court patronage and ministerial influence. That perception made distance a more serious problem than merely the delays and communication hindrances which would result. Could even principled Americans of high virtues resist temptation so far from home in so different a moral culture?[57] Their constituents, after all, "could have no Opportunity of knowing or directing the Conduct of their Delegates" or of evaluating their service.[58] John Adams outlined some problems of distance by asking a series of questions: "6. Could American representatives, possibly know the sense, the exigencies, &c. of their constituents, at such a distance, so perfectly as it is absolutely necessary legislators should know? 7. Could Americans ever come to the knowledge of the behaviour of their members, so as to dismiss the unworthy?"[59] Not only were the answers "no," but just thinking about distance taught colonial whigs another argument against parliamentary legislation. Parliament was too far away.[60]

Americans also had institutional and national grounds for refusing representation in Parliament. Representation, colonial whigs argued, was "unnecessary, because they have legislatures of their own, which answer all their purposes,"[61] and, besides, they were a separate, distinct people who were properly represented in separate legislatures.[62] It was not unreasonable either, for Americans to think their representation in local assemblies more complete than any they could obtain in Parliament. There American representation would have been limited to the House of Commons with no American peers sitting in the House of Lords. That was not an immaterial consideration, after all, as the Lords were an equal part of the legislature, passing on money bills, as well as framing and amending all other kinds of law.[63]

Had all these objections not existed, there was one more that settled the question for most Americans: a fundamental objection to representation in Parliament, so serious that the colonists would never have agreed to it. Even in the single branch of the House of Commons, American representation would not be equal, indeed, it would never be close to equal. "We are far however from desiring any Representation" in Parliament, the Massachusetts House of Representatives explained in December 1765, "because we think the Colonies cannot be equally and fully represented; and if not equally then in Effect not at all."[64]

To some extent it was a matter of practicality. "Great Britain will never offer us such a number of representatives in the house, as would give us any considerable weight or influence there," a correspondent told the *Pennsylvania Journal*. "To allow the colonies such a number of members in the house of commons, as would enable them to carry points against the mother country, when a competition of interests arises, would be in effect to resign her own independency, which we may be assured she never will do."[65] In fact, it was as much a matter of constitutional theory as of political practicalities. British constitutional theory with its emphasis on the legitimacy, even the necessity of vicarious or virtual representation, just could not attribute the importance to equal representation that American constitutional theory did.[66] Even in 1778, after Parliament had renounced the authority to tax and the administration was inclined to satisfy most American demands, peace commissioners were instructed that if American representation in Parliament was stipulated in the treaty the numbers were "to be very small."[67]

Americans knew that representation in Parliament would have to be by British constitutional theory and on British terms. About all it would have accomplished constitutionally would have been to make stronger Parliament's claim to the authority to legislate for the colonies in all cases whatsoever.[68] "It is indeed hard to conceive of a worse system of government than that to which we shall subject ourselves, if we accept of a representation in parliament," the *Pennsylvania Journal* argued at the time of the Stamp Act crisis.

> Our dependence on Britain, instead of being lessened, will be vastly increased. We shall have indeed the shadow of liberty, but be destitute of the substance. Our influence in the British legislature will in reality by no more than it is now, but instead of being free from its jurisdiction, we shall be regularly and properly subject to it. They will have a right by the very constitution, to command our purses and

persons at pleasure. Our liberties, our lives, and every thing that is dear, will be at their mercy.

That was why John Adams would say that an American representation in the House of Commons would "be a snare rather than a blessing." It would have solved Great Britain's constitutional problem. It would have compounded America's constitutional grievance.[69]

CHAPTER EIGHT

INTERMEDIATE SOLUTIONS

It would have been easier to resolve the controversy over Parliament's authority to bind the colonies in all cases whatsoever had it been possible for Americans to be represented in the House of Commons and had they been willing to accept representation on British terms. Unable to utilize the representation solution, political theorists sought alternatives somewhere between absolute parliamentary sovereignty and absolute colonial legislative autonomy. Some of the schemes they came up with would have resolved very little. One, for example, wanted American representatives sitting for limited purposes, such as to address the Commons when colonial taxes were debated or to vote on questions of trade regulation only.[1] Another suggestion, was to suspend for a year execution of statutes affecting North America, so the colonies could raise objections to injudicious laws or provisions. A third idea was to have colonial assemblies enroll statutes, making them binding on their people by giving them direct consent.[2] With any of these proposals Parliament would have remained the sovereign supreme legislature and the American representation grievance would have been unrelieved.

Historians have given most attention to the schemes of Edmund Burke. It is probably because of who he was. It cannot be due to the merits of his ideas for he offered American whigs little except good intentions. Burke would have had Parliament as supreme as ever, but with supremacy un-exercised. His imperial legislators would have been wise enough to leave local matters to the colonial assemblies and, guided by custom and established institutions, would eschew experimentation and innovation.[3] The proposal made more sense in the eighteenth century than it would today. English constitutionalists often hoped for the best when there was no institutional mechanism to guarantee results. It might have worked, too, had all members of Parliament been Edmund Burkes.

The eighteenth century probably gave more attention to the solutions of Thomas Pownall than to those of Burke. At least, no one published more pages on how the controversy over the authority to legislate might be resolved than did the former governor. It is possible that his ideas hold some interest for other types of history, such as the history of eighteenth-century political theory or the history of British imperialism. It is strikingly strange, however, that this man, who was an expert on the governance of the British colonies and who gave more thought to ending the revolutionary controversy than almost anyone else, contributed nothing to constitutional history. He may have wanted an American accommodation on American terms, but he credited only one American grievance. Let the colonies have legislative autonomy, he said, they "have of right, internal government, both in jurisdiction and legislation, perfectly free in all cases whatsoever." That was all. American assemblies would be autonomous, because the supreme, sovereign British Parliament would respect their jurisdiction. By 1774, passage of the Coercive Acts had taught American whigs they had to have much more constitutional security than that.[4]

Somewhat more promising, and certainly more original and more imaginative, were the many formulae for dividing legislative authority concurrently between Parliament and autonomous, independent colonial assemblies, two spheres of supremacy rather than one, with Parliament supreme only in imperial affairs. General Henry Seymour Conway's Bill for Conciliation with the Colonies, for example, would have divided the authority to legislate, giving the assemblies "full power and authority" to regulate their "internal government." Parliament would be restricted to "the power of ordering and enacting such things as concern the maintenance of the said charters and constitutions, the general weal of the empire, and the due regulation of the trade and commerce thereof."[5] Although the concept of divided sovereignty was contrary to the eighteenth-century British political truism that sovereignty had to exist whole and be exercised by one individual or one institution,[6] it had the merit of reflecting the American whig constitutional doctrine that trade and general superintendence of the empire were within the exclusive jurisdiction of Parliament and internal police belonged exclusively to the regional legislatures. Indeed, the earl

of Abingdon, who may have been thinking more of Ireland than of the
colonies, practically codified the American whig constitution in his proposed Bill for a Declaration of Right over the British Dependencies. He
vested in Parliament the "power to make and enact laws and statutes to
regulate and controul the external commerce or foreign trade" of the entire empire. His proviso, restricting this legislative authority was so close
to the American whig argument that it is worth examining as a reminder
of the terms upon which the Continental Congress would have kept the
American colonies under British rule.

> Provided nevertheless, that the said laws and statutes so made and
> enacted, with power to regulate and controul the external commerce
> or foreign trade of Great Britain and its empire, are not meant or in-
> tended directly or indirectly, as laws and statutes for the purpose of
> raising a revenue, nor for any other internal use whatever in or over
> those kingdoms, or countries, parts or places, of whose external com-
> merce or foreign trade such regulations and controul shall be had, but
> as mere provisions of enlargement to, or matters of restriction upon
> such trade or commerce as may tend to the common advantage and
> general good of the whole.

Abingdon's imperial constitution was actually more restrictive on Parliament than the constitution of the American whigs. Abingdon limited the
authority to regulate trade to the "general good of the whole." The Continental Congress, it will be remembered, conceded Parliament authority
to regulate colonial trade "for the purpose of securing the commercial advantages of whole empire to the mother country."[7] There was little chance
Parliament would have adopted plans such as Conway's and Abingdon's
after it had rejected the more generous American formula. It could not
have mattered, however, for they were proposed too late. Conway offered
his bill in May 1780 and Abingdon's bill was debated in July 1782.[8]

Governor Pownall said there were three possible solutions to the controversy over Parliament's authority to legislate for the internal affairs of
the colonies. One was his own scheme of a sovereign Parliament which,
knowing why colonial assemblies had been created and respecting that
purpose, did not intrude into their sphere of jurisdiction. The second was
American representation in Parliament. And the third was for the colonies
to have a "Parliament of their own under an American union."[9] That last
seems to have been the proposal most frequently suggested for resolving
the constitutional crisis. The idea was to place an intermediate legislature
between the Parliament of Great Britain and the American assemblies.
This institution could have been the extant Continental Congress,[10] but

more often mentioned was "an American Parliament," a new legislative body,[11] one that would be created by Parliament and subordinate to the sovereignty of Great Britain,[12] although Edmund Burke told members of the Commons that it should not be "founded upon your laws and statutes here, but grounded upon the vital principles of English liberty."[13]

Burke meant that if created by a parliamentary statute, the new legislature would not solve the problem of parliamentary supremacy. It would be more in keeping with English liberty if the American parliament grew indigenously, as the Continental Congress had grown out of the whig movement, or if the new parliament was called first by the thirteen assemblies authorizing it by legislation enacted in regular session, submitted to and approved by the crown. Another way that an American parliament could be "grounded upon the vital principles of English liberty," some observers suggested, would be if its delegates were elected by the colonial assemblies from their own membership. That procedure would preserve the autonomy of the assemblies. Whatever the assemblies gave up by becoming subordinate to the American or continental parliament, they would gain by each being an equal member of that parliament, and by having that parliament to shield them from the British Parliament.[14] Just by being in existence, an American parliament would preserve colonial legislative liberty by keeping the British Parliament from legislating for continental affairs in which provincial assemblies would not be competent. Thus, not only would Americans keep local control, the constitutional doctrine of consent would remain inviolate.[15]

There were also British reasons for creating a continental parliament. A generation earlier Martin Bladen had suggested that an American parliament could be used by the imperial government to keep better informed of American affairs and attitudes, and Governor Pownall thought that as the British Parliament would dominate a continental legislature, it would be the means of securing British legislative control over North America.[16] Americans, of course, could hope for the opposite, that a continental legislature would become a buffer against imperial power, more independent than the Irish Parliament, perhaps the constitutional equal of the legislature at Westminster. "One special business of this convention," a New Yorker wrote, "should be to keep a vigilant and careful watch over the designs and transactions of the British Ministry and Parliament, that so by an early watch word it may prevent tyranny in its embrio." As it would be enacting statutes for the continent, the king's veto would be an active part of the process, to be used to protect the provincial assemblies from the American parliament just as that parliament protected the assemblies from the British Parliament.[17]

There were alternatives suggested that could have accomplished some of the purposes of an American parliament. One was an imperial privy council representative of both North America and Great Britain. Another was a variation of the American parliament idea with perhaps a second house, most likely an appointed senate, or a lord lieutenant on the Irish model. Although some of these schemes were advanced by well-known individuals, such as the whig-loyalist William Smith of New York,[18] and others were elaborate enough to be published as pamphlets,[19] there is no profit detailing them. Only one deserves discussion, not so much because it made a contribution to the debate on Parliament's authority to legislate for the colonies in all cases whatsoever, but because of the light it sheds on the difficulties in formulating intermediate solutions. It was Joseph Galloway's plan submitted to and voted on by the first Continental Congress.

THE GALLOWAY PLAN

Joseph Galloway drafted several plans for an Anglo-American union.[23] As they were all basically the same, it is necessary to consider only the first, the one that Galloway presented to the American public and which was debated by the delegates to the first Continental Congress.

Galloway is remembered as one of the leading and most militant loyalists of the Revolutionary War. The title of a recent biography, *The Loyalist Mind*, sums up his place in history. It is that fact, that he was a loyalist who sacrificed much for his principles, that makes his constitutional and jurisprudential theories important to us. We may wonder, however, whether there was a loyalist legal mind. Certainly when dissected in terms of concepts rather than results, the legal mind of this loyalist is no different from the legal mind of the average American whig.

Although Galloway may have based his loyalty to Great Britain on the doctrine of parliamentary supremacy, he did not confound parliamentary supremacy with parliamentary sovereignty. His definition of law should interest historians, as evidence of how close the jurisprudence of American loyalists could be to the jurisprudence of American whigs. Like Thomas Hutchinson who relied on forensic history and the second original contract to support his version of the British constitution, Galloway did not define law as sovereign power.

Galloway never wrote on jurisprudence, yet we can gather from his support of the Continental Congress that, like most Americans, he thought right existed independently of power. "A Congress of Delegates," Galloway argued at a time when whigs were urging a continental convention to consider the Coercive Acts, was "the first proper Step to be taken. . . . In this Congress composed of the Representatives, constitutionally chosen, of all concerned, and who would of Course act with Weight and Authority, something might be produced by their united Wisdom, to ascertain our Rights, and establish a political Union between the two Countries with the Assent of both, which would effectively secure to Americans their future Rights and Privileges."[21]

The language that Galloway selected to explain his plan, both to his fellow delegates and to the rulers of Great Britain, tells us as much about his theory of law as does anything that he said directly about legal philosophy. A practicing lawyer, Galloway knew that for members of Parliament a continental congress would be either illegal or extralegal. Yet he referred to his proposed congress as constitutional, composed of representatives "constitutionally chosen," who would act with "Authority." Moreover, he wanted the congress "to ascertain our Rights," suggesting that he understood rights existed independently of Parliament's sovereign command.

Galloway was elected a delegate to the Continental Congress from Pennsylvania and at one of the earliest sessions attempted to set its direction. The controversy between Great Britain and the colonies, he believed, could be reduced to a single issue: American representation in the House of Commons. "This, and this only," he told the Congress, "is the source of American grievances. Here, and here only, is the defect; and if this defect were removed, a foundation would be laid for the relief of every American complaint."[22] Americans, he said, were deprived of their right to consent, a right that existed independently of the will and pleasure of the sovereign. He did not say so directly, but in his remarks to Congress Galloway implied that he located sovereignty in constitutional law, not in Parliament. Certainly, it was in the constitution that he found the right to consent. "It is the Essence of the English Constitution," he contended, "that no Law shall be binding, but such as are made by the Consent of the Proprietors [landowners] in England."[23] It is evident that in Galloway's jurisprudence the right to consent not only existed as an entity independent of sovereign command, but that it could not be forfeited and remained viable even when unexercised.[24] A word he used in this context was "restore." He referred to Americans being restored to their "antient and essential right of participating [in] the power of making the laws,"[25] and to Great Britain "restor[ing] to her American subjects, the enjoyment of the right of assenting to, and dissenting from, such bills as shall be proposed to regulate their conduct."[26] Galloway may have been aware of the argument that by migrating to North America the English settlers of the colonies had voluntarily relinquished their right to consent in Parliament. If so, he refuted it.[27] "I have ever thought We might reduce our Rights to one," he told his fellow delegates. "An Exemption from all Laws made by [the] British Parliament, made since the Emigration of our Ancestors. It follows therefore that all the Acts of Parliament made since, are Violations of our Rights." It was a surprisingly extreme statement for 1774, a theory of law that went beyond the boldest claims of the more militant whigs, and Galloway knew it. "I am well aware," he concluded, "that my Arguments tend to an Independency of the Colonies, and militate against the Maxim that there must be some absolute Power to draw together all the Wills and strength of the Empire."[28]

Galloway's authority for the autonomy of rights was the same as the American whigs' authority for the autonomy of law. It was constitutional. Like the rebellious whigs against whom he would soon be at war, Galloway rejected the notion that civil rights depended upon natural law for authority. "I have looked for our Rights in the Laws of Nature—but could not find them in a State of Nature, but always in a State of political Society," John Adams quoted Galloway as telling the Continental Congress. "I have looked for them in the Constitution of the English Government, and there found them. We may draw them from this Soursce [sic] securely."[29] No further explanation is quoted, but we do not have to guess as to what Galloway meant. Fourteen years earlier in an anonymous pamphlet he had asserted the right of Pennsylvanians to have judges with the tenure *quamdiu se bene gesserint*. It was a right that had always been denied the colonies by the British government, a right, therefore, that Americans could not say they had enjoyed. Yet it was a right, it existed, and it belonged to Pennsylvanians as much as to the British who did exercise and did enjoy it. It belonged to them, Galloway explained, by constitutional law, and he included all of the classical common-law explanations why the English had rights: custom, ownership, inheritance, contract, and reason.

> [L]et me entreat you to insist on the enjoyment of this your native, your ancient, and indubitable right. 'Tis yours by the usage and custom of ages; 'tis yours by the rules of reason; 'tis yours by covenant with the first founder of your government; 'tis yours by the united consent of King, Lords, and Commons; 'tis yours by birthright and as *Englishmen*. Complain, and remonstrate to your representatives incessantly, until they shall, like the great and good ALFRED, make a restitution of this your most important and essential right.[30]

Galloway's explanation of how the British constitutional insistence on Parliament's supremacy was fundamentally incompatible with the American doctrine of government by direct representation is quoted in Chapter 6.[31] He thought the two positions "so repugnant, that they cannot be reconciled of themselves, without some intermediate proposition *which shall include the affirmative of both*—or which shall leave the parliamentary authority *supreme* over the Colonies, and at the same time give the Colonies a *representation.*"[32] Galloway had the answer, an intermediate American parliament, which he wanted the Continental Congress to adopt, if not as the solution to the controversy with the mother country, at least to furnish "the ground of negotiation" with Parliament.[33] The constitutional theory from which Galloway would have Congress negotiate was striking, for it was based on American notions of representation and implied that the British doctrine of vicarious, virtual, constructive representation was unconstitutional. Listening to Galloway were delegates who within two years would vote for American independence. They would disagree with his plan, but could have had little quarrel with his constitutional reasoning.

> Having thus briefly stated the arguments in favour of parliamentary authority . . . I am free to confess that the exercise of that authority is not perfectly constitutional in respect to the Colonies. We know that the whole landed interest of Britain is represented in that body, while neither the land nor the people of America hold the least participation in the legislative authority of the State. Representation, or a participation in the supreme councils of the State, is the great principle upon which the freedom of the British Government is established and secured. I also acknowledge, that that territory whose people have no enjoyment of this privilege, are subject to an authority unrestrained and absolute; and if the liberty of the subject were not essentially concerned in it, I should reject a distinction so odious between members of the same state, so long as it shall be continued.[34]

Galloway's plan was that a "legislature for regulating the administration of the general affairs of America be proposed and established in America including all the said colonies, within and under which government each colony shall retain its present constitution and powers of regulating and governing its own internal police in all cases whatsoever."[35] This legislature would be called the "Grand Council." It would exercise jurisdiction over "Laws in which more than one Colony are concerned,"[36] and its members would be elected by the provincial assemblies. It would be, Galloway intended, not an intermediate legislature, but a "new Branch" of Parliament.[37] The descriptive words would have been "king, Lords, Commons, and General Council." Together with a president-general appointed by the crown, the Grand Council would "be an inferior and distinct branch of the British legislature united and incorporated with it" for purposes of continental legislation. Statutes were to be promulgated by a two-stage procedure. Bills were to "originate and be formed and digested either in the Parliament of Great Britain or in the said Grand Council and, being

prepared, transmitted to the other for their approbation or dissent, and . . .
the assent of both shall be requisite to the validity of all such general Acts
or Statutes."[38]

Galloway's plan is one of the most striking instances on record illustrating the devotion of eighteenth-century Americans to British constitutional
law principles. One provision, for example, was "[t]hat the Grand Council shall have power to choose their Speaker and shall hold and exercise
all the like rights, liberties and privileges as are held and exercised by
and in the House of Commons of Great Britain."[39] Galloway was making
certain that centuries of parliamentary struggle for autonomy from the
crown were grafted into American constitutional law and that underlying
the new continental constitution were the constitutional customs of Great
Britain. Moreover, in the provision that regulations promulgated by the
British Parliament obtain the approbation of the American Grand Council,
he was codifying two of the most basic principles of British constitutionalism, consent and balanced government. The requirement of colonial assent
meant that "no law to bind America could be made without her consent,
given by her representatives."[40] Galloway had also designed this provision
to extend the British doctrine of balanced government into the imperial
constitution. "It is this joint consent," he explained, "which constitutes
the unity of the British, and of every other mixed form of government."[41]
The balance was especially strengthened by the joint veto. On any matters affecting both Great Britain and America, or at least in the case of
parliamentary legislation if Parliament conceded that the colonies were
affected, each representative body had a check upon the other. Finally, it
should be noted that Galloway incorporated into his plan the doctrines of
local knowledge, shared interests, and shared burdens. Great Britain, he
contended, "ought not in Equity to exercise a Law-making Authority over
the Colonies, while they are destitute of any Opportunity or constitutional
Mode of communicating that Knowledge of their Circumstances, which is
indispensably necessary to the right forming of Laws."[42] The Grand Council created that mode of communication, especially with the instrument
of withholding assent which, it must be assumed, would be explained by
a statement of principles and reasons. Moreover, by providing that the
delegates to the Grand Council would be elected "by the representatives
of the people of the several colonies in their respective Assemblies once in
every three years," Galloway assured that they would be local men who
shared the interests of the people affected by any legislation enacted, and
would share the burden of any taxes imposed. This would be true even for
taxes originating in the House of Commons.[43]

Galloway's plan incorporated one other fundamental principle of the
British constitution: the supremacy of Parliament. "I would," he told the

Continental Congress, "acknowledge the necessity of the supreme authority of Parliament over the Colonies, because it is a proposition which we cannot deny without manifest contradiction, while we confess that we are subjects of the British Government."[44] In fact, he wanted the Congress to adopt the doctrine of parliamentary supremacy as a principle of American constitutional law. The ninth section of his plan stated that the Grand Council was "an inferior and distinct branch of the British legislature."[45]

From the perspective of customary English constitutionalism, Galloway's plan was a remarkable blending of seventeenth- and eighteenth-century theory. It was a bit old-fashioned in that it reached back to the constitution that was primarily concerned with checking power rather than enacting legislation. In fact, in the text of the plan, Galloway did not refer to legislating or statutes. His Grand Council was to "originate" and "form" "general regulations."[46] By contrast, the plan belonged to the eighteenth century by adopting the American concept of actual, universal representation of the geographical unit, and specifically rejected the British concept of virtual representation. It was a difference that Galloway appreciated and stressed, when later he recalled that his plan "would have given the Colonists a perfect representation in America; a representation by far more popular and perfect than that in Great Britain."[47] Galloway's plan departed from British constitutional law in one important aspect. He gave the veto to Parliament on one side and the Grand Council on the other, but not to the crown. Although it is unlikely, there is a possibility that this was one reason why some members of the Continental Congress voted against the plan. In 1774, American whigs were still looking to the king as their check on Parliament. Galloway, instead, made Parliament a check on American legislation.

Galloway's plan obtained support, not only among future loyalists[48] but also from future rebels. In the Continental Congress, however, delegates who at first saw merit to it had second thoughts and it was expunged from the minutes.[49] The grounds on which individual delegates opposed it are not known. It may be that some had already determined on independence and would not consider any scheme for resolving the constitutional controversy.[50] There was certain to be some opposition based on local legislative autonomy. Patrick Henry made an argument against Galloway's plan that sounded very much like his later opposition to the United States Constitution. "We shall liberate our constituents from a corrupt House of Commons," he warned, "but throw them into the arms of an American Legislature, that may be bribed by that nation which avows, in the face of the world, that bribery is a part of her system of government."[51] It is likely that uncertainty about what an American Grand Council would become—what powers it might assume and how independent it would remain—made some delegates hesitate. They could have had the same doubts that antifederalists would have fourteen years later. One question they must have asked themselves was what would be the consequences of admitting Parliament's supremacy. Galloway did this not by calling Parliament "supreme" but by calling the Grand Council "inferior,"[52] though he softened the implications by also calling it a "branch" of Parliament. It was still an admission of supremacy, something that the colonies had been resisting since 1765. Except for a resolution of the assembly of Nova Scotia, it would have been the only significant admission of parliamentary supremacy voted by any representative body on the North American mainland. Even had Galloway been able to persuade them that the admission would be harmless, we can imagine it would have stuck in the throats of most whigs.

The delegates who were voting, it should be remembered, had been sent to the Continental Congress to deal with the Coercive Acts, and Galloway's plan did not address that issue. Rather, it distracted from it, especially in view of the virtual certainty that Parliament would reject the plan. Adoption by Congress would have only delayed resolution of the conflict and probably would have strengthened the parliamentary forces in the colonies as anger over the Coercive Acts receded in time. Finally, it may be that Galloway solved the wrong problem. He implied there was a deficiency in the colonial constitution, but American whigs thought the issue was Parliament's attempt to usurp authority to legislate in all cases whatsoever. Galloway tried to soften a constitutional shock by invoking the old constitutional remedy of an absolute check on power. What American whigs wanted was to end parliamentary innovations, not to make parliamentary innovations constitutional.[53]

There was one consideration that scholars tend to overlook but which may have troubled members of the Continental Congress. Galloway's plan provided for a president-general appointed by the crown. The plan is vague on details but the ninth section does say that the "President-General and the Grand Council" together formed the new, inferior branch of the British Parliament. One reading of the ninth section is that when acts of Parliament were submitted to the Grand Council for its "approbation or dissent," the president-general had to concur or even a unanimous Grand Council could not exercise its veto. Put more bluntly, although Galloway gave the Grand Council a veto over acts of Parliament, he may also have given a royal appointee, certain to be a British imperialist, a veto over the veto.

CHAPTER NINE

PARLIAMENTARY SOLUTIONS

The earl of Chatham was full of plans. He had led Great Britain in the last war that added Canada to the British empire, and more than most imperial leaders was alarmed by the threat the American controversy posed to that empire. He was also a man torn by conflicting considerations. Perhaps coached by his friend Earl Camden, he was persuaded of the essential constitutionality of the American cause, and early in the contest he had opposed parliamentary taxation of the colonists for purposes of revenue. He had even formulated an argument, based on certain unique features of the British constitution, why it was unconstitutional for Parliament to tax Americans. But when it became evident late in 1774 that all of the colonies refused obedience to the Coercive Acts, Chatham realized that the Americans were but a step from declaring independence, and he drew a line.[1] In fact, he drew two lines. One was against independence. The second was around the sovereignty of Parliament. These two principles were not negotiable. On the day after Christmas, 1774, Chatham spoke with Arthur Lee of Virginia. "His opinion," Lee reported, "is that a solemn settlement of the question, by a renunciation of the right to tax, on one part, and an acknowledgment of supremacy on the other, might be made."[2] Thirty-six days later, in the House of Lords, Chatham introduced his plan for peace in the form of a "Provisional Act for settling the Troubles in America."[3]

Chatham offered several motions for peace, all of which were extensively debated in the House of Lords. He may have made the last significant attempt by the opposition to end the war in May 1777, but it came to nothing.[4] Earl Gower, for one, complained "that the motion held out nothing new, and was nothing more than a repetition of what had come from the noble Lord on former occasions."[5] He was right. Chatham's "Provisional Act," moved in the Lords on 1 February 1775, had incorporated all of his proposals for reforming the imperial constitution, and as he would not compromise on either Parliament's sovereign power to legislate for the colonies in all cases whatsoever except taxation, and he would not hear of independence, he added nothing of substance over the next three years before he died.[6]

Despite its obvious shortcomings, we must give attention to that lengthy bill that Chatham offered for "settling the Troubles in America." It is important just because it was Chatham's plan. He was the most influential statesman of that day, he cared deeply about the survival of the empire, unlike most members of Parliament he thought of Americans as equal citizens entitled to equal rights, and he understood that the controversy tearing apart the empire he had rebuilt was a constitutional conflict. That his plan was bankrupt of viable solutions tells us much of why the controversy resulted in civil war. Of course, Chatham had to deal with a constituency, the two houses of Parliament. He knew the members would not go far toward appeasing the Americans. Still, the new empire he envisioned was much, much closer to the empire of Lord North and the earl of Mansfield than it was to the empire envisioned by the delegates to the first and second Continental Congress.

In the preamble, Chatham addressed what he knew was the overriding issue in dispute, Parliament's authority to bind the colonies in all cases whatsoever. He hoped to change the language yet save the principle of the Declaratory Act by providing that Parliament "had, hath, and of right ought to have, full power and authority to make laws and statutes of sufficient force and validity to bind the people of the British colonies in America, in all matters touching the general weal of the whole dominion of the imperial crown of Great Britain, and beyond the competency of the local representative of a distant colony." Perhaps to be certain that there was no dispute whether "the general weal" included foreign, imperial, and domestic commerce, he inserted a clause stating that Parliament's authority to legislate included "most especially an indubitable and indispensable right to make and ordain laws for regulating navigation and trade throughout the complicated system of British commerce."[7]

Scholars of the American Revolution sometimes wonder how closely London was listening to American whigs and their constitutional arguments. Often it seems that the members of Parliament were paying no attention. The earl of Chatham should provide one answer, for it would be expected that if anybody was reading the colonial petitions it was he, but considering the way he stated Parliament's authority to legislate we cannot be certain. When dealing with the colonial grievance against the stationing of standing armies on the continent without consent of the local assemblies, Chatham referred to a petition from the Continental Congress to the king, indicating he was heeding what the Congress said, but how closely? It is not relevant that he rejected the standing army complaint for he was determined to keep matters of defense in the hands of the imperial administration and, as a former wartime prime minister, felt there was no ground for compromise.[8] He did, however, want to accommodate American whigs on the issue of Parliament's authority to legislate in all cases whatsoever. A quick reading of what he said of the authority could leave the impression that he was adjusting Parliament's claim to meet colonial objections. When he limited the authority to legislate to "all matters touching the general weal of the whole dominion of the imperial crown of Great Britain, and beyond the competency of the local representative of a distant colony," Chatham could be read as adopting the position of some American whigs who, at least before the Continental Congress met, conceded to Parliament a general power of superintendence over the empire. What Chatham failed to do was to give consideration to the words of the Continental Congress which, he knew, spoke for all thirteen colonies. The Congress, it will be recalled, had limited Parliament's jurisdiction "to the regulation of our external commerce, for the purpose of securing the commercial advantages of the whole empire to the mother country, and the commercial benefits of its respective members."[9] That Chatham did not utilize this language may only reflect the fact that his main purpose was not to resolve the controversy, but to have Parliament adopt a plan reasonable enough to provide the basis for negotiation. Specific wording could be left to those negotiations.

Possibly Chatham adjusted his plan to meet another part of the Continental Congress's statement of constitutional principles. Claiming legislative autonomy for the colonial assemblies, Congress asserted that as Americans could not be represented in Parliament, "they are entitled to a free and exclusive power of legislation in their several provincial legislatures, where their right of representation can alone be preserved, in all cases of taxation and internal polity, subject only to the negative of their sovereign." Perhaps Chatham was thinking of this claim when limiting Parliament's authority to legislate to matters "touching the general weal . . . and beyond the competency of a distant colony." If his intention was to imply what the Continental Congress said explicitly, he put some of the implication back in a later section of his provisional bill where he provided "that the colonies in America are justly entitled to the privileges, franchises, and immunities granted by their several charters or constitutions; and that the said charters or constitutions ought not to be invaded or resumed, unless for misuser, or some legal ground of forfeiture."[10]

It is the constitutional theory of authority, much more than specific provisions, that divides Chatham's plan from the solutions proposed by the Continental Congress. By saying charters "ought not to be invaded or resumed," and saying that they were answerable to "misuser, or some other legal ground of forfeiture" in England's courts of common law, Chatham's constitutional premise was that Great Britain possessed sovereign authority. What his plan did was explain how Parliament limited or renounced some of that authority. This theory—that right was determined by sovereignty and sovereignty was vested in Parliament—underlies Chatham's solution to the standing army grievance. The imperial authority over the standing army within the jurisdiction of a colony was undisputed and complete. The British army was constitutional once Parliament authorized it and could legally be posted in the empire anywhere the crown directed. Chatham, however, respected American apprehensions that the army might be used to police them. So he told them not to worry. Although the authority existed, it would not be abused. "Nevertheless," his plan provided, "in order to quiet and dispel groundless jealousies and fears, be it hereby declared, that no military force, however raised, and kept according to law, can ever be lawfully employed to violate and destroy the just rights of the people."[11] Before concluding that Chatham was offering Americans at least as much security as enjoyed by eighteenth-century Britons, remember that large army units were not stationed in Great Britain. In the European part of the empire, the standing army was kept in Ireland, not in England or Scotland.

The divergence between the earl of Chatham's constitutional theory of imperial authority and that of colonial whigs deserves close attention because on this matter Chatham was speaking for just about every person of significance in London, administration and opposition, whig or tory. Again, the difference stems from opposite definitions of authority. This fact can be gleaned by considering the main topic of this book—Parliament's authority to legislate for the colonies—and by returning to the question on which the Continental Congress made its most significant constitutional decision. After an extensive debate, it will be recalled, Congress had resolved that Parliament could exercise legislative authority over Americans because "from the necessity of the case, and a regard to the mutual interest of both countries, we cheerfully consent to the operation of such acts of the British parliament" as regulate "our external commerce." The Continental

Congress was saying more than that Parliament had authority to regulate American trade. It also was saying that Parliament's authority to legislate was derived from the consent of the governed. Chatham was saying that Parliament's authority was inherent. "[A]ll subjects in the colonies," his plan provided, "are bound in duty and allegiance duly to recognize and obey (and they are hereby required so to do) the supreme legislative authority and superintending power of the parliament of Great Britain." The constitutional theories not only were opposed, they were incompatible. It is difficult even to imagine how the conflict might have been compromised had both sides been willing.[12]

The remaining parts of Lord Chatham's plan may be passed over more quickly. One provision, perhaps what made the bill unacceptable to most members of the House of Lords, renounced Parliament's right to tax the people of the colonies for purposes of revenue. No taxes were to be levied on a colony "without common consent, by act of provincial assembly there." He sought to soften opposition by also authorizing Congress to make "a free grant to the King, his heirs, and successors, of a certain perpetual revenue, subject to the disposition of the British parliament." It was a clever solution to a serious conflict between American and British constitutional needs. By providing that payments were to be made to the king, not to Parliament, Chatham satisfied the American requirement that requisitions for revenue come from the crown and not from Parliament. By providing that Parliament and not the king dispose of the revenue, Chatham met the British constitutional imperative that money not pass from the colonies to the crown. Why he wanted a "perpetual" revenue, once controversial in English constitutional law, is uncertain. Perhaps Chatham intended the provision as a sop to Parliament and, expecting the colonies to make only a token offer, wanted questions of requisition and grant to arise only once, permitting the taxation issue to then lie buried in the perpetuity clause.[13]

The significant part of Chatham's taxation solution was that the grant to the king came from the Continental Congress. Adoption of Chatham's plan would have provided Great Britain's first official recognition of the Continental Congress. It was not quite what American whigs were looking for, however, as the plan gave Congress no authority except to vote a grant to the king, allocate the payments among the individual colonies, and "to take into consideration the making due recognition of the supreme legislative authority and superintending power of parliament over the colonies." If that expectation seems farfetched, we may again wonder if Chatham was thinking more of getting his bill through Parliament rather than of securing the "due recognition" from Congress. The plan said nothing of what would occur should Congress refuse. It appears, however, that Chatham thought it possible Congress or the colonial assemblies would give "due recognition." His plan contains another clause providing for repeal of all parliamentary statutes to which Congress objected, including the five Co- ercive Acts, to take effect "from the day that the new recognition of the supreme legislative authority and superintending power of parliament over the colonies, shall have been made on the part of the said colonies."[14] It does not make sense to put in such a stipulation unless Chatham hoped there was some chance it would be met.

It could be that Chatham thought the Continental Congress could afford to acknowledge Parliament's supremacy because in another section of his bill he had Parliament renounce authority to legislate on matters to which American whigs had objected. It would have provided

> that the powers of Admiralty and Vice-Admiralty courts in America shall be restrained within their ancient limits, and the trial by jury, in all civil cases, where the same may be abolished, restored: and that no subject in America shall, in capital cases, be liable to be indicted and tried for the same, in any place out of the province wherein such offence shall be alleged to have been committed, nor be deprived of a trial by his peers of the vicinage; nor shall it be lawful to send persons indicted for murder in any province of America, to another colony, or to Great Britain, for trial.

Together with the renunciation of the authority to tax, these promises covered only some of the grievances of American whigs. If the list is in- dicative that Chatham thought he had covered the entire constitutional controversy concerning Parliament's authority to legislate, it is a sorry comment on communication between Philadelphia and London.[15]

There is a final feature to Chatham's bill that may be obvious but is worth mentioning because it was found in almost all the other plans sub- mitted by members of Parliament for resolving the American controversy. It is the element of wishful thinking. Unable to entrench the rule that mur- der trials must be at the venue, for example, Chatham said it would not be "lawful" to send defendants to another forum. At best he was expressing the hope that if Parliament enacted another statute of Henry VIII, and was reminded of the promise made in Chatham's Provisional Act, it would rectify the mistake and repeal the legislation.[16]

Although Chatham's bill received the most votes that the friends of America ever managed to muster in the House of Lords, it went down to overwhelming defeat.[17] The only aspect of sovereignty it surrendered was taxation, but that was too much for most members. As seen by imperialists it was not a plan for preventing war and uniting Great Britain and America under a supreme Parliament, but one for setting America free from Great Britain. "In what circumstances," it was asked of the colonies, "would they differ from independent kingdoms, allied by treaty, and regulating their political or commercial intercourse in such a manner, as that each might derive the greatest advantage from both?"[18]

On the other side of the Atlantic many whigs rejected Chatham's plan out of hand, wondering how it differed from that of Lord North.[19] In recent years, scholars have suggested that a sticking point may have been the commercial aspects of the plan. "For its main intention was to preserve the material sovereignty—Britain's control over imperial industry and commerce—and it is far from certain that the American radicals would have accepted this."[20] Industry might have been a problem if it meant further restriction of manufacturing, an authority Chatham insisted belonged unconditionally within Parliament's supreme jurisdiction. But aside from that, the Continental Congress had already conceded more than Chatham asked, and as he would have repealed all offensive statutes enacted since 1763, the old Trade and Navigation Acts would have been enforced by the ineffective laws that George Grenville had sought to reform when he started the revolutionary controversy.[21]

Chatham's retention of trade regulation would not have troubled many American whigs. In fact the plan was favorably received by some colonists hopeful it would at least furnish grounds for discussions. "Lord *Chatham's* bill, on the one part, and the terms of Congress on the other," Virginia's House of Burgesses voted, "would have formed a basis for negotiation, which a spirit of accommodation on both sides might, perhaps, have reconciled."[22] Other Americans said the same,[23] but we may wonder if they looked closely at the plan. It is possible they were momentarily misled by the hopes that all colonists had in Chatham's good wishes and his leadership. There could have been negotiations, of course, but they would not have gotten very far had Lord Chatham taken part. His plan was not similar to that of the Continental Congress. He wanted peace and he wanted Parliament to stop legislating for the internal affairs of the colonies, but he also insisted that the colonists recognize "the supreme legislative authority" of Parliament. American whigs could not do that.

THE REPEAL SOLUTION

In his plan Lord Chatham wanted Parliament, in addition to suspending the Boston Port Act, two of the Massachusetts Acts, and the Quebec Act, to repeal six statutes that the Continental Congress and other American whig bodies had identified as grievances. As he explained on another occasion, repeal of the laws that offended the colonists should be the first step toward redressing injuries. "The people of America," he charged, "look

upon parliament as the authors of their miseries; their affections are es-
tranged from their sovereign. Let, then reparation come from the hands
which inflicted the injuries; let conciliation succeed chastisement; and I
do maintain, that parliament will again recover its authority."[24] Chatham
wanted America's "fears" repealed in order to restore her "love."[25]

John Wilkes would have repealed the laws to which American whigs
objected because they were "undoubted badges of slavery," Henry Cruger
because, as "an unsurmountable bar to reconciliation," they kept Americans "in union" against Parliament,[26] and William Jolliffe because repeal
would "convince America, that we are in earnest in our declarations of
amity."[27] For a brief moment it appeared as if repeal might be official administration policy. In their proclamation to the colonists as British peace
commissioners, Richard Viscount Howe and General William Howe had
announced in September 1776 that the king was prepared to join Parliament "in the revisal of all his acts by which his subjects there may think
themselves aggrieved." After reading that promise, Lord John Cavendish
moved in the House of Commons, "the Revisal of all Acts of Parliament, by
which his Majesty's subjects in America think themselves aggrieved." This
was the repeal solution, and Cavendish said it would show that Parliament
was "in earnest, and wished sincerely" for peace. The date—6 November
1776—was too early, however, and the motion was defeated by a vote of
more than two to one.[28]

Several other peace plans besides Lord Chatham's provisional bill incorporated the repeal solution.[29] One practice was to list those acts of Parliament the Continental Congress, in its Declaration of 14 October 1774,
had termed "infringements and violations of the rights of the colonists."
Their repeal, Congress had voted, "is essentially necessary in order to restore harmony between Great-Britain and the American colonies."[30] With
the exception of the standing-army complaint, all the grievances voted by
American assemblies were statutory and could have been satisfied by parliamentary action alone.[31] One demand, however, went further. It was the
famous instructions drafted by John Dickinson for Pennsylvania's delegates
to the first Congress—perhaps the most widely circulated document of its
kind[32] except for the Declaration of the Continental Congress. These instructions pushed to the edge of the American whig constitutional position,
requiring renunciation by Great Britain

> of all powers under the statute of the 35 Henry the 8th, chapter the
> 2d.—Of all powers of internal legislation—of imposing taxes or duties
> internal or external—and of regulating trade, except with respect to
> any new articles of commerce, which the Colonies may hereafter raise,
> as silk, wine, &c. reserving a right to carry these from one Colony

to another—a repeal of all statutes for quartering troops in the Colonies, or subjecting them to any expence on account of such troops—of all statutes imposing duties to be paid in the Colonies, that were passed at the accession of his present Majesty, or before that time; which ever period shall be deemed most advisable—of the statutes giving the Courts of Admiralty in the Colonies greater power, than the Courts of Admiralty have in England—of the statu[t]es of the 5th of *George* the 2d, chapter the 22d [the Hat Act], and of the 23d of George the 2d, chapter the 29th [the Iron Act], of the statute for shutting up the port of Boston—and of every other statute particularly affecting the province of *Massachusetts-Bay,* passed in the last session of Parliament.[33]

These instructions demanded more freedom of trade than the Continental Congress would ask. Also, the Continental Congress did not include the Hat Act or the Iron Act among the statutes it wanted repealed, but it did mention the Quebec Act[34] over the protests of James Duane who thought that if the thirteen colonies wanted Parliament to keep its hands off them, they should keep their hands off Quebec.[35]

There was a way to have the repeal solution without arguing which statutes to include. When, in 1777, the earl of Chatham moved to end the war by removing "accumulated grievances," Lord Gower complained that the motion "was worded in so vague and indistinct a manner, that it was impossible to know what set of measures it described, under the general charge of grievances." Chatham explained: "I wish for a repeal of every oppressive act which your lordships have passed since 1763. I would put our brethren in America precisely on the same footing they stood at that period."[36] Everyone knew what he meant. The 1763 solution was the best known, best understood, and most frequently suggested proposal for ending the controversy with the colonies.

"Their friends," Lord North observed of American whigs in October 1775, "have said that they only wished to be put on the same footing on which they were in 1763. He wished to God, if it were possible, to put the colonies on the same footing they were in in 1763." Sir George Savile thought 1763 was everyone's solution. "I ask gentlemen on the other side of the House, what are their wishes?" he told the Commons, referring to the administration. "I am answered 'Would to God we were in the situation of 1763.' I ask the colonies. I am answered 'Would to God we were in the situation of 1763.'" That generally was what the friends of America thought the colonial whigs wanted. "[T]heir language to us has been," Richard Price asserted, "'Restrict us, as much as you please, in *acquiring* property by regulating our trade for your advantage; but claim not the disposal of that property after it has been acquired.—Be satisfied with the authority you exercised over us before the present reign. —PLACE US WHERE WE WERE IN 1763.'" When John Wilkes submitted a bill in the House of Commons "for the repeal of the whole system of new statutes and regulations respecting America since 1763," he explained that, "I fix on that period, because the Congress complain of nothing prior to that era."[37]

Some members of Parliament believed that the 1763 solution had once been adopted as government policy. In their protest against the Massachusetts Government Act, some dissentient lords argued that the legislative intent behind repeal of the Stamp Act had been to return the American constitution to 1763. "This principle of repeal was nothing more than a return to the ancient standing policy of this empire," they contended. "To render the colonies permanently advantageous, they must be satisfied with their condition. That satisfaction there is no chance of restoring, whatever measures may be pursued, except by recurring, in the whole, to the principles upon which the stamp-act was repealed."[38]

The dissentient lords stated what most proponents thought the basic strength of the 1763 solution. It would remove the cause of the controversy. "Is this not proposing a plan of accommodation?" a Philadelphian asked. "Yes Sir," he answered, "and the only constitutional plan that can be devised." Serjeant James Adair thought it a solution without costs or risks. "Make the experiment," he urged in the House of Commons. "Take them at their word. Repeal the acts that have passed since sixty-three, and put them on the footing of their old system of colonial administration. Surely, Sir, it is a less expensive and dangerous experiment, than that which we are now so strongly urged to make [meaning, war]. If it should fail, Sir, how are we injured? Will our blood be spilt by it?"[39]

At first, the administration did not want to hear of the 1763 solution. Interpreting facts the opposite of how Wilkes saw them, Lord North protested that a blanket repeal back to 1763 would encourage Americans to demand that, first, the Navigation Act, and then every other restrictive statute be repealed.[40] Belittling the 1763 solution, North complained that it would have no substantial effect on constitutional law. "[B]efore the year 1763, the authority of the British legislature was not denied in America," he claimed, "the repealing thirteen acts of parliament would not consequently place us in the same situation in which we then were." Joseph Galloway made the same argument in the Continental Congress. The 1763 solution he argued was no solution. "[I]t points out no ground of complaint—asks for a restoration of no right, settles no principle, and proposes no plan for accommodating the dispute." Besides, he contended, and here he made two points of law with which most of his fellow delegates strongly disagreed, "[t]here is no statute which has been passed to tax or bind the Colonies since the year 1763, which was not founded on precedents and statutes of a similar nature before that period; and therefore the proposition, while it expressly denies the right of Parliament, confesses it by the strongest implication."[41]

Galloway was against the repeal solution in general, not just the 1763 solution. Any repeal would prove the colonies could intimidate the mother country, and America would be "immediately lost." That was the major objection voiced against solving the revolutionary controversy by a selective repeal of designated statutes. The argument was that the Americans would never be satisfied, that they were really after independence, not legislative autonomy, so repeal of one statute would just encourage them to demand more. There was also the contention that repeal would be argued as a precedent, that it would become authority for the general surrender by Parliament of the right to legislate. What would be the consequence of repealing the Tea Act, George Rice asked the House of Commons in April 1774. "I am sorry to say," he complained, "that, if we look back to the conduct of America, we shall find that hitherto whenever we have made any concession they have made that the ground of fresh demands. . . . Taxation and supreme authority [are] inseparable. If you repeal this . . . I believe it will be difficult to find any argument by which we shall maintain the right to make laws binding [on the colonies]."[42]

We may think the argument too forced, a twist of reasoning convenient to imperialists who were opposed to granting any concession to the upstart colonists. But it did fit eighteenth-century constitutional theory that the best defense of a legal position was to avoid unfavorable precedents. The leading lawyer of the day, the lord chief justice, the earl of Mansfield, examined the statutes that the Continental Congress wanted repealed and warned the House of Lords that "any one of which, if repealed, would be a total renunciation of the sovereignty." The attorney general said much the same about the 1763 solution and so did the solicitor general about repeal of the Tea Act.[43] Of course there were members in opposition who denied the conclusion, but what is interesting is that most argued that the conclusion could be avoided by saving the right to legislate. The Tea Act was "neither very commercial nor very productive" and could be repealed on expediency grounds, the member for Lincoln City told the Commons. "Taking away [and] not exercising are two very different things. Let the right remain."[44] It was partly in response to such arguments that Lord North formulated the rule that American acknowledgment of the right was a condition precedent of the repeal solution. "[A] revisal of all acts, by which his Majesty's subjects in that country think themselves aggrieved," he claimed, "was the great principle that pervaded the conduct of administration from the beginning." But "why enter into deliberation about what you are willing to concede, till we know first that they acknowledge our authority. . . . Let them acknowledge the right once; let them fairly point out the constitutional abuse of it, and the grievances flowing from that abuse, and I shall be ready . . . to adopt the most efficacious and speedy measures, not only to remedy real grievances, but even to bend to their prejudices in some instances."[45]

North spoke after independence had been declared, in November 1776, and for the next two years he did not have to be concerned that Parliament would repeal before America acknowledged. The reason was because there was no agreement about what to repeal. In fact, there was more agreement about what could not be repealed. There was at first, for example, solid resistance to repealing the Tea Act both because it was the legislation Americans had challenged so aggressively, which would make repeal a precedent for conceding the right, and because it had become the embodiment of Great Britain's claim to legislative sovereignty. "If you give up this duty you give up the whole of your authority," the solicitor general of England warned the Commons. "I shall advise giving up a great deal more. Don't keep a lingering contest. . . . With regard to America give up the rest."[46] He seemed to be saying that the precedent had to be retained as a precedent even without the substance.

Four years later the fortunes of war had drastically altered constitutional perceptions in London. By February 1778, Lord North was ready to adopt the 1763 solution. When he sounded out opinion, however, he learned that most of his colleagues favored a "declaration by Parliament that we will not tax them" rather than the 1763 solution. "Both measures, they say, are equally mortifying," he told Dartmouth, "but the former is much the more likely to induce the Americans to enter into a treaty with Great Britain."[47] Three bills were introduced by the administration and quickly enacted into law. The first repealed the Massachusetts Government Act.[48] The second declared that "the King and Parliament of *Great Britain* will not impose any duty, tax, or assessment whatever, payable in any of his Majesty's colonies, provinces, and plantations, in *North America* or the *West Indies;* except only such duties as may be expedient to impose for the regulation of commerce" with any revenue paid to the treasury of the colony where collected.[49] The third authorized appointment of commissioners to go to North America and negotiate a peace that would keep the colonists in the empire by giving up what just three years before most members of Parliament had thought was the sovereign power of Great Britain.[50]

The peace commissioners, Lord North explained when introducing the third bill, would be given authority to suspend acts of Parliament. "The colonies have demanded to be put in the situation they were in [in] 1763," he explained. "I doubt if they will ever be placed exactly in the same situation, but perhaps they may be placed in one not much less advantageous." Of the statutes enacted since 1763, "many ought to be repealed, all perhaps should be revised. I would give the commissioners full power to take them all into their consideration, and to suspend such as should be repealed."[51]

It was too late. The battle of Saratoga had been fought and lost, and soon the former colonies would have European allies supporting their war effort. Nevertheless, the British Parliament in February 1778 adopted the 1763 solution. Peace commissioners were authorized "to suspend, in any places, and for any times during the continuance of this act, the operation and effect of any act or acts of parliament which have passed since the tenth day of *February*, one thousand seven hundred and sixty-three, and which relate to any of his Majesty's said colonies, provinces, or plantations in *North America*, so far as the same does relate to them."[52] There were only three exceptions: the Declaratory Act, which everyone agreed had now become meaningless[53] but had to be saved for constitutional reasons;[54] the Quebec Act, with the borders of that province no longer extending across the back country of the middle colonies;[55] and 4 George III, cap. 34, the act regulating and restraining paper bills of credit. Although the Americans had not made bills of credit a serious constitutional grievance, treating that matter as part of Parliament's authority to regulate trade, the administration knew the law had to be altered but did not want it suspended without negotiation. The purpose was to prevent Americans from using suspension to pay debts in inflated continental currency.[56]

The peace commissioners were instructed to tell the Americans that Parliament not only renounced the power exercised by the Massachusetts Government Act, but would never again alter colonial charters except when requested "by their General Assemblies."[57] They also were to say that persons accused of treason committed in North America would no longer be threatened with trial in England, and they were instructed to negotiate a statute "authorizing a trial out of the country where the treason hath been committed but in some place adjoining where justice may conveniently be administered."[58]

Although Parliament did not specifically enact a provision recognizing colonial legislative autonomy, that appears to have been the intent, for the peace commissioners proposed to the Continental Congress that they "perpetuate our union" by exchanging legislative deputies. The American assemblies would each send at least one agent to Parliament, and Great Britain would send agents to the colonial assemblies. Apparently those agents would be members as they were "to have a seat and voice," but their chief function was "to attend to the several interests of those by whom they are deputed." It would seem that their primary duty would be to inform and warn, providing some unity of purpose among what otherwise were autonomous legislative bodies.

> In short to establish the power of the respective legislatures in each particular state, to settle its revenue, its civil and military establishments, and to exercise a perfect freedom of legislation and internal government, so that the British states throughout North America, acting with us in peace and war under one common Sovereign, may have the irrevocable enjoyment of every privilege that is short of a total separation of interests or consistent with that union of force on which the safety of our common religion and liberty depends.[59]

The British Parliament had satisfied what just four years earlier had seemed the most drastic demand made by any American whigs. That had been stated in instructions to Pennsylvania's delegates that the Continental Congress required Parliament to renounce "all powers of *internal* legislation."[60] For the British it may have seemed that Americans had forced them to the limit of the constitution and that they had made every concession possible short of independence. Two years later another peace commission attempted to persuade the Americans that there was nothing more they could ask for, when, in a proclamation, the commissioners asserted that Great Britain had "manifested the sincerity of her affectionate and conciliatory intentions in removing for ever your pretended grounds of discontent by repealing among other statutes those relating to the duty on tea and the alterations in the government of Massachusetts Bay, and by exempting for ever not only the continental but the insular colonies from Parliamentary taxations."[61]

Those last peace commissioners were wrong. The grounds of discontent were not removed. At this late date, 29 December 1780, American whigs could be content with nothing short of independence. But even if the date had been 1774, when colonial whigs still wanted to remain in the empire, governed by the ancient British constitution, there would have remained unresolved the issue that had commenced the revolution controversy: the sovereignty of Parliament. After all, the parliamentary solution to the "autonomy" demand was exactly that, a *parliamentary* solution. Peace commissioners could offer it because they had been authorized by Parliament. They spoke in the name of George III but by authority of Parliament. Lord Osborne had correctly summarized the constitutional effect of the three Conciliatory Bills of 1778 when telling the House of Lords they were "well suited" for peace. "Every material objection to claims of this country were removed. Taxation was relinquished farther than it depended on the duty and generosity of the Americans themselves. On the other hand, the supremacy of this country was asserted, and would, if accommodation took place, be preserved."[62] Parliament was still supreme.

CHAPTER TEN

"RIGHT," "ACKNOWLEDGMENT," AND "RENUNCIATION" SOLUTIONS

We must return to 1774. Parliament's Conciliatory Acts of 1778 might have been a solution to the "autonomy" grievance had they been offered four years earlier, but even had they been, the constitutional controversy would not have been resolved. As Edmund Burke had argued during the debates on the Conciliatory Bills, to make peace with the Americans, "parliamentary rights must be negotiated upon." The supremacy issue would have remained. It would not have been solved even by full colonial legislative autonomy.[1]

There was no misunderstanding. Government leaders in London knew that the supremacy issue was best left unaddressed by Parliament, to work itself out over the coming decades, even better, over the nineteenth century. The British suspected any resolution might lead too far. That had been the administration's fear in 1774 when it rejected the 1763 solution, as either meaningless or as likely to make America independent. Colonial whigs, by contrast, had been certain that a return to 1763 could have been their constitutional salvation, and that neither it nor legislative autonomy meant independence. "Consider the Statutes prior to 1763, to which *America* concedes obedience," a Pennsylvania whig explained in March 1775, referring to parliamentary legislation that would have remained enforceable after implementation of the 1763 solution, such as the

Hat Act and the White Pine Acts. "[C]onsider the acknowledged prerogatives of the King of *Great Britain,* in all the Colonies; the appeal to the King and Council from judicial determinations; his negative to laws; and let any impartial man say, whether this is a system of independence." Even under the constitution of the pre-1763 empire, if Great Britain acknowledged that colonial legislative autonomy included authority over stationing the army within a colony and Parliament no longer promulgated internal legislation such as the Iron Act or the Post Office Act, Parliament would still exercise a jurisdiction of significant general superintendency. "[B]y the Authority of Parliament are the various branches of the Empire connected," another observer searching for a constitutional solution wrote in 1776. "Parliament is the regulator of commerce: it is the highest court of appeal, and natural arbiter of the differences which may arise between the colonies themselves, or between them and the ministers. In these benign and respectable lights only, has it in times past been viewed by the Americans." Whether these paltry powers added up to *de jure* parliamentary supremacy or *de facto* American independence was never an issue. As mentioned at the conclusion of chapter 3, the abstraction of supremacy had become more important than the substance. The ultimate sovereignty of Parliament had to be acknowledged. It did not have to be exercised.[2]

There is an odd feature to this stage of the controversy. The Americans were divided between thirteen separate colonies yet their constitutional strategy was uniform and had not changed. The British had the unity of speaking through a majority of Parliament guided by a single ministry, yet their constitutional strategy, although focused toward one end, was uncertain about procedures and confused about purpose. The Americans knew they would not acknowledge Parliament's right to legislate in all cases whatsoever and wanted the issue left unresolved. The British wanted Americans to acknowledge Parliament's right but were not agreed what to do once the right was acknowledged. The administration knew that the controversy resulted from a series of constitutional steps, the consequences of which had not been anticipated. Looking back, it was evident that it would have been better to have avoided all innovations, a tactic that American whig leaders seem to have always understood. After the Massachusetts General Court answered Governor Thomas Hutchinson's challenge in the debate of 1773 and denied Parliament's right, Thomas Cushing, speaker of the House of Representatives, almost apologized to Benjamin Franklin. "In justice to the Americans," he wrote, "the colonies from the first of this dispute . . . were disposed to confine the dispute to that of taxation only and entirely to waive the other as a subject of too delicate a nature but the advocates for the supreme authority of Parliament drove us into it."[3] That complaint illustrates the difficulties faced by imperial government and local, colonial opposition alike under the unwritten British constitution. Once a thing had been done, it could not be undone. Massachusetts would have avoided claiming the right. Once it was claimed, Massachusetts could not back down.

The British strategy, that the right not only had to be maintained by Parliament but had to be acknowledged by the colonial assemblies, was as certain as the American strategy of avoidance, but its purposes, objectives, and motivations were varied and confusing. There were, of course, the demands of those British imperialists who could be termed "hardliners," such as the lord president of the Council. They rejected even the American solution to the regulation of trade—that they "cheerfully consent"—"because it totally excludes every substantial idea of right on one side, or submission on the other; of dependence and subordination to powers constitutionally created, and legally and justly exercised." Other, more compromising positions, went off in so many directions that, unless considered as constitutional law, they seem inconsistent today. When appointed a peace commissioner under the Conciliatory Acts of 1778, Governor George Johnstone "looked upon the establishing of the independency of America, as entailing ruin upon this country," yet wanted "the repealing the Declaratory Law; which was downright nonsense, as it now stood in our statute books, after the repeals we have already made." By contrast, Edmund Burke wanted Parliament to return to 1763 but opposed repeal of the Declaratory Act, a law, he admitted, that claimed for Parliament an "obnoxious power."[4] Burke's reason why he would not repeal the Declaratory Act was probably Rockinghamite politics—the Act was the major legislation of Lord Rockingham's administration—but his explanation or excuse is as clear a statement of the dangers of surreptitious precedents as any made in the eighteenth century. "If this act were repealed," he claimed, "it would be a *denial* of legislative power, as *extensive* as the *affirmation* of it in the act so repealed." Burke "was averse to doing anything upon speculations of right. Because when Parliament made a *positive* concession, the bounds of it were clear and precise; but when they made a concession founded in *theory and abstract principles*, the consequences of those principles were things out of the power of any legislature to limit."[5]

Burke's analysis was a summary of both why Great Britain had gotten into this constitutional quagmire and why every imperialist agreed that Parliament's supremacy had to be maintained while disagreeing about how to maintain it. There was only one common theme running through all the arguments—what Henry Goodricke called "our joint and equal submission to the one supreme legislature." There was much less agreement, however, as to what submission meant and how supremacy was to be effected. On the one hand, Goodricke, who was both anti-American and, during his short term in Parliament, opposed to Lord North's leadership, believed that Great Britain should give up every other claim but had to maintain the supremacy of Parliament. On the other hand, General Thomas Gage, who was on the front line defending that supremacy in Boston, believed nothing could be given up without, as a consequence, giving up all claims of right. After the Tea Party, Parliament could not yield to one demand "unless some submission is shown on the part of the colonies."[6]

Gage may have been fearful that Americans would interpret any concession as a sign of British weakness, but he was also fearful of surreptitious precedents. There was far greater respect for the authority of surreptitious precedents than most historians credit. "[B]y declaring them exempt from one statute or law," Lord Lyttelton had warned the upper house during the Stamp Act crisis, "you declare them no longer subjects of Great Britain, and make them small independent communities not entitled to your protection." Lyttelton was a man of such good sense, and so many of his contemporaries were on guard against surreptitious precedents, that we cannot be certain that he knew he was exaggerating.[7]

There seemed to be a middle ground, or at least Lord North thought there was. It was to shift the constitutional controversy from the very fine point of law that was called "the question of right"[8] to an even finer point, the acknowledgment of the right. To repeal all "the acts complained of by the Americans," North asserted, "would be of no use in terminating the present contest, while the Americans deny the right we have to make those acts."[9] The legal explanation was concisely stated by Governor Hutchinson.

> They have petitioned for the repeal of a law, because Parliament had no right to pass it. The receiving and granting the prayer of such petition, would have been considered as a renunciation of right; and from a renunciation in one instance, would have been inferred a claim to renunciation in all other instances. The repealing, or refraining from enacting any particular laws, or relieving from any kind of service, while a due submission to the laws in general shall be continued, and suitable return be made of other services, seems to be all which the Supreme Authority may grant, or the people or any part of them, require.[10]

That was the solution that Lord North seized as a way out of the predicament of maintaining the right but not exercising it: acknowledgment. "How is it possible to treat . . . [with] those, who both as subjects and independent states, have all along disputed our power and right of legislation?" he asked in the House of Commons. North answered: "Let them acknowledge the right once; let them fairly point out the constitutional abuse of it, and the grievances flowing from that abuse, and I shall be ready . . . not only to remedy real grievances, but even to bend to their prejudices in some instances." Almost two years earlier, the earl of Suffolk, a secretary of state and one of the leaders in the cabinet opposed to any concessions to the colonists, had explained the "acknowledgment" solution. The mother country, he had strongly insisted, "should never relax till America confessed her supremacy; and that as soon as America had dutifully complied, she would meet with every indulgence consistent with the real interest of both countries; but that any concession on our parts, till the right on which all our pretensions were founded, was allowed, would be to the last degree impolitic, pusillanimous, and absurd." It was up to American whigs. If they were sincere about wishing to remain in the empire, all they had to do was acknowledge the "right." Once they acknowledged the right any constitutional arrangement was possible.[11]

THE ACKNOWLEDGMENT SOLUTION

When Lord North submitted to Parliament his proposal of 27 February 1775 for resolving the controversy over the authority to tax,[12] influential members of the House of Commons demanded that settlement of the taxation controversy not become a surreptitious precedent for the controversy about the authority to legislate in all cases whatsoever. Welbore Ellis, who had been secretary at war at the time of the Stamp Act and who would be the last secretary of state for the colonies before the Treaty of Paris, wanted an American concession to precede Parliament's renunciation of the authority to tax. "I must expect to meet with," he told the Commons, "as the first step in the business, an express and definitive acknowledgment from the Americans, of our supremacy. Without that point first settled, I can neither receive nor consent to any other propositions." The leader of the Scottish members in the House, Henry Dundas, then solicitor general and about to be appointed lord advocate of Scotland, also insisted that acknowledgment precede any settlement of the taxation controversy. He "could never accede to any concessions," Dundas declared, "until the Americans did, in direct terms, acknowledge the absolute supremacy of this country."[13]

The "acknowledgment" solution had been broached many times before Lord North introduced the first of his conciliatory proposals. Most notably, it was the basic condition laid down by Lord George Germain who would direct the war effort after succeeding the earl of Dartmouth as secretary of state. "Support your supremacy; whatever you do," he had urged during the debate on the Massachusetts Government Bill. "It has been observed, that we negotiated about *Falkland's Island;* I wish, Sir, we could negotiate with the *Americans* upon the same terms. If they would do as the *Spaniards* did, that is, disown the fact, and give up the point in question, we might then negotiate."[14]

Until the passage of the Conciliatory Acts of 1778, "acknowledgment" was the official administration solution to the legislation controversy. At the time that he was offering to settle the taxation controversy by having Americans pay requisitions instead of direct parliamentary assessments, Lord North announced his intention to interdict the trade of New England and the right of New Englanders to fish off the Newfoundland Banks "till they returned to their duty." However, he promised, "whenever they should acknowledge the supreme authority of the British legislature, pay obedience to the laws of this realm, and make a due submission to the King, their real grievances, upon their making proper application, would be redressed."[15] North implied that if the Americans first conceded the right almost any concession by Parliament would be possible. "He did not mean to tax America," North explained in the Commons, "if they would submit, and leave to us the constitutional right of supremacy, the quarrel would be at an end."[16] Governor George Johnstone interpreted North's proposal by paraphrasing him. "Why not petition first, and acknowledge the right, and then we will grant relief."[17]

It must be understood that the acknowledgment condition asked American whigs to concede the constitutional argument. It is simply wrong to think that Lord North was magnanimously offering them a face-saving sop—to say, for example, that "'Submission' was all that was expected," or to call it "the empty gesture of 'submission'."[18] Nor is it right to suspect that the Americans distrusted the administration's motives, to suppose they were afraid "that something more than a point of honor is proposed in their acknowledgment of an unlimited right in Parliament."[19] Although there were members of Parliament who said that to maintain a right Parliament had to enforce it, the majority view was that a right which was acknowledged by those on whom it would operate was not lost under the doctrine of nonuser even if, by constitutional design, it was not executed.[20] It really did not matter. Even if American whigs understood and believed that the Parliament intended never again to assert the authority to legislate for the internal police of the colonies, they would not have acknowledged the right. And, again, the reason was constitutional. Under the doctrine of parliamentary sovereignty, one Parliament could not bind a later Parliament, one session of Parliament could not even bind a second session of the same Parliament.

The American whigs had no constitutional room to maneuver. Their answer to the acknowledgment condition was determined by the dynamics of parliamentary supremacy. It was the same in 1775 as it had always been. Alexander Wedderburn, bencher of the Middle Temple, future solicitor general, and future lord chancellor, had stated it during the Stamp Act crisis. "I shall read a resolution of [the] assembly of Massachusetts Bay," he announced in the Commons during February 1766. "Resolved that we will never dispute the right, unless Great Britain should ever think proper to exercise it."[21]

By February 1775, therefore, when Lord North made his proposal and two months before the battle of Lexington, the ultimate claims had been articulated on both sides of the controversy over the authority to legislate for the internal affairs of the colonies in all cases whatsoever. The British constitutional limit was that Parliament must claim the authority, the colonists must acknowledge Parliament's authority, and Parliament must not surrender the authority.[22] Whether Parliament had to exercise the right was a question the administration answered in two stages.[23] In February 1775 it admitted that it did not have to exercise the authority to tax. In February 1778, with the Conciliatory Acts, Lord North added that the authority to legislate internally did not have to be exercised.

It does not seem that the Americans made the opposite demand on London. They apparently did not ask Parliament to renounce the authority to legislate. Rather they articulated the constitutional doctrine that left the administration no choice but to insist that they first acknowledge Parliament's right before Parliament renounce its exercise. Again the American doctrine was not new. It was seldom, however, stated officially by a whig governmental body until passage of the Coercive Acts forced the Americans to articulate it. Earlier it had been mentioned in privately published arguments, as by a New York newspaper in February 1766: "The Parliament which represents the people of England, who choose them, have no right of sovereignty over us; but the King has a constitutional right, and that we always have submitted to, and always shall. We want no submission from the Parliament: We never invaded their rights: and if they invade ours, they ought to recede."[24]

Whatever restraints American whig governmental bodies had felt against articulating this doctrine were removed at the local and provincial level by passage of the Coercive Acts. "*Resolved*," Worcester County, Massachusetts, voted in August 1774, "That we bear all true allegiance to his majesty King George the third, and that we will, to the utmost of our power, defend his person, crown, and dignity, but at the same time, we disclaim any jurisdiction in the commons of Great Britain over his majesty's subjects in America."[25]

The American prerogative solution will be examined in the next chapter. The lesson to understand now is that it was an extreme return to the old, customary constitution of the seventeenth century, the most radical repudiation possible of the new constitution of Parliament's sovereignty. Colonial whigs not only wanted to go back to the constitution of checks and balances, they put it in terms of preserving the king's prerogative rights as much as preserving their own constitutional rights. A sample of the argument is found in a series of three resolutions passed by the Georgia Provincial Congress during July 1775. (1) "That those who now would subject all America, or this province, to dependency on the Crown and Parliament, are guilty of a very dangerous innovation which in time will appear as injurious to the Crown as it is inconsistent with the liberty of the American subject." We risk misunderstanding the constitutional nature of the American Revolution if we think this resolution unique. It is less familiar than it should be for historians have not given this aspect of the colonial whig case the attention it deserves. Many have not even noticed that colonial whigs said some surprising things in defense of the crown's prerogatives—at least when they thought those prerogatives eroded by Parliament's pretensions to sovereignty. (2) "That, that part of the American continent which we inhabit was originally granted by the Crown and the charter expressly from Charles the 2nd, makes its constitution dependent on the Crown only." The Georgia Congress surely knew this principle of constitutional law no longer made sense in London. The resolution was, for the time and circumstances, an extraordinarily extreme argument, a fact that may indicate how extreme these Georgians thought the Coercive Acts to be, as it was against the Coercive Acts that they were reacting. (3) "That this province bears all true allegiance to our own rightful Sovereign, King George III, and always will and ought to bear it agreeable to the constitution of Great Britain, by virtue of which only the King is now our Sovereign, and which equally binds Majesty and Subjects."[26] We will never know if many British leaders read what these Georgians said. It may not matter. Other American whigs told them the same thing, convincing some members of Parliament that the crown was the potent British institution in American constitutional theory.[27] It was this belief that forced Parliament, or at least some members, to demand that the colonies acknowledge Parliament's supreme authority before Parliament could consider renouncing its exercise.

As the crown was no longer the player in the British constitution that colonial whigs would have made it in the American constitution, it is not surprising that most British observers failed at first to understand that the colonists were threatening constitutional government and constitutional liberty as they functioned in Great Britain. It was easier for them to suppose the controversy was becoming too intransigent—that "this point of honor on one side, and distrust on the other, increase the difficulties of treating: one dare not, and the other will not make the first advance."[28]

In truth, conflict between two constitutions, the English constitution of customary, prescriptive right, and the British constitution of legislative command, left no ground for advance. The dispute had become too legal once it was understood "that the Idea of *Right* form'd the Groundwork upon which both Parties meant to stand."[29] The earl of Shelburne spoke too late when, in April 1778, he suggested that "the lawyers and *commis*, the present conductors of public business, must be sent back to their proper vocations, or their original obscurity." Four years later, with the war lost and American independence a certainty, Charles James Fox lamented the authority of a legalism. "The obstinate adherence to the word *right*," he told the Commons, "has made us lose the substance—power."[30]

THE RENUNCIATION SOLUTION

It is time for historians to accept the fact that the eighteenth-century British empire was pulled apart not only by opposing interpretations of the constitution, but by conflicting dynamics of constitutional law that could not be reconciled. On one side was the dynamics of the new constitution unable to restrain a sovereign Parliament in the way the old constitution supposedly had restrained a customary government. On the other side was the fundamental constitutional principle that British liberty depended on Parliament's supremacy over the crown. Parliament's problem with the crown made America's problem with parliamentary supremacy almost unsolvable. It was because of the crown that Parliament had to insist on the acknowledgment condition before it could relinquish the exercise of supremacy, and it was because Parliament could not constitutionally relinquish the exercise that America could not acknowledge but had to insist that Great Britain recognize independence.

There was a poverty of ideas. Some participants in the controversy such as Samuel Adams, Richard Jackson, and John Wilkes, could think only of repealing the Declaratory Act, of enacting an American bill of rights, or of Parliament unilaterally setting bounds to its own power—solutions that failed to solve the constitutional predicament.[31] Others, such as Edmund Jenings—Maryland born, educated at Eton, Cambridge, and the Middle Temple, and possibly a double agent in the war—realized that there was no constitutional solution. He wanted the Americans to "make the first concession, by acknowledging the right of parliament; but as that concession is giving up the question, which she cannot afterwards retract, it is hardly credible she will at any time make it, without some assurance, or certain hope, that such concession will not in future operate against her. Any advance or concession on the part of Great Britain, on the other hand, may, in the plentitude of power, be retracted."[32]

Two of Jenings's words summed up the constitutional predicament— "hope" and "retract." America would hope that Parliament would not retract. "[W]hen Great Britain offers to America every thing but independence," he later wrote following passage in 1778 of Lord North's Conciliatory Acts, "*she gives every thing, only to gain the right and power of retracting every thing.*" That constitutional reality was why the colonists could not rely on a bill of rights or on Parliament setting some "boundary" or drawing some "line" to limit its claim to right. "You could not say that supremacy shall exist for such and such purposes, and shall be restrained in its exercise in such and such cases," the duke of Grafton explained to the House of Lords, "because the very instant you set limits to its [Parliament's] right of taxation, you would annihilate the principle on which that right is founded, and would consequently leave the question as open and undecided as ever." The constitutional predicament seems to have been better understood in America than in London, certainly it was among those colonists who read James Cannon's *Cassandra* articles in the newspapers. "I call upon you to prove that Great-Britain can offer *any plan of constitutional dependence* which will not leave the future enjoyment of our liberties to *hope, hazard,* and *uncertainty,*" Cannon challenged a loyalist. "By the constitution of *Great-Britain* the present Parliament can make no law which shall bind any future one. . . . Is it wisdom then, or is there *safety* in entering upon terms of accommodation with a power which cannot stipulate for the performance of *its* engagements?"[33]

The first of North's 1778 Conciliatory Acts, renouncing the authority to tax, illustrates the constitutional dynamics. Just by renouncing the right Parliament was asserting it,[34] if not claiming it or reserving it for the future. Even worse, if the American "states" were to "treat under the said bill," the Continental Congress feared, "they would indirectly acknowledge that right, to obtain which acknowledgment the present war hath been avowedly undertaken and prosecuted on the part of Great Britain." The Congress explained one problem when it compared the Renunciation Act to North's Conciliation Motion of February 1775.[35] There was no substantive difference "excepting the following particular, viz. that by the motion, actual taxation was to be suspended so long as America should give as much as the said parliament might think proper; whereas by the proposed bill, it is to be suspended as long as future parliaments continue of the same mind with the present."[36]

Security under the British constitution of the 1770s had become a matter of politics and not of law. Should Congress so much as "treat" with Great Britain on the terms of the tax Renunciation Act, and, as a result, the "pretended right [to tax] be so acquiesced in, then, of consequence, the same might be exercised whenever the British Parliament should find themselves in a different *temper* and *disposition.*" It is little wonder that these delegates, who could have these constitutional fears and uncertainties, recommended to the states that they adopt *written* constitutions.[37]

American discussion of the constitutional predicament was endless, but it was never carried beyond the problem to the solution because the Continental Congress did not dare negotiate with the British on the premise of Parliament's supremacy. The Irish had to do so, however, and it is the Irish debates, more clearly and authentically than historical speculation, that demonstrate how insolvable was the constitutional predicament. "How can England treat with Ireland, until the English Parliament relinquishes her claim of binding Ireland in all cases whatsoever?" the remarkable Francis Dobbs, Dublin barrister, leader of the Volunteer movement, and brother of a former North Carolina governor, asked Lord North two years after the Conciliatory Acts had failed to restore peace with America. "Is it not a contradiction in terms, that an English Parliament should enter into a treaty with an Irish, if an Irish Parliament is to be subject to the will of an English; and if an English act can bind Ireland in all cases whatsoever."[38] There is no need to speculate about the American possibilities when we have the Irish reality. All the constitutional questions that the American whigs avoided were covered in the Irish debates.

What Ireland needed, Charles Francis Sheridan argued, was a constitution in "every Particular the exact Counterpart of that of Great Britain." Sheridan, who was a barrister and a member of the Irish Parliament, did not mean exactly like Britain's for he was a chief critic of Blackstone's theory of arbitrary parliamentary sovereignty and a defender of the old constitution of customary rights.[39] He wanted a return to the constitutional security of contractarian and prescriptive rights which had been superceded in his country by the Glorious Revolution and the Irish Declaratory Act. That Act claimed for the sovereign, supreme British Parliament authority over Ireland and the Irish Parliament.[40] Yet he knew Ireland could never go back to the old constitution, and, certainly, it could not by asking the consent of the British Parliament. Sheridan indicated the strength of the new constitutionalism when he asked what would happen if the Irish House of Commons passed a resolution denying the constitutionality of the Irish Declaratory Act, and the British Parliament, instead of ordering the repeal of the Irish resolution or reenacting the Irish Declaratory Act, took no notice of the vote by the Irish Commons, appearing to acquiesce in it. Sheridan's reluctant conclusion that nothing would have changed, even applying the norms of the old constitution, is one of the finest exposés of the constitutional predicament that the Continental Congress had faced.

> In this Case, I doubt not, it would be concluded we had gained an important Victory; but if we do not admit, (as we certainly do not) that *our* having appeared so long to acquiesce, in the declaratory Act of 6th Geo. I. by having taken *no Notice* of it, was to be construed by *them* into a Surrender of what we hold to be *our Rights;* neither could *their* apparent Acquiescence on a similar Occasion, be considered by *us,* as a Surrender of what *they* deem to be *theirs;* and if we deny that *their* Claim could be rendered valid, in Consequence of a solemn Act of *their* Legislature, they certainly will not allow that *ours* can acquire Validity from a declaratory Resolution of *one* of the Branches *only* of *our* Legislature: For such and nothing more would be our Declaration of Right.[41]

Sheridan wanted the Irish Declaratory Act nullified. His problem was how to effect it. The Irish Parliament could not ask the British Parliament to repeal it for that would be an admission of British parliamentary supremacy. The very act of repealing was an assertion of the right. His solution was to fall back on the prescriptive right of practice despite its shortcomings in a constitution of sovereign command. One doctrine of the old constitution that Sheridan thought could be revived was nonuser. He contended that except for trade regulation, the British Parliament usually did not enact legislation binding on Ireland. Irish statutes were passed by the Irish Parliament. As the Irish Declaratory Act had been a usurpation, Sheridan argued, the failure of the British Parliament to enact Irish statutes was nonuser of the Declaratory Act and effectively a renunciation of it. "It certainly is not in the theoretical Right to this Power, but in the Practical Exercise of it, in which consists the Grievance," Sheridan explained. "Will not therefore their having ceased to *exercise* this Power, equally prove a Rule of Conduct to future Parliaments; will it not equally prove the *Inexpediency* of those Parliaments resuming it." Most critics did not think so. "[T]he theorical [sic] is a very likely method of giving rise to the practical exercise of it," one observed. "This is just as if a man should tell me, sir, I assure you I will not cut your throat, but I insist upon holding a razor to it."[42]

The obvious solution was for the British Parliament, responding to a petition from some Irish group other than the Irish Parliament, to repeal the Irish Declaratory Act. There were, however, more arguments against that solution than arguments supporting it. How, for example, could you repeal a declaratory act? If the Act was meaningless, repeal would have been meaningless, or, if the Act had meaning, its repeal would have meant nothing. If the British Parliament "did not *derive* the Right in Question from that Act," Sheridan contended, "the *Repeal* of that Act could not take it from them; if it be a *Right* inherent in them, they cannot renounce it—for no Act of one Parliament, could, in that case, be binding to a subsequent Parliament."[43] In fact, as another Irish commentator observed, repeal could be worse than no repeal for the implication of repeal is that the law being repealed is valid. "If they never had a right to make, they need not repeal, because there is consequently no law;—but by assuming a power to repeal, they imply a right to have made."[44]

The British Parliament did repeal the Irish Declaratory Act. Despite knowing repeal meant little in law and might even be harmful, most Irish wanted it repealed. Perhaps the best argument was that, although repeal offered the Irish no constitutional security, it would help restore political "confidence" between the two kingdoms.[45]

What we might think had been a great triumph for the Protestants of Ireland probably brought them little satisfaction, knowing as they did that the constitution remained unchanged. Ireland's new liberty rested on British good intentions. The Irish Parliament was in the same constitutional limbo American assemblies would have been in had the British Parliament repealed the American Declaratory Act in 1774. There can be little doubt that American whigs would have been as dissatisfied with that constitutional predicament as was Henry Flood with the Irish predicament following repeal of the Irish Declaratory Act. Flood, a barrister of the Inner Temple, was the leading champion of an independent Irish parliament. "It is a first principle of law," he told the Irish House of Commons shortly after repeal, "that a Declaratory Act only declares the law to be what it was before; that is to say, that it only declares, and that it does not alter the law. —What follows? That as making a Declaratory Act does not alter the law, so neither can the mere unmaking alter the law."[46] Flood was criticizing what he called "simple repeal," which, although a precedent was not the only precedent. "Many acts have been made by the British Parliament binding Ireland," he explained, "some of them before the Declaratory Law of George the 1st. Now whilst one of these remains, there is an exercise and a proof of right, stronger by much than the Declaratory Law."[47] Indeed, even if the repeal statute had been the only precedent it would not have been a strong precedent since London could at any time have claimed it had been extorted under duress at a moment when the Irish Volunteers were armed and Great Britain was at war with France, Spain, the Low Lands, and America.

Flood, it must be understood, was distinguishing the repeal of the Declaratory Act from the repeal of other legislation.[48] Here is how he summed up the rule: "The claim is a claim of right, or the legal principle either real or assumed. The simple repeal takes away the declaration only, but leaves behind the claim or legal pretension." The legal consequence, Sheridan explained, was that nothing had changed. "[I]f it be a *Right* inherent in them [the British Parliament]; they cannot renounce it—for no Act of one Parliament could in that case be binding to a subsequent Parliament."[49]

On that last point the lawyers disagreed. Sheridan thought it was as meaningless for Parliament to renounce a right as it was for Parliament to repeal a declaration that it had the right. Flood believed the British Parliament could renounce a right, and, therefore, contended that Ireland had to demand that Parliament renounce the Irish Declaratory Act. By the very fact that "the mere repeal of a Declaratory Act does not renounce the principle of it," Flood insisted, it was obvious that some other action was needed. He wanted a renunciation act. "[N]othing but a final renouncing of the principle of this law, is adequate to our security." Flood reminded the Irish Commons that Americans had been told that the American Declaratory Act "was a sacrifice to British pride, and that it never would be exercised. But how long was it before it was exercised? Is there a man in England that would ask America now to be content with the bare repeal of that Declaratory Law? Then why should he ask it of Ireland?"[50]

Henry Grattan, a barrister of the Middle Temple and a leader of the popular party in the Irish Parliament, replied that it was constitutional folly to ask the British Parliament for any pronouncement of Irish autonomy. "You are made to say to England, 'We are independent of you; give us liberty,'" he told the Commons. "Such security is not liberty, but dependency under the appellation of liberty." Flood's answer was that although simple repeal was meaningless, a renunciation act had the force of a promise. If Great Britain "does not renounce the claim," he asserted, "she certainly may revive it; but if she does renounce it, she certainly cannot revive it."[51] Grattan knew better. "There are certain rights inherent in parliaments which they cannot relinquish or give up," he pointed out. "Now, though the present Parliament of Great Britain has renounced all claims to bind Ireland, yet a man who has a mind to argue with impossibilities, may say, We are not secure, because a future English parliament may think themselves entitled to exercise a power which their predecessors could not relinquish."[52] It was foolish to give the British Parliament a precedent of being asked to exercise jurisdiction over the Irish Parliament to solve such a speculative possibility.

Henry Flood must have known he stood on unconvincing constitutional ground. His analysis of what he expected from a renunciation act shows how little security Americans could have obtained from either a repeal of the Declaratory Act or the 1763 solution. Although he was promising the Irish that a renunciation act would make them more confident that the

British Parliament would never again claim the authority to legislate in all cases whatsoever, he was not offering the guarantee of an entrenched constitutional right. "Because," Flood explained, "a renunciation will in the first place give all the legal security that the cause is capable of: and because in the next place, it will pledge the good faith of Great Britain expressly, and when it is expressly pledged, I shall be ready to confide in it."[53] An Irish Protestant might have to make do with that assurance, but it would not have been enough for American whigs.

Henry Grattan's warning that any British statute set a dangerous precedent was well taken, but his solution to the supremacy problem was no more persuasive than Flood's. Grattan wanted the Irish Parliament to claim a constitutional amendment on the basis of contractarian right. Legal weight, he argued, should be accorded to the fact that, in addition to the Declaratory Act, the British Parliament had repealed several other statutes to which the Irish had objected. It had also renounced the right of the English House of Lords to hear Irish judicial appeals, removed commercial restrictions long imposed on Ireland, and had not objected when the Irish Parliament repealed Poynings Act,[54] the law that had given the British executive control of Irish legislation. As these steps had been taken in response to Irish demands, Grattan concluded, they amounted to an implied yet "sealed" treaty between Great Britain and Ireland. "On the one side: —the restoration of the final judicature, the extinction of her legislative claim, of her privy council, of her perpetual mutiny bill, the repeal of the act of legislative supremacy: . . . thus are the two nations compacted for ever in freedom and in peace." Grattan theorized that this "treaty" guaranteed the Irish Parliament perpetual legislative independence by international law, a higher law than Parliament's law and superior to any renunciation act. "The municipal law, or the principles of the municipal law, are no standard; but the law of nations is: it is known to both countries, supersedes the particular customs of both nations, binds the respective states with regard to each other; is above their judges, and above the legislature: the Parliament makes the municipal law, but is itself bound by the law of nations."[55]

Giving the Irish the ultimate legislative concession, the British Parliament passed a Renunciation Act. We learn much about why it was so difficult to resolve the American constitutional controversy by considering its provisions and what they meant in constitutional law: "That the said right claimed by the people of *Ireland* to be bound only by laws enacted by his Majesty and the parliament of that kingdom, in all cases whatever . . . shall be, and it is hereby declared to be established and ascertained for ever, and shall, at no time hereafter, be questioned or questionable."[56] Under the constitution of parliamentary sovereignty, this statute imposed a moral obligation on future British Parliaments. It did not, however, promulgate an entrenched right. The renunciation was not secured against changing legislative will and pleasure. American whigs never asked for a colonial renunciation act. They well might not have asked even had Parliament repealed the American Declaratory Act. A renunciation act, like repeal, would have left them constitutionally where they had been before.

THE DERNIER SOLUTION

There were differences between the American and Irish solutions because there were differences in the American and Irish concepts of constitutional supremacy. American whigs assumed that they were fighting for a constitution under which the ultimate supremacy lay beyond will and pleasure and where people were governed by the rule of law. Under Irish constitutional theory the ultimate supremacy lay with the sitting parliament. Americans wanted a revival of the constitution of customary, prescriptive rights. Except for Charles Francis Sheridan, most Irish Protestants seemed satisfied with the Blackstonian constitution. "Acts of parliament derogatory from the power of subsequent parliaments bind not," Sir William Blackstone stated definitively. "Because the legislature, being in truth the sovereign power, is always of equal, always of absolute authority: it acknowledges no superior upon earth, which the prior legislature must have been, if its ordinances could bind the present parliament."[57] Blackstone would never have admitted it, but for centuries this principle of the sovereignty of the sitting parliament had undermined the English search for constitutional security and the rule of law. When people in 1647 complained that the good laws passed that session of Parliament might be repealed by a succeeding parliament, Judge David Jenkins scoffed at the "very weak" objection. "That feare is endlesse and remedilesse," he insisted, "for it is the essence of parliaments, being compleat, as they ought to be . . . to have power over parliaments before."[58]

Lord North knew that he could not constitutionally offer American whigs the entrenched security that they needed. When he introduced his taxation Conciliatory Bill in February 1775, promising not to tax the colonies if Americans accepted certain obligations, North admitted that his promise had to be kept by majorities of future parliaments. North, therefore, gave the colonists the only assurance anyone could give. "Others perhaps will say, it is proper that parliament should bind itself," North told the House of Commons. "I answer, that whenever parliament confirms an agreement, it always does bind itself."[59] It is not clear North meant the British Parliament was bound or only that session of Parliament. John Erskine, the

Scottish theologian who edited and published for British readers the works of Jonathan Edwards and other American clergymen, pointed out that it did not matter if the sitting session thought itself bound by the promise. "The present parliament, however willing" he wrote, "can give no security, that the power of taxing shall not be thus abused, because no rules or limitations fixed by them, can restrain subsequent parliaments from suspending or altering these rules."[60] The best the Americans could expect from Lord North's plan, a second writer pointed out, would be for subsequent parliaments to feel "honour bound: to adhere to the promise. "I say, in *honour* bound, because the *power*, or *authority*, can in neither case be restrained or limited. This being all the security which, from the nature of government, can be given, must content them. More than this no minister can propose, no Parliament can approve."[61]

The constitutional rule restricting Lord North was the same rule that restricted the choices of Flood and Grattan. American whigs had been told seven years before that what Flood and Grattan would attempt in 1782 was constitutionally impossible. "[S]hould any parliament give up, renounce, and for ever quit claim to the right of making laws to bind us in any case whatever," *Cassandra* wrote in the *Maryland Gazette*, the renunciation would not have much meaning, for "it can constitutionally stipulate for no longer than that one sitting." The colonists might accept Lord North's offer to enter into agreements guaranteeing American rights or colonial legislative autonomy, but they should not put all their constitutional reliance on them. "If we are foolish enough to do this, must not our *future* security depend entirely on the *will* of a *British parliament*, i.e., of a *British ministry*."[62]

In the quest to find solutions to the revolutionary controversy, American whigs were learning lessons to be written into future American constitutional law. To discover that Parliament could not be restrained even by its own promises told them of much more than the need for direct representation. It said something about legislative power and constitutional security. "A constitution that affords no check against its own servants," *Cassandra* warned, "can yield no *security* to us."[63] Long one of the key elements of English and British liberty,[64] the right to security was one of the fundamental constitutional rights then in dispute between the colonies and the mother country.[65] It would be a reason why Americans would write constitutions. They would want the security of legislatures that can constitutionally bind themselves.

CHAPTER ELEVEN

PREROGATIVE SOLUTIONS

Generally it is not useful to single out for criticism assertions of history that are obviously false. Occasionally, however, there are claims so erroneous their very restatement serves to clarify the record just by being completely wrong. An instance, dealing with the authority of Parliament to bind the colonies in all cases whatsoever, has recently been published. "The British located sovereignty in Parliament," it is claimed, "not because they could not imagine locating it anywhere else, but because they were persuaded that the consequences of doing so would lead to the loss of their claim to control over the colonies."[1]

It would be difficult to formulate another sentence demonstrating a greater misunderstanding of eighteenth-century British constitutional government. The fact is that the British located sovereignty in Parliament not to control the colonies, but to control the king. The colonies were immaterial. Had they been susceptible to control it would not have mattered if they were controlled by the war office, the Board of Trade, or a secretary of state reporting to Parliament. What mattered was that they not be controlled by the crown or that they not be associated with the crown independently of Parliament. That was why all the leaders of Parliament, whigs, tories, Rockinghamites, and Chathamites demanded that Americans first acknowledge Parliament's "right" and then Parliament would agree to limit or not to exercise the right.

Parliament was caught in the same uncertainty of British constitutional dynamics in which American whigs were caught. The Americans could not agree to even a *pro forma* acknowledgment of the right when one parliament could not bind another parliament and no one could predict when some future parliament might take advantage of the acknowledgement and exercise the right. American liberty required that Parliament first renounce the right and then the colonists could discuss what powers Parliament possessed for the regulation of trade and the general superintendence of the empire. Parliament, however, could not renounce its authority for that would have left the populous, wealthy thirteen colonies constitutionally linked to the crown, independent of Parliament in all matters except the regulation of all foreign and some intraempire trade. Any revenues or requisitions would have been paid to George III as king of Georgia or king of Connecticut. The constitution had left the Parliament as few choices as it had left the Americans. Parliament either had to require that the colonies acknowledge its theoretical authority, declare them independent, or fight a civil war.

Once more it is necessary to make what by now is a familiar point. The prerogativism of American whigs was not an intellectual inconsistency forced on them when the Coercive Acts left them nowhere else to turn except to natural law. American monarchism was the logical product of their attachment to the principle of the old English constitution, the proof of their sincerity to constitutionalism. It was not new, but even though muted until 1774, it had always been part of their constitutional solution to the controversy concerning Parliament's authority to legislate in all cases whatsoever, should Great Britain push them that far. It had never been concealed, but had been stated throughout the controversy, and even earlier, as by the Council and House of Burgesses of Virginia, in 1764, before passage of the Stamp Act. "[A]t this time," the councilors and burgesses said in a petition to George III,

> they implore Permission to approach the Throne with humble Confidence, and to intreat that your Majesty will be graciously pleased to protect your People of this Colony in the Enjoyment of their ancient and inestimable Right of being governed by such Laws respecting their internal Polity and Taxation as are derived from their own Consent, with the Approbation of their Sovereign or his Substitute: A Right which as Men, and Descendants of *Britons*, they have ever quietly possessed since first by Royal Permission and Encouragement they left the Mother Kingdom to extend its Commerce and Dominion.

Ten years later, the Continental Congress was making the same constitutional connection. It did not petition Parliament. It did petition the king.

"We ask but for peace, liberty, and safety," Congress told George III. "We wish not for a diminuation of the prerogative, nor do we solicit the grant for any new right in our favour. Your royal authority over us and our connexion with Great-Britain, we shall always carefully and zealously endeavour to support and maintain." These three sentences were the most revolutionary statements made by the first Continental Congress. If American whigs were prepared to support what was said, they were risking civil war. The argument was phrased with great care, but no words could soften the constitutional reality. Congress said it did not wish "a diminuation of the prerogative," for that was what it meant to say from the American perspective. From the British perspective, however, Congress appeared to be asking an increase of the prerogative, or even a revival of the prerogative. For Congress wanted the king to assume an active role in the imperial constitution. "We therefore most earnestly beseech your majesty," the Congress petitioned, "that your royal authority and interposition may be used for our relief and that a gracious answer may be given to our petition."[2]

The Americans solved the legislative grievance by placing all connection between Great Britain and the colonies in the executive branch of the government. "That the executive power," whigs of a North Carolina county explained, "constitutionally vested in the Crown and which presides equally over Great Britain and America, is a sufficient security for the due subordination of the Colonies without the Parliament's assuming powers of Legislation and Taxation which we enjoy distinct from, and in equal degree with them."[3] That statement is what the eighteenth century would have called a "constitutional" resolution to the legislation controversy. All that Parliament had to do was "relinquish all pretence of right to govern the *British* Colonies in *America*, and leave that to whom it solely and exclusively belongs, namely, the King, our lawful Sovereign, with his Parliament in the respective Colonies, and the *Americans* have a Constitution without seeking further."[4] Considered in the perspective of the supremacy controversy, Americans defended the prerogative link not as a change in constitutional law but a restoration of constitutional security. When the Lords and Commons attempted to usurp legislative authority over the colonies, they also usurped the position of the king. "To me," Benjamin Franklin wrote in a private letter,

> those Bodies seem to have been long encroaching on the Rights of
> their and our Sovereign, assuming too much of his Authority, and be-
> traying his Interests. By our Constitution he is, with his plantation
> Parliaments, the sole Legislator of his American Subjects, and in that
> Capacity is, and ought to be, free to exercise his own Judgment, un-

restrained and unlimited by his Parliament here [Great Britain]. And our Parliaments have right to grant him Aids without the Consent of this Parliament, a Circumstance, which, by the way, begins to give it some Jealousy.[5]

Franklin meant that London was jealous—suspicious or "suspiciously fearful" as the word was then defined—of American suggestions that colonial assemblies had a right to pay taxes directly to the king without any parliamentary check. The jealousy was that this "right" could make the king independent of Parliament, not that it would make the colonies independent of Great Britain. After all, as Americans like Franklin understood the constitutional situation, they were contending for the restoration of their constitutional connection with the king, not for constitutional separation. It could not be said, Alexander Hamilton pointed out, "that an English colony is independent, while it bears allegiance to the King of Great-Britain." "By recognizing as their King, a King resident among us and under our influence," Richard Price told his fellow Britons, the Americans "gave us a negative on all their laws. By allowing an appeal to us in their civil disputes, they gave us likewise the ultimate determination of all civil causes among them.—In short. They allowed us every power we could desire, except that of taxing them, and interfering in their internal legislations."[6]

The twentieth century may no longer understand what was going on in the 1770s. American whigs were pushing against the republican grain. They wanted the certainty of the restrained, balanced constitution, not experimentation with civic virtue. We see this by considering not what we think they should have wanted, but what they said they sought: a revived monarchy with a king who, in imperial government at least, would exercise the balance of the balanced constitution. George III was asked to veto bills by Parliament legislating for the colonies and to prorogue sessions or call elections when Parliament threatened American rights.

Few turns of the revolution controversy have eluded historians more than the apparent royalism of American whigs. They were supposed to be guided by something called "republicanism," and to see them appealing for protection to the prerogative has provided scholars who doubt they could have been guided by constitutional ideology with convincing evidence of their insincerity. The doubts were summarized recently by a critic:

One may question the strength of the American commitment to the constitutional position sketched out in 1774 by the colonial pamphleteers and argue that the colonists were merely casting about in

desperation for a way to reconcile two apparently contradictory im-
pulses—a desire to remain within the empire and a determination
to deny parliamentary authority. The inflation of the king's imperial
role, one might observe, was simply a hasty colonial solution to the
dilemma, quickly seized upon and just as quickly abandoned.[7]

The appeal to the prerogative was no more quickly abandoned than it had
been quickly seized upon. George III rejected the American argument,
declared the colonists rebels, and put them beyond the royal protection,
before they abandoned the prerogative solution—Tom Paine's antimonar-
chical writings notwithstanding.

The evidence should be reexamined not only from the perspective of
"republicanism," "Namierism," and related considerations, but also from
the perspective of constitutional law. Recall the constitutional predicament
that existed at the time the American whigs turned to George III and asked
him to reassert his prerogative on their behalf. Putting aside the question
whether there were solutions other than legal solutions, and considering
only narrow issues of law, with the passage of the Coercive Acts, the controversy between the colonial whigs and Parliament had reached a legal
impasse. Parliament had set the condition precedent of acknowledgment
by American assemblies of its right to legislate in all cases before it would
renounce exercise of the right. The Continental Congress, in turn, wanted
all supremacy statutes repealed with the implication that Parliament renounced the right, a step Parliament could not take constitutionally as it
would have strengthened the potential power of the King by leaving the
crown as the chief link between the colonies and the mother country. To
find a solution around this impasse the American whigs had two theories
they could have adopted as a basis for formulating arguments. They could
have turned to natural law and asserted "the rights of man," the rights of
nationalism, or that Parliament, by violating the constitution, had placed
them in a state of nature. This approach, favored by a small minority of the
delegates to the Continental Congress, notably Patrick Henry and John
Sullivan, was rejected by the majority and by almost every American whig
of whom we know. The American case against parliamentary sovereignty
had been stated as constitutional law in 1765 at the start of the controversy, and it remained constitutional to the end, even in the writing of the
Declaration of Independence.

Unwilling to depend on the shifting sands of natural law or to abandon
their claims to rights under the British constitution, American whigs had
only one place to turn once the Coercive Acts made it impossible for them
to continue their strategy of avoiding the issue of Parliament's right to
legislate. They turned to the English constitution, especially to the prin-

ciples of the seventeenth-century English constitution, that is, to the royal prerogative.

It was less a matter of constitutional choice than of choosing the constitution. The Coercive Acts had been the constitutional moment of truth, telling American whigs that Parliament irrevocably rejected their constitutional arguments of customary restraints on legislative power. After that, American whigs had no other constitutional option. They had to abandon the constitution or appeal to the crown. George III was their last constitutional resort.

In a constitutional history of Parliament's authority to legislate, it is not possible to explore in detail the richness, the implications, or the logic of the prerogative solution. It belongs more fully with the American whig constitutional case against Great Britain's assertion of the authority to govern as distinguished from merely the authority to legislate. The best that can be done is to provide an outline of the evidence, and no aspect of the evidence reveals more of the constitutional logic and consistency of the prerogative solution than the fact that it was also being pursued in contemporary Great Britain.

Much has been made in recent years of the influence upon American whigs of the so-called "radicals" in eighteenth-century British politics. They are also called "commonwealthmen" and various kinds of whigs. Their program for government reform was varied, with individuals pursuing different concerns or reacting to different causes of unhappiness, such as foreign entanglements, military adventurism, creeping taxation, bloated bureaucracy, decreasing agrarian influence, new sources of money, novel methods of investment, and the rising influence of trade, manufacturing, and the major cities. What interests us is that the most vocal complaints and the most pressing demands for change were largely focused on Parliament, particularly on the House of Commons. Some of the objectives of the reformers were unrelated to the American constitutional controversy, such as demands for annual or triennial elections, or for the enactment of "place" bills that would exclude royal pensioners and executive or military officeholders from the House of Commons. Other objectives more closely paralleled American political ideas, as, for example, a growing movement for direct, more equal representation.[8] Still others arose from a realization that parliamentary supremacy was being converted into parliamentary sovereignty and that Parliament was exercising arbitrary power, a lesson taught in part by the constitutional controversy between Parliament and American whigs.

British radicals in the age of the American Revolution had a peculiar way of looking at institutions and of expressing their concerns, one that makes them appear not to have been radical at all. They argued for annual elections, for example, not only in terms of policy or principle, of ending court corruption and crown influence in the House of Commons, but also of restoring the constitution, of purifying the present by going back to an ancient constitution, based on custom and contract, to a constitution that Parliament long had disregarded but which they said still was "law." This appearance of nostalgia makes these reformers seem "conservative" today. In fact, they were not. When calling for a return to first principles they were not so much going back in time for the authority of law, but using an imagined past to reject the present. If they wanted equal representation, they said it had been an element of the ancient constitution and called for its "restoration." They should be thought of as constitutionalists rather than as conservatives, for, using the idealism of a more perfect constitution, they softened the impact of radical change by clothing it in constitutional dress.

A central element of the "radicals" political unhappiness was opposition to arbitrary authority. It drove them to restore (or was it to create?) constitutional restraints on the exercise of legislative power. This was what linked British radicals to the American whig efforts to activate the prerogative solution. Students of the American Revolution should look at the British reformers from this point of view. The fact that they too asked George III again to become an active weight in a balanced constitution provides some evidence that there was legal logic to the prerogative solution and that it may have been not only the best, but the only solution remaining in English-British constitutional law.

If anything, British reformers went further than American whigs. They not only asked for resurrection of the royal prerogative, they pretended to ask the House of Commons to resume at least one of its dormant balancing functions, the power of impeaching royal officials. Complaining that there were persons who advised the king not to hear London's petitions and to exercise arbitrary power against the American colonies, the livery of London in July 1775 instructed London's members in the House of Commons, "to move for an impeachment of the authors and advisers of those measures." It was an anachronistic idea, to rectify in 1775 the grievances of the Americans by exercising a procedure belonging to the seventeenth-century constitution of the Stuart era, a process of the old constitution that had existed before the Glorious Revolution.[9]

The prerogative the king most frequently was asked to exercise was the veto. We are not concerned with objections to specific legislation but with requests that the king act because Parliament abused or exceeded its authority. Students of the American Revolution should give close attention to these petitions, heeding not just what they sought but how they were worded. Not to be missed is the fact that the antiparliamentary petitions drafted in Great Britain, praying the king check the power of Parliament by exercising the veto, read like American petitions praying the king protect the colonies from parliamentary legislation. The arguments were not what we would expect: that Parliament had sent to the king unwise and unjust legislation. They said that Parliament was abusing authority or was endangering the rights of the people. An example was the petition from the common council of London asking George III to veto the cider and perry excise of 1763. The excise affected only the arboricultural sections of the nation, not London, yet the common council "beseech[ed] your Majesty, to protect their Liberty, and to keep them happy, and at Ease, free from the Apprehension of being disturbed in their Property." The grievance was against power, the arbitrary power exercised by Parliament and the power granted to excise officials to enter private homes. The appeal was to the old constitution of restraints on power by the rule of law and to the customary constitution of the king's veto.[10]

Given the conditions of constitutional law in the 1760s and 1770s, the most extreme demands were those praying King George to dismiss Parliament and call new elections. Several times during the Middlesex election controversy, opponents of Parliament petitioned that the House of Commons be dismissed for disclaiming the voice of the people and expelling John Wilkes.[11] The politics of the situation need not concern us for it is the wording of these petitions and remonstrances that tells us of the constitutional perceptions that British reformers or radicals shared with American whigs. In March 1773, the lord mayor, aldermen, and livery of London, complained in an address delivered in person to the king that, "Our representatives, who were chosen to be the guardians of our rights, have invaded our most sacred privileges," in various ways including the expulsion of Wilkes and the arrest of the London officials.

> We therefore, your remonstrants, again supplicate your Majesty to employ the only remedy now left by the constitution, the exercise of that salutary power with which you are intrusted by law, the dissolving of the present parliament, and the removal of those evil counsellors, who advised the measures so generally odious to the nation; and your Majesty, as the true guardian of our rights, shall ever reign in the hearts of a grateful people.[12]

The expression to mark is that the king was asked "to employ the only remedy now left by the constitution," a remedy with which he was "intrusted by law." This constitutional helplessness—of having no alternative to the king—was a recurring theme in petitions, as, for example, when London's common council complained that, by expelling Wilkes, the ministry had deprived the voters of Middlesex of the franchise, and "have thereby taken from your Subjects all Hopes of parliamentary Redress, and have left us no Resource, under GOD, but in your Majesty."[13]

Parliament was the constitutional problem, and the prerogative was the constitutional solution. At least that was what British opponents of Parliament in the 1760s and 1770s were telling their king. It was claimed that 2445 freemen of Bristol signed a petition to George III saying that they had no recourse but to beg prerogative relief. "We sought parliamentary redress," they asserted,

> but the base and unworthy conduct of your Majesty's ministers, who have exerted their utmost efforts to conceal the fears and apprehensions of your people, have blasted our pleasing expectations. We have now no other resource under God, but in your Majesty. . . . [G]rant us redress of those intolerable grievances, by bringing to a strict account those evil counsellors and servants who have endeavoured to deceive their royal master—abused the public trust—[and] violated the freedom of our constitution.[14]

At the risk of being repetitive, one additional point must be made. The politically and constitutionally disaffected in Great Britain drafted similar petitions making similar arguments on behalf of what they called American "rights." They warned the king that constitutional grievances had driven his colonial subjects "to despair" and asked him to veto legislation coercing the Americans,[15] including the Massachusetts and Quebec Bills.[16] "Your petitioners," the lord mayor, aldermen, and livery of London prayed in 1775, "beseech your Majesty, to dismiss your present ministers and advisers from your person and counsels for ever; to dissolve a parliament, who, by various acts of cruelty and injustice, have manifested a spirit of persecution against our brethren in America, and given their sanction to Popery and arbitrary power."[17]

There was more form than substance to these petitions, a touch of constitutional unreality coloring the political infighting of that day. No one expected George III to veto a bill that had passed the two houses of Parliament or to call elections unless asked by either the ministry or a majority of the members of the House of Commons. The main function of these petitions was political, to state grievances formally, in an attractive, semi-official guise assuring their publication by newspapers and magazines, and thus getting their arguments before a wider public than just the king. Even so, they had a constitutional function, for they often elicited at least a defense on the constitutional merits, sometimes forcing the administration to admit the arbitrary reach of parliamentary power. Robert Macfarlane reported that a Middlesex petition of 1768, imploring the king to save the constitution by dissolving Parliament, was ridiculed by the ministry, "as soliciting his majesty to overturn the constitution, and to encroach upon the privileges of the democratical branch of the legislature, whose resolutions he could not annihilate without endangering the whole system of our liberty, and assuming that despotic authority against the exercise of which they clamoured with such violence."[18]

It is not necessary to dwell on what Macfarlane had the ministers saying. Equating liberty with parliamentary supremacy and the prerogative with "despotic authority," they were repeating the best-known clichés of the eighteenth-century constitution. It is the Middlesex petitioners who deserve attention. They did not think they were "endangering the whole system of our liberty." They were questioning the reality of British liberty and, almost alone in the eighteenth-century, faulting the cherished British constitution. If they wanted a different constitution, they did not want what today would be called a radical constitution, only what the eighteenth century would have called a radical remedy for constitutional injury. They sought constitutional security from the sovereign supremacy of an unrepresentative Parliament, and to obtain it appealed to the apparatus of the seventeenth-century constitution to put checks and balances back into the eighteenth-century constitution. We may suspect they knew it was too late, that the British constitution could no longer contemplate institutional restraints on legislative discretion, but can we be sure?

Most constitutional commentators of the 1760s and 1770s wrote of the veto as a viable prerogative power. But they were British, and the British, or at least the English, luxuriated in constitutional archaisms. It took a touch of realism not characteristic of English legal thought to admit that "though still existing in name," the royal veto was "extinguished in fact."[19] We may be certain that every lawyer knew that no Hanoverian king had ever exercised the veto, and we may suspect that every competent lawyer knew that no Hanoverian king—or any British monarch in the future— would ever again veto an act of Parliament.

There was also substantial opinion, constitutionally unrealistic perhaps but frequently asserted, that the king could dismiss parliaments and call elections at his discretion. "It is idle to pretend, that your majesty cannot dissolve the parliament," Macfarlane argued. "The septennial act gives you a positive right to the exercise of this prerogative."[20] It is immaterial that most legal experts probably agreed with Macfarlane. What is material is that George III understood the power was either unconstitutional or constitutionally dubious. "[T]here is a time, when it is morally demonstrable that men cease to be representatives," the lord mayor, aldermen, and livery of London told him. "That time is now arrived. The present House of Commons do not represent the people." The argument did not matter. The king was not going to dissolve Parliament. Told that he had a constitutional duty to act, George III implied that the constitutional authority was gone. "I shall always be ready to receive the requests, and to listen to the complaints of my subjects," George told the London officials. But he would do nothing "injurious to my parliament, and irreconcilable to the principles of the constitution." From the perspective of today George III was acting constitutionally, taking the crown out of politics and preparing the way for the responsible government of Parliament and cabinet. "I have ever made the law of the land the rule of my conduct, esteeming it my chief glory to reign over a free people," he explained. "With this view I have always been careful to execute faithfully the trust reposed in me, as to avoid even the appearance of invading any of those powers which the constitution has placed in other hands."[21] We in the twentieth century not only know what the king meant, we approve, for he was moving Great Britain toward today's constitution. It would be well, however, to consider the perspective of those eighteenth-century Americans and Britons apprehensive of Parliament's arbitrary power. George III was saying more to them than that he would keep himself out of politics. He was taking the crown out of government. Constitutional law no longer would be protected from the caprice of an arbitrary Parliament, even in theory. The prerogative was not available to enforce the rule of law.

It was an odd moment in constitutional history that we do not fully understand, a time when the followers of John Wilkes pleaded for a revival of the prerogative and the head of the house of Hanover defended the right of the "democratic" branch of the government to do as it pleased.[22] The ambiguity of the constitution, in fluctuation between two very different definitions of law, right, and power was reflected in the unexpected maneuverings to which politicians were pushed as parliamentary supremacy was being transformed into parliamentary sovereignty. "It is a Matter of Indignation," a political commentator complained in 1770, "to observe the Persons who at present imprudently call themselves *Whigs* endeavouring to exalt the Prerogative of the Crown in the most absolute and essential Manner; by petitioning the King to *dissolve the Parliament*, and annihilate the Power of the House of Commons, which is the only true, great, and constitutional Bulwark of our Liberties."[23] The constitutional irony is what he meant by the Commons being a bulwark of the people's liberties. In another of those eighteenth-century constitutional clichés, Parliament was a bulwark protecting liberties from the prerogative power of the crown.

In the American controversy, the same inexplicable shifting of political parties occurred, a realignment of arguments reflecting the constitutional realization that arbitrary power had come to be vested in the houses of

Parliament. "The contest with America," a "Revolution Whig" observed in 1775, "seems to have produced a strange overturn in the political systems of the two great parties who divide this kingdom.—The Tories, by acknowledging the supreme power of the British parliament over the whole British empire, appear to be turned Whigs; and the Whigs, in attempting to extend the power of the King's prerogative beyond the controul of his parliament, shew themselves to be Tories." [24]

Our lesson, however, is not of inconsistency but of consistency. It is that American whigs were not abandoning the British constitution when they turned to the prerogative for a solution to their constitutional predicament. They were not dissembling their political objectives or revealing the insincerity of their earlier claims to constitutional principle. They were, in fact, doing precisely what the radical-reformist whigs of Great Britain were doing and for the same reason. They had encountered the fundamental finality of the new constitution, the sovereignty of Parliament, and had no legal alternative except to appeal to the crown to revive the prerogatives of the old seventeenth-century balanced constitution. What we will never learn is whether, like the followers of John Wilkes and the parliamentary reformers in Great Britain, they knew from the beginning that the appeal would fail.

CHAPTER TWELVE

CONCLUSION

The prerogative solution was constitutionally impossible. British tories as well as British whigs could not allow American colonists to secure their constitutional liberty at the expense of British constitutional liberty. There can be no mistaking where British constitutionalists located liberty and which institution everyone, even members of the ministry, identified as the one serious threat to liberty. Liberty was located in Parliament and the threat was from the crown.

After George III rejected petitions that he dissolve Parliament for ignoring the wishes of the people in the John Wilkes affair, Attorney General William De Grey, who had prosecuted Wilkes, reminded his colleagues in the House of Commons of the constitutional necessity to "preserve the independence of our own body, as involving the liberty of the people, and defend it against the people themselves misguided and inflamed by faction and self-interest, with no less activity and perseverance than against the Crown or the Lords." Therefore, he said, the House should praise the king for avoiding constitutional temptation. "Let us," De Grey urged, "look up with affection and gratitude to the prince, who, knowing the value of our constitution, as well to himself as to his subjects, has nobly rejected an opportunity which the late Petitions have given him, of destroying the equilibrium of the constitution by increasing his own power, which a sovereign less virtuous and less wise would have embraced." [1]

Five years after De Grey lauded George III for not using the Wilkes controversy to increase "his own power," members of all factions in both houses of Parliament commended the king for his fidelity to the eighteenth-century constitution by rejecting American petitions praying that he revive seventeenth-century prerogativism. Even the king's first minister, Lord North, said the American war was being fought not just to establish parliamentary supremacy over the colonies, but to defend the constitution against American monarchism. Charles James Fox had irritated North by reminding the Commons of the "political distinctions" between "Whig and Tory," and calling North and the other ministers "tories." "His lordship then said," a London newspaper reported, "that if he understood the meaning of the words Whig and Tory, which the last speaker had mentioned, he conceived that it was the characteristic of whiggism to gain as much for the people as possible, while the aim of toryism was to encrease the prerogative. That in the present case, administration contended for the right of Parliament, while the Americans talked of their belonging to the crown. Their language therefore was that of toryism."[2]

Two hundred years of parliamentary supremacy have clouded our hindsight. We cannot take Lord North as seriously as did his contemporaries because we cannot appreciate the degree to which the eighteenth-century British constitutional mind thought that the potential of prerogative power was the ultimate menace to the perfect liberty established at the Glorious Revolution. Long before the American Revolution ended, John Dunning, former solicitor general of England, earned himself a permanent sentence in British constitutional history by moving in the House of Commons, "that it is necessary to declare, that the influence of the crown has increased, is increasing, and ought to be diminished."[3] Over the strong objections of Lord North, the motion carried by 233 to 215. Influence meant something quite different than constitutional authority, but it was the possibility of royal power not the likelihood of actual power that raised alarms among British constitutionalists when American whigs sought protection from an active royal prerogative. One did not have to know precisely what constitutional changes would be wrought to think the risk not worth the gain of peace with the colonies.[4] One possibility was on everyone's mind. Suppose that the colonies and Great Britain were united only by common interest and allegiance to a common king, a commentator wrote in the *Boston Evening-Post*. "When the King wants the Assistance of his American Subjects, he must apply to their Houses of Commons for Grants, in the same Way he now does to his Parliaments in Britain."[5] Some people thought that the reality of the danger was proven by what had happened with the revenues of Ireland. In fact, when Josiah Tucker argued that total American independence, with all connections broken to both crown and Parliament would strengthen British liberty, other people said Great Britain should also separate from Ireland, "to *preserve our present happy constitution.*" The reason: "Our connections with Ireland invests the king with an amazing degree of power, by giving him the disposal of many places both in church and state; not to mention the pensions which are liberally bestowed to silence the opposers of government in England. It is sufficient to hint at this, to shew how much the constitution will be benefited by such a separation."[6] People who drafted plans for continual union under which Parliament would no longer possess authority to legislate for the colonies, generally provided either that requisitions paid the king by the colonies be controlled by Parliament or that revenue raised in one of the dominions for the use of the king could not be remitted or spent in another of the king's dominions.[7]

The American prerogative solution seemed so fraught with constitutional peril that it inspired some rather extreme, sometimes surprising arguments. The archbishop of York, for example, accused American whigs of wanting "to throw the whole weight and power of the colonies into the scale of the crown."[8] One reason James Duane voted for Joseph Galloway's plan of union was to reassure Great Britain that America could never do that. By giving to Parliament and to the colonial Grand Council a mutual veto over legislation binding on the colonies, the Galloway plan, Duane contended, would have guarded Great Britain "against all attempts of the Sovereign to unite with one part of the Empire . . . to oppress or injure her."[9]

No matter what policy was pursued or program undertaken, someone thought it held hidden potentials for reviving royal power. Some people praised George III for supporting the war with America in order to increase the authority of Parliament, even though it meant he ran "a risk of diminishing his own."[10] Others thought the war could not help but make the king more powerful not only in colonial affairs, but at home. "We cannot," the lord mayor, aldermen, and livery of London warned the electors of Great Britain, "discover any real Object or possible Event of this Dispute, (should we be successful) but that of establishing the arbitrary Power of the Crown over our Fellow-Subjects in *America,* which must greatly endanger the Constitution here, and encreasing the Number of Placemen and Pensioners already so enormous, as to threaten the utter Destruction of Freedom and Independence among us."[11] Later, the ministry was accused of the opposite, of knowing that the Americans would always keep up a resistance, and of not making peace in hope that the fighting would continue for years. "A standing army, the species of force they would employ, though distant from the seat of empire, is always a formidable engine, and would be particularly so in this instance, as by its means that encreased influence, which the crown acquires, and perhaps necessarily enjoys, during a state of hostility, would be perpetuated."[12] Even when the administration sent peace commissioners to North America, there was concern that the peace mission could increase the prerogative. The commissioners might surrender everything but the power and patronage of the crown, Edmund Burke charged, they "would increase the prerogative as they diminished" the areas of the empire that were subject to Parliament's supremacy.[13]

There is but one final point to be made. It is the major lesson of this study. The constitutional necessity to check prerogative power shaped the course of the American Revolution controversy much more than has been credited in this century. "Even a Burke, who boasts of his Philanthropy and Love of Liberty, would have bound America to unlimited Subjection," Thomas Northcote wrote the Irish Reform Committee. The fact was not surprising to Northcote in 1783, and it should not be to historians living in a different constitutional epoch.[14] It may have been a power Burke would not have exercised, but he, too, would have used the word "unlimited" to describe it. The colonists understood why. British officials made certain of that by frequently telling colonial leaders that their liberty depended on Parliament, not on the king. William Samuel Johnson, writing the governor of Connecticut, used quotation marks to indicate he was quoting directly the words of the earl of Hillsborough, secretary of state for the colonies. "It is essential to the constitution," Hillsborough told Johnson, "to preserve the supremacy of Parliament inviolate; and tell your friends in America . . . that it is as much their interest to support the constitution and preserve the supremacy of Parliament as it is ours. Neither of us can be safe but upon that ground."[15] That constitutional ground was Parliament's institutional role as a check on arbitrary power.[16]

For us the eighteenth-century need for proportional constitutional structure may appear as an overemphasis on symmetry. For members of Parliament and the educated British public, it was a matter of constitutional balance. The taught articulation was as familiar among military officers as it was among barristers. "[T]he whole of our political system," General John Burgoyne has been quoted as observing, "depends upon the preservation of its great and essential parts distinctly, and no part is so great and essential as the supremacy of the legislation."[17] Political thought in the second half of the eighteenth century was different than in later centuries. We should not conclude that British leaders thought more narrowly. It was, rather, that they thought more constitutionally.

Charles Howard McIlwain was not sure of the distinction. He believed that British leaders had thought narrowly. In his study, *The American Revolution: A Constitutional Interpretation*, McIlwain concluded that the controversy became too legal, for which he blamed the lawyers. It was the lawyers, he claimed, such as the lord chief justice, the earl of Mansfield, the government's chief legal advisor, who, unable to comprehend the controversy except from the narrowness of law, prevented the administration from seeing that the solution was a commonwealth of independent legislatures joined in union only by a common allegiance to the crown. "The rigorous logic of his theory of sovereignty compelled Mansfield to demand one ultimate and undivided authority and he could brook no exception even of a practical kind," McIlwain wrote, claiming that Mansfield's jurisprudence anticipated that of John Austin who, in 1832 under a much different constitution, taught the following generations of British lawyers not to confuse law with morality. Austin defined "law" as general commands of a superior enforced by sanctions. "But Austinianism is logic, and logic is not all of life," McIlwain complained. "So, happily, an illogical modern Empire has arisen not unlike the modern limited monarchy for the realm itself, in defiance of Austin and in the teeth of Lord John Russell's repetition of Mansfield's dictum: no dependence, no sovereignty; with its futile logic, always so soothing to the timid souls who live in constant dread of surrendering their 'sovereignty' to somebody or other." [18]

McIlwain was right. Mansfield dreaded surrendering sovereignty to somebody. He is wrong, however, to think that somebody was the colonial assemblies. "For Lord Mansfield," McIlwain continued, "the sovereignty of the Parliament and the dependency of the dominions must continue to coexist. They must stand or fall together." John Adams, who believed that colonial assemblies could be autonomous from Parliament yet remain in allegiance to the king, was praised by McIlwain for seeing the practical situation much more clearly than Mansfield, that is, less like a lawyer. "Adams, Austinian though in a certain sense he was, looked further into the future, and saw what Mansfield could not, that for a working empire his theory must be modified in practice by a voluntary concession. Such a compromise, however, was too advanced for the rigorous logic of the eighteenth century." [19]

McIlwain must be approached with caution. His error was not just to be anachronistic, it was also that he professed to be discussing law when in fact he was treating it with contempt. He ignored law when saying that the British Commonwealth of Nations solution to the American Revolution controversy was too "advanced" for the eighteenth century. In terms of law, that solution could have retarded, not advanced, British liberty. It would have been difficult for Lord Mansfield—or any other member of Parliament or lawyer—to have seen the solution "advancing" anything except the autonomy and power of the crown. Keep in mind points just made: that fear of an increase of royal authority saturated the constitutional thinking of that day,[20] that there was, for example, much concern about the influence that George III derived from the revenue of Ireland and of the pensions he was able to award on the Irish establishment.[21] "[F]rom the perspective of Britain's own internal constitutional development during the previous century," Jack P. Greene has pointed out, "colonial theories about the organization of the empire seemed dangerously retrograde. By placing the resources of Ireland and the colonies directly in the hands of the Crown and beyond the reach of Parliament, those theories appeared to strike directly at the root of the legislative supremacy that, for them, was the primary legacy of the Glorious Revolution."[22]

Sir Lewis Namier, a historian not given to overemphasizing ideology, wrote that the commonwealth solution was unacceptable to many more Britons than just Lord Mansfield and other narrow-minded common lawyers. Royalty, he noted, "was still an active factor in British politics, and to eighteenth-century Englishmen any exercise of its attributes apart from the British Parliament would have seemed a dangerous and unconstitutional reversion to 'prerogative'."[23] By the year of the Declaration of Independence, royal power seemed so extensive that otherwise harmless programs caused apprehension among constitutionalists. The *Annual Register*, for example, reported that a Scottish militia bill, part of the administration's preparations for war, was criticized on the grounds that it would increase "the dangerous and unconstitutional power of the crown, which was already greater than had ever hitherto been deemed consistent with public liberty."[24] There was even fear of what could happen if Great Britain won the war and the Americans submitted unconditionally. "The consequences of so enormous an additional power thrown into the hands of the crown," the *Annual Register* warned, "are . . . too melancholy to be dwelt upon with pleasure. The English constitution will inevitably perish in the same grave, into which our pride and injustice had a little before precipitated the liberties of America."[25]

We must be cautious. It would be wrong to think all these warnings due to antiadministration politics, but of course many were. Some writers, for example, even argued that the ministry pursued the war expecting that military victory over the Americans could be converted into constitutional victory over Parliament. "A part of them might hope at least," one pamphlet charged in 1777, "that by a decisive blow, an extension of the power of the crown might follow a reunion with the colonies, brought about by victory; and to be maintained by a MILITARY force alone."[26]

Such talk seemed a lot less farfetched in the 1770s than it would today. Events occurring during the first years of that decade were widely interpreted as warnings that constitutional government was in danger. "No equal portion of time," the *Annual Register* said of 1772 alone, "has been so fatal to public liberty, and the rights of mankind, as that which comprehends the overthrow of the constitution, in those great and extensive countries, of France, Sweden, and Poland."[27] Until that year, Sweden had "been considered among the freest governments in Europe. It has been even thought to approach to a perfection in that respect, superior to any other of the modern states."[28] The newspapers and magazines reprinted accounts of how the Swedish king, using his standing army, suppressed the nobility, disbanded the assembly, and assumed the powers of government into his own hands.[29] "Never forget," New Yorkers were warned, "that about two years ago a crowned miscreant compelled the states of *Sweden*, the Parliament of that Country, to release him from his coronation oath! His success may tempt others to commit the same sacrilege."[30]

Of course warnings of what could happen if America were conquered were known to be exaggerated. Parliament would have been aware of the danger and should have been able to protect its constitutional supremacy over the crown. There was less certainty, however, about how Parliament could have preserved its independence if, instead of war, peace had been made on the commonwealth solution, leaving the colonies tied to Great Britain only through allegiance to the king. People wondered what checks would then symmetrize the constitutional balance. As late as 1778, John Moreton, member for Wigan, chief justice of Chester, attorney general to the queen, and consistent supporter of the administration, warned the House of Commons "of the danger of raising money in America by requisitions from the crown; by which revenue, so raised, the King might be enabled to govern this country without parliaments."[31] He was voicing the ultimate constitutional nightmare of the eighteenth century: fear of an independent royal revenue. It was a worry that went beyond crown control of standing armies or of the king dominating Parliament through the corrupting influence of pensions and places. If the king obtained sufficient funds, he or the ministry could reduce the constitutional importance of Parliament or ignore it altogether. There had even been concern in some quarters, for example, that the real intent of taxing the colonies had been to obtain an independent revenue.[32]

A sense of how seriously the threat was taken may be gathered by considering the importance people then gave to the case of *Campbell* v. *Hall*. It had involved a temporary tax only, proclaimed by the king following the conquest of Grenada. Today the intent appears constitutionally harmless for instead of promulgating a new tax, the crown had decreed that the former French revenue system be retained, but only until Parliament or an assembly could vote permanent British taxes. The action smacked, however, of prerogative taxation and in a widely acclaimed ruling, Lord Mansfield declared it unconstitutional.[33] The lord chief justice's decision in

Campbell v. *Hall* must be measured by the reaction of the day, and not by how insignificant the danger of prerogative taxation may appear from our vantage point of hindsight. "[A] more important cause than this has not been litigated since that of Hampden," the *Scots Magazine* suggested.[34] "Indeed," another observer added, "since the cause of ship money, no point of equal consequence has ever been brought before any British court of judicature for decision; nor will the liberties of Britain be much less affected by the determination."[35] It was not possible for an eighteenth-century constitutionalist to make a stronger claim than that.

There is a nagging question that must be considered. If the threat to the constitution most feared in eighteenth-century legal theory was the specter of prerogative revenue, why did Parliament pass the Irish Renunciation Act? If in 1775, the British could not consider leaving the American imperial connection to the crown alone, how could they afford in 1782 to renounced the authority to legislate for Ireland leaving that kingdom connected to London mainly through the crown? The answer is that Ireland was less wealthy than was North America, and the crown already had control of as much of the Irish revenue as it was likely to get. Parliament had little to lose by giving Henry Flood his Renunciation Act in addition to repealing the Irish Declaratory Act. The colonies were quite a different proposition. The 1700s were a century filled with predictions that Americans would soon outnumber the British, would surely be the richest people in the world, and that eventually the capitol of the empire would be Philadelphia. Parliament would have assumed grave constitutional risks had it granted to the Americans the solution to the constitutional predicament that it granted to Ireland. From the perspective of both the constitutional vision of the eighteenth century and the survival of Glorious Revolution principles, an American Renunciation Act could have been the undoing of the British constitution. Even members of Parliament who understood that both repeal of the Declaratory Act and passage of a renunciation of legislative supremacy were constitutionally meaningless, would have been reluctant to vote for either without also developing some new constitutional mechanism for controlling the king's dealings with the colonies.

It may be objected that the wrong fear is being stressed. Today we may think that the eighteenth-century Parliament and constitutionalists could not have been concerned about the king. Surely it was the ministry that worried them. In light of how the ministry developed into the cabinet and became the executive branch of government in the nineteenth century, this suggestion is plausible. There were people in the 1770s who realized that the ministry could become much more powerful if the colonies remained in the empire but independent of Parliament. Lord North, for example, was praised for refusing to consider the American whig solution to the taxation controversy, royal requisitions paid by the colonies directly to the crown, with Parliament having no role either setting the amounts or receiving the revenue.[36] "Had Administration entertained tyrannical schemes," it was pointed out, "they certainly would have rather chosen to draw supplies from *America* by Royal requisition, in the disposal of which they would be unaccountable, than by a mode in which it will be appropriated by Parliament."[37]

We must separate ourselves from the twentieth-century constitution and return to the constitution of the eighteenth century. If we think as eighteenth-century constitutionalists thought, we would think that the king was a danger. Most likely, however, we might not think the ministry had much potential for constitutional mischief. Historically, it had always been the monarchy that had threatened the constitution.[38] Moreover, in the 1770s, the ministry was not yet independent of the crown. There were still many constitutional theorists saying that the balance of the constitution required that ministers be the king's personal selections. In fact, most people thought of the ministers as the king's, not as Parliament's servants. "In other times," *Junius* complained, "the interest of the King and people of England was, as it ought to be, entirely the same. A new system has not only been adopted in fact, but professed upon principle. Ministers are no longer the public servants of the state, but the private domestics of the Sovereign."[39]

It probably would not have mattered if the members of Parliament who rejected the American whig scheme for a prerogative solution to the controversy were more worried about the ministry than the king, or were concerned about both. They were not constitutionally willing to risk any increase of executive power at the expense of Parliament's supremacy. In fact, there does not seem to have been anyone who would so much as consider the American solution. Ministers such as Lord North and the earl of Dartmouth called it "dangerously Tory in its implications," threatening "a revival of the independence of the royal prerogative" and the destruction of the Glorious Revolution constitution.[40] Certainly the king was not tempted. He preferred the constitution that had placed his ancestors on the thrones of England, Ireland, and Scotland, and, William Knox recorded, "very early declared it to be his determination rather to cast off the revolted Colonies entirely, than consent to give up the authority of the Supreme Legislature over them."[41]

Lord Mansfield deserves better than to be tarred with the Austinianism with which Charles Howard McIlwain smeared him. He may have been narrow, but he was narrow on the side of British constitutional liberty, not narrow on the side of denying Americans a premature commonwealth of nations. "I seek for the liberty and constitution of this Kingdom no farther back than the Revolution," Mansfield said, referring to 1688 and the Glorious Revolution. "There I take my stand." [42] He stood there with every other British statesman, lawyer, constitutionalist, and member of Parliament.

Had Lord Mansfield agreed that sovereignty could be divided, and that Parliament could renounce its supremacy over colonial assemblies while Americans remained in allegiance to the king, he risked taking the same constitutional step backward from the Glorious Revolution that American whigs had already taken. Given the British constitution of 1775 and the legacy of the Glorious Revolution, the choice was not only between the supremacy of Parliament and American legislative autonomy, it was also between the supremacy of Parliament and the king's prerogative. If sovereignty was divided by giving the colonial assemblies supremacy within their jurisdictions, and limiting the imperial jurisdiction of Parliament, a potential sphere of power was created for the king to fill.

It does not do to think of the twentieth century and of Elizabeth II, to say as McIlwain would, that George III could have been the head, the cement, the binding link of empire and nothing else. It is possible for us to imagine a British commonwealth of nations; it was not possible for Lord Chief Justice Mansfield and his colleagues in the British government. They could not foresee the twentieth-century commonwealth as easily as McIlwain suggests. George III was the monarch then, not Victoria or George V. The eighteenth-century constitution of 1775 was less than a hundred years removed from the Glorious Revolution and the struggle against the House of Stuart. George III was still a powerful monarch, and he was powerful mainly through the exercise of what was called influence. To have provided him with the leverage of being the link of empire, constitutionally risked the chance that his influence would be increased. The concern was not that his influence would certainly increase in imperial affairs; that was not the risk. The risk was that as a result of his enhanced role in the governance of the empire, his influence in Great Britain would have been increased. It was not until the nineteenth century—after the Reform Act, the final demise of the royal prerogative, with the establishment of what the British refer to as responsible government, with the crown out of politics and a party system selecting the nation's leaders—that dominion status within the empire with allegiance to the queen became constitutionally possible. [43]

These constitutional considerations explain why the controversy became too legal; why the British insisted that the Americans first had to acknowledge "the right" before there could be a renunciation of "the exercise." If the Americans had acknowledged an abstract supremacy, Parliament could then have devised a constitutional mechanism to check any threat from the crown should the colonies provide the king with revenue. But the Americans could not acknowledge without risking their constitutional security to the whims and changing politics of some future parliament. The controversy, therefore, became too legal not in an abstract sense, but because the procedures or the mechanics of constitutional advocacy provided no opportunity for a political solution unless either the British or the Americans surrendered a constitutional principle they thought essential for their constitutional liberty. The dynamics of the eighteenth-century British constitution had produced a constitutional dilemma. American liberty—the right to be free of arbitrary power—could not be secured under parliamentary supremacy. British liberty—the representative legislature over the crown—could not be secured without parliamentary supremacy.

Of course, the Declaration of Independence would indict George III and not Parliament. Under the constitution for which the Americans fought a civil war, their allegiance had been to the king. The crown therefore, not Parliament, broke the contract with the colonists, and it was against the king that they rebelled. A little piece of history that has generally been forgotten is that, during the year of war between the battle of Lexington and the Declaration of Independence, the army of New England militia that besieged General Thomas Gage in Boston had called itself the "King's Troops" and had referred to the British soldiers as the "Parliaments."[44] And in London for a while, the American war had been called "the War of Parliament."[45] It might as aptly have been called "the war of the two constitutions." For the tension between the two eighteenth-century British constitutions remained until the end of the controversy. True, the British were thinking only of the constitution of sovereign command when insisting that the condition for any constitutional settlement was that the Americans acknowledge Parliament's authority to legislate in all cases whatsoever. In fact, they were acting under the old constitution as well. For they were protecting their Glorious Revolution constitution of parliamentary supremacy against the prerogatives of the crown. It was, after all, in the old constitution of customary, prescriptive, contractarian rights that were to be found the customary prerogatives and prescriptive powers belonging to the crown by the terms and stipulations of the original contract.

ACKNOWLEDGMENTS
SHORT TITLES
NOTES
INDEX

ACKNOWLEDGMENTS

Research for this study, as well as for the previous three studies in this series, was supported by a fellowship from the John Simon Guggenheim Memorial Foundation and by a Huntington Library–National Endowment for the Humanities Fellowship. Leave from teaching responsibilities at New York University School of Law was provided by the Filomen D'Agostino Greenberg and Max E. Greenberg Faculty Research Fund at the School of Law, and by John Sexton, dean of the School of Law. The manuscript was written amid the beauty and scholarship of the Huntington Library where Virginia Renner guarded against distractions, Martin Ridge kept an eye out for coyotes, and Leona Schonfeld saw to it that the word processors were not thrown through the windows. In fact, if it were not for Leona Schonfeld's patience and expertise, this book might well have been published without its list of Short Titles. It hardly seems possible, but perhaps in some inexplicable fashion this study benefitted by being read by that premier band of American legal historians, the members of the New York University School of Law Colloquium in Legal History: Martin Flaherty, Robert J. Kaczorowski, Eben Moglen, Richard B. Bernstein, Lawrence Fleischer, and William E. Nelson. As with the previous volumes in this Revolution-era series, the index was prepared by Carol B. Pearson of the Huntington Library, cite and substance checking was done by Barbara Kern of Ninth Street, and the editing by Lydia Howarth of Nashville, Tennessee.

This volume is the last in this series, *Constitutional History of the American Revolution*. Previous volumes have dealt with *The Authority to Tax, The Authority of Rights*, and *The Authority to Legislate*. In a sense this volume, *The Authority of Law*, is a sequel to *The Authority to Legislate*, as it completes the account of the constitutional issues and difficulties raised by Parliament's claim of authority to bind the American colonies by legislative fiat in all cases whatsoever. Only two other topics remain to complete the constitutional history of the American Revolution. One is the "Authority to Govern," which would expand on such topics as the question of the king's role as the "link" of empire, the threat that both British whigs and tories feared from a strengthened crown, the matter of salaries and judicial tenure, the doctrine of "balance" in the constitution, and, most important, the problem of ministerial instructions to colonial governors as that was the method by which London may well have attempted to govern the colonies had Parliament established its authority to legislate in all cases whatsoever. The other topic requiring study is the Declaration of Independence. That book need not be part of a series entitled *Constitutional History of the American Revolution*. But a constitutional history of the Declaration of Independence is badly needed, both to restore the Declaration to its original understanding, and to rescue it from the mythical fabrications that characterize twentieth-century scholarship. Finally, a word of appreciation should be mentioned of Gordon Morris Bakken of the California State University, Fullerton. Unfortunately, it was not until these pages had been set in type that he discovered that in 1844 Franklin Pierce had cast doubt on the main thesis of this book. According to Bakken's research, in an address to the Dover Chamber of Commerce, in New Hampshire, Franklin Pierce said: "The reason that the American Revolution controversy was never resolved was not due to the fact that the debate became too legal. The problem was that not enough of the leaders on either side were lawyers. Too many of the decision makers like Lord North, Benjamin Franklin, George III, and Thomas Hutchinson never went to law school."

New York University School of Law

SHORT TITLES

Abercromby, "De Jure"
James Abercromby, "De Jure et Gubernatione Coloniarum, or An Inquiry into the Nature and the Rights of the Colonies, Ancient, and Modern." ca. 1780. HM 518, Huntington Library, San Marino, Calif.

Abingdon, *Dedication*
Willoughby Bertie, earl of Abingdon, *Dedication to the Collective Body of the People of England, in which the Source of our present Political Distractions are pointed out, and a Plan proposed for their Remedy and Redress.* Oxford, England, 1780.

Abingdon, "Speech on Right"
"Lord Abingdon's Speech on Introducing his Bill for a Declaration of Right over every Part of the British Dependencies," reprinted in *Celebrated Speeches of Flood,* pp. 34–38.

Abingdon, *Thoughts on Burke's Letter*
Willoughby Bertie, earl of Abingdon, *Thoughts on the Letter of Edmund Burke, Esq; to the Sheriffs of Bristol, on the Affairs of America.* 6th ed. Oxford, England, [1777].

Adams, *Legal Papers*
Legal Papers of John Adams. Edited by L. Kinvin Wroth and Hiller B. Zobel. 3 vols. Cambridge, Mass., 1765.

Adams, "Novanglus"
> John Adams, "Novanglus," reprinted in *The American Colonial Crisis: The Daniel Leonard–John Adams Letters to the Press 1774–1775.* Edited by Bernard Mason. New York, 1972.

Adams, *Writings*
> *The Writings of Samuel Adams.* Edited by Harry Alonzo Cushing. 4 vols. New York, 1904–8.

Addresses and Petitions of Common Council
> *Addresses, Remonstrances, and Petitions; Commencing the 24th of June, 1769, Presented to the King and Parliament, from the Court of Common Council, and the Livery in Common Hall assembled, with his Majesty's Answers: Likewise the Speech to the King, made by the late Mr. Alderman Beckford, When Lord Mayor of the City of London.* London, [1778].

Addresses of the Common Council
> *Addresses Presented from the Court of Common Council to the King, On his Majesty's Accession to the Throne, and on various other Occasions, and and his Answers. Resolutions of the Court. . . . Instructions at different Times to the Representatives of the City in Parliament. Petitions to Parliament for different Purposes. . . . Agreed to between the 23rd October, 1760, and the 12th October, 1770.* London, [1770].

Allen, *American Crisis*
> William Allen, *The American Crisis: A Letter, Addressed by Permission to the Earl Gower, Lord President of the Council, &c. &c. &c. On the present alarming Disturbances in the Colonies.* London, 1774.

American Archives
> *American Archives, Fourth Series. Containing a Documentary History of the English Colonies in North America From the King's Message to Parliament, of March 7, 1774, to the Declaration of Independence by the United States.* Vols. 1 and 2. Washington, D.C., 1837.

American Gazette
> *The American Gazette. Being a Collection of all the Authentic Addresses, Memorials, Letters, &c. Which relate to the Present Disputes Between Great Britain and her Colonies. Containing also Many Original Papers Never Before Published.* London, 1768.

Ammerman, *Common Cause*
> David Ammerman, *In the Common Cause: American Response to the Coercive Acts of 1774.* Charlottesville, Va., 1974.

[Anderson,] *Free Thoughts*
> [James Anderson,] *Free Thoughts on the American Contest.* Edinburgh, 1776.

Anderson, *Interest of Britain*
 James Anderson, *The Interest of Great-Britain with Respect to her American Colonies Considered.* London, 1782.

Anglo-American Political Relations
 Anglo-American Political Relations, 1675–1775. Edited by Alison Gilbert Olson and Richard Maxwell Brown. New Brunswick, N.J., 1970.

Annual Register 1772
 The Annual Register or a View of the History, Politics, and Literature, for the Year 1772. London, 1773.

Annual Register 1774
 The Annual Register, or a View of the History, Politics, and Literature, for the Year 1774. London, 1810.

Annual Register 1776
 The Annual Register, or a View of the History, Politicks, and Literature, for the Year 1776. 5th ed. London, n.d.

Anon., *Address to Junius*
 Anonymous, *An Address to Junius, Upon the Subject of his Letter in the Public Advertiser, December 19, 1769.* London, [1770?].

Anon., *Address to People of Britain*
 Anonymous, *An Address to the People of Great-Britain in General, the Members of Parliament, and the Leading Gentlemen of Opposition in Particular, on the Present Crisis of American Politics.* Bristol, 1776.

Anon., *America Vindicated*
 Anonymous, *America Vindicated From the High Charge of Ingratitude and Rebellion: With a Plan of Legislation, Proposed to the Consideration of Both Houses, For Establishing a Permanent and Solid Foundation For a just constitutional Union Between Great Britain and her Colonies.* Devizes, England, 1774.

Anon., *American Resistance Indefensible*
 Anonymous, *American Resistance Indefensible. A Sermon, Preached on Friday, December 13, 1776, Being the Day appointed for a General Fast. By a Country Curate.* London, [1776].

Anon., *Answer to Sheridan*
 Anonymous, *Answer to a Pamphlet, Written by C. F. Sheridan, Esq; Entitled, A Review of the Three Great National Questions . . . Part the First, Declaration of Right.* Dublin, 1782.

Anon., *Appeal to Reason and Justice*
 Anonymous, *An Appeal to Reason and Justice, in Behalf of the British Constitution, and the Subjects of the British Empire. In which the present Important Contest with the Revolted Colonies is impartially considered,*

the Inconsistency of Modern Patriotism is demonstrated, the Supremacy of Parliament is asserted on Revolution Principles, and American Independence is proved to be a manifest Violation of the Rights of British Subjects. London, 1778.

Anon., *Argument in Defence*
Anonymous, *An Argument in Defence of the Exclusive Right Claimed by the Colonies to Tax Themselves, with a Review of the Laws of England, Relative to Representation and Taxation. To Which is Added, An Account of the Rise of the Colonies, and the Manner in which the rights of the subjects within the realm were communicated to those that went to America, with the exercise of those rights from their first settlement to the present time.* London, 1774.

Anon., *Candid Thoughts*
Anonymous, *Candid Thoughts; or, an Enquiry into the Causes of National Discontents and Misfortunes Since the Commencement of the Present Reign.* London, 1781.

Anon., *Case Stated*
Anonymous, *The Case Stated, on Philosophical Ground, Between Great Britain and her Colonies: or the Analogy between States and Individuals, Respecting the Term of Political Adultness, Pointed Out.* London, 1778.

Anon., *Characters*
Anonymous, *Characters, Containing an Impartial Review of the Public Conduct and Abilities of the most Eminent Personages in the Parliament of Great-Britain: Considered as Statesmen, Senators, and Public Speakers.* London, 1777.

Anon., *Common Sense Conferences*
Anonymous, *Common Sense: in Nine Conferences, Between a British Merchant and a Candid Merchant of America, in their private capacities as friends; tracing the several causes of the present contests between the mother country and her American subjects; the fallacy of their prepossessions; and the ingratitude and danger of them; the reciprocal benefits of the national friendship; and the moral obligations of individuals which enforce it: with various anecdotes, and reasons drawn from facts, tending to conciliate all differences, and establish a permanent union for the common happiness and glory of the British empire.* London, 1775.

Anon., *Conciliatory Bills Considered*
Anonymous, *The Conciliatory Bills Considered.* London, 1778.

Anon., *Considerations on Expediency*
Anonymous, *Considerations on the Expediency of Admitting Representatives From the Colonies into the British House of Commons.* London, 1770.

Anon., *Considerations on National Independence*
Anonymous, *Considerations on National Independence, Suggested by*

Mr. Pitt's Speeches on the Irish Union. Addressed to the People of Great Britain and Ireland. By a Member of the Honourable Society of Lincoln's Inn. London, n.d.

Anon., *Considerations on the Imposition*
Anonymous, *Considerations on the Imposition of 4 ½ per Cent. Collected on Grenada, and the Southern Charibbee Islands, by Virtue of His Majesty's Letters Patent, Under Pretence of the Prerogative Royal, Without Grant of Parliament.* London, 1774.

Anon., *Considerations Upon Rights of Colonists*
Anonymous, *Considerations Upon the Rights of the Colonists to the Privileges of British Subjects, Introduc'd by a brief Review of the Rise and Progress of English Liberty, and concluded with some Remarks upon our present Alarming Situation.* New York, 1766.

Anon., *Constitutional Advocate*
Anonymous [Richard Goodenough], *The Constitutional Advocate: By Which, From the Evidence of History, and of Records, and from The Principles of the British Government, Every Reader may form his own Judgement concerning the Justice and Policy of the present War with America. Addressed to the People at Large, And humbly submitted to the Consideration of their Representatives.* London, 1776.

Anon., *Constitutional Considerations*
Anonymous, *Constitutional Considerations on the Power of Parliament to Levy Taxes on the North American Colonies.* London, 1766.

Anon., *Constitutional Right*
Anonymous, *The Constitutional Right of the Legislature of Great Britain, to Tax the British Colonies in America, Impartially Stated.* London, 1768.

Anon., *Defence of Resolutions*
Anonymous, *A Defence of the Resolutions and Address of the American Congress, in Reply to Taxation no Tyranny.* London, [1775].

Anon., *Examination into the Conduct*
Anonymous, *An Examination into the Conduct of the Present Administration, From the Year 1774 to the Year 1778. And a Plan of Accomodation with America.* London, 1778.

Anon., *Experience preferable to Theory*
Anonymous, *Experience preferable to Theory. An Answer to Dr. Price's Observations on the Nature of Civil Liberty, and the Justice and Policy of the War with America.* London, 1776.

Anon., *Free Thoughts on the War*
Anonymous, *Free Thoughts on the Continuance of the American War, and the Necessity of its Termination. Addressed to the Inhabitants of Great Britain. By a Gentleman of Lincoln's Inn.* London, 1781.

Anon., *General Opposition*
Anonymous, *The General Opposition of the Colonies to the Payment of the Stamp Duty; and the Consequence of Enforcing Obedience by Military Measures; Impartially Considered. Also a Plan for uniting them to this Kingdom, in such a manner as to make their Interest inseparable from ours, for the future. In a Letter to a Member of Parliament.* London, 1766.

Anon., *History of Lord North*
Anonymous, *The History of Lord North's Administration to the Dissolution to the Thirteenth Parliament of Great-Britain.* London, 1781.

Anon., *History of North and South America*
Anonymous, *The History of North and South America, Containing an Account of the First Discoveries of the New World, the Customs, Genius, and Persons of the Original Inhabitants, and a particular Description of the Air, Soil, natural Productions, Manufacturers and Commerce of each Settlement. Including a Geographical, Commercial, and Historical Survey of the British Settlements, From the Earliest times to the present Period. With an Account of the West Indies and the American Islands, to which is added an Important Enquiry into the Present American Disputes.* 2 vols. London, 1776.

Anon., *Honor of Parliament*
Anonymous, *The Honor of Parliament and the Justice of the Nation Vindicated. In a Reply to Dr. Price's Observations on the Nature of Civil Liberty.* London, 1776.

Anon., *Inquiry into the Nature*
Anonymous, *An Inquiry into the Nature and Causes of the Present Disputes Between the British Colonies in America and their Mother-Country; and their reciprocal Claims and just Rights impartially examined, and fairly stated.* London, 1769.

Anon., "Introduction" to *Lords Report*
Anonymous, "Introduction" to *The Report of the Lords Committees, Appointed by the House of Lords to Enquire into the Several Proceedings in the Colony of Massachuset's Bay, in opposition to the sovereignty of His Majesty, in His Parliament of Great Britain, over the Province; and also what hath passed in this House relative thereto, from the First Day of January, 1764.* London, 1774.

Anon., *Letter*
Anonymous, *A Letter to the People of Pennsylvania, &c.* reprinted in Bailyn, *Pamphlets*, pp. 257–72.

Anon., *Letter to Doctor Tucker*
Anonymous, *A Letter to Doctor Tucker on his Proposal of a Separation Between Great Britain and her American Colonies.* London, 1774.

Anon., *Letter to Lord Camden*
Anonymous, *A Letter to the Right Honourable Lord Camden, on the Bill for Restraining the Trade and Fishery of the Four Provinces of New England.* London, 1775.

Anon., *Letter to Mansfield*
Anonymous, *A Letter to the Right Honourable Lord M[ansfield], on the Affairs of America: From a Member of Parliament.* London, 1775.

Anon., *Letter to North on Re-election*
Anonymous, *A Letter to Lord North on his Re-election into the House of Commons.* London, 1780.

Anon., *Letter to People of America*
Anonymous, *A Letter to the People of America, Lately Printed at New York; now Re-Published by an American. With a Postscript by the Editor, Addressed to Sir W[illiam] H[owe].* London, 1778.

Anon., *Letter to Rev. Cooper*
Anonymous, *A Letter to the Rev. Dr. Cooper, on the Origin of Civil Government; in Answer to his Sermon, Preached before the University of Oxford, on the Day appointed by Proclamation for a General Fast.* London, 1777.

Anon., *Magna Charta Opposed to Privilege*
Anonymous, *Magna Charta, Opposed to Assumed Privilege: Being a complete View of the Late Interesting Disputes between the House of Commons and the Magistrates of London.* London, 1771.

Anon., *Observations of Consequence*
Anonymous, *Some Observations of Consequence, In Three Parts. Occasioned by the Stamp-Act, Lately imposed on the British Colonies.* [Philadelphia,] 1768.

Anon., *Observations on Quebec*
Anonymous, *Observations and Reflections on an Act passed in the Year, 1774, For the Settlement of the Province of Quebec.* London, 1782.

Anon., *Old Constitution*
Anonymous, *The Old Constitution and Present Establishment in Church and State Honestly Asserted.* London, 1718.

Anon., *Plain Question*
Anonymous, *The Plain Question Upon the Present Dispute with our American Colonies.* 4th ed. London, 1776.

Anon., *Plan for Conciliating*
Anonymous, *A Plan for Conciliating the Jarring Political Interests of Great Britain and her North American Colonies, and for promoting a general Re-union throughout the Whole British Empire.* London, 1775.

Anon., *Plan of Reconciliation with America*
Anonymous, *A Plan of Reconciliation with America; Consistent with the Dignity and Interests of Both Countries. Humbly inscribed to the King.* London, 1782.

Anon., *Political Reflections*
Anonymous [Richard Wells], *A Few Political Reflections Submitted to the Consideration of the British Colonies, by a Citizen of Philadelphia.* Philadelphia, 1774.

Anon., *Power and Grandeur*
Anonymous, *The Power and Grandeur of Great-Britain, Founded on the Liberty of the Colonies, and The Mischiefs attending the Taxing them by Act of Parliament Demonstrated.* New York, 1768.

Anon., *Proposals for Union*
Anonymous, *Proposals for a Plan Towards a Reconciliation and Re-Union with the Thirteen Provinces of America, and for a Union with the other Colonies.* London, 1778.

Anon., *Proposition for the Peace*
Anonymous, *A Proposition for the Present Peace and Future Government of the British Colonies in North America.* London, [1775].

Anon., *Prospect of the Consequences*
Anonymous, *A Prospect of the Consequences of the Present Conduct of Great Britain Towards America.* London, 1776.

Anon., *Reasons For*
Anonymous, *Reasons for a Declaration of Rights, in answer to what hath been advanced on that Subject, in a Pamphlet lately published, entitled, a review of the Three Great National Questions.* Dublin, 1782.

Anon., *Reflections on Critical Situation*
Anonymous, *Reflections on Our Present Critical Situation. In a Letter from a Landed Proprietor.* London, 1777.

Anon., *Reflections on the Contest*
Anonymous, *Reflections on the American Contest: In which the Consequence of a Forced Submission, and the Means of a Lasting Reconciliation are pointed out, Communicated by Letter to a Member of Parliament, Some Time Since, and now Addressed to Edmund Burke, Esq.* London, 1776.

Anon., *Reflexions on Representation*
Anonymous, *Reflexions on Representation in Parliament: Being an Attempt to shew the Equity and Practicability, not only of establishing a more equal Representation throughout Great Britain, but also of admitting the Americans to a Share in the Legislature.* London, 1766.

Anon., *Remarks on Conduct*
Anonymous, *Remarks on the Conduct of Opposition with Regard to Amer-*

ica; Shewing their Inconsistency, by a Short Review of their own Measures.
London, 1777.

Anon., *Remarks on Price's Observations*
Anonymous, *Remarks on Dr. Price's Observations on the Nature of Civil Liberty, &c.* London, 1776.

Anon., *Remarks on the New Essay*
Anonymous [John Gray], *Remarks on the New Essay of the Pen[n]sylvanian Farmer; and on the Resolves and Instructions Prefixed to that Essay; By the Author of the Right of the British Legislature Vindicated.* London, 1775

Anon., *Remarks upon a Discourse*
Anonymous, [Henry Barry?], *Remarks upon a Discourse Preached December 15th 1774. Being the Day recommended by the Provincial Congress: And afterwards at the Boston Lecture. By William Gordon, Pastor of the third Church in Roxbury.* [New York,] 1775.

Anon., *Resistance No Rebellion*
Anonymous, *Resistance No Rebellion: In Answer to Doctor Johnson's Taxation no Tyranny.* London, 1775.

Anon., *Review of Present Administration*
Anonymous, *A Review of the Present Administration.* London, 1774.

Anon., *Serious and Impartial Observations*
Anonymous, *Serious and Impartial Observations on the Blessings of Liberty and Peace Addressed to Persons of all Parties. Inviting them also to enter into that Grand ASSOCIATION, which is able to secure the Safety and Happiness of the British Empire. By a CLERGYMAN in Leicestershire.* London, 1776.

Anon., *Some Candid Suggestions*
Anonymous, *Some Candid Suggestions Towards Accommodation of Differences with America. Offered to Consideration of the Public.* London, 1775.

Anon., *Some Fugitive Thoughts*
Anonymous, *Some Fugitive Thoughts on a Letter Signed Freeman, addressed to the Deputies, assembled at the High Court of Congress in Philadelphia.* South Carolina, 1774.

Anon., *Some Reasons for Approving Gloucester's Plan*
Anonymous, *Some Reasons for Approving of the Dean of Gloucester's Plan, of Separating from the Colonies; with a Proposal for a Further Improvement.* London, 1775.

Anon., *Some Seasonable Observations*
Anonymous, *Some Seasonable Observations and Remarks upon the State of our Controversy with Great Britain; And of the Proceedings of the Continental Congress: Whereby many interesting Facts are related, and Methods proposed for our Safety and an Accommodation.* [Boston,] 1775.

Anon., *Speech in Behalf*
Anonymous, *A Speech in Behalf of the Constitution Against the Suspending and Dispensing Prerogative, &c.* London, 1767.

Anon., *Summary of Important Arguments*
Anonymous, *A Brief Extract, or Summary of Important Arguments Advanced by Some Late Distinguished Writers, in Support of the Supremacy of the British Legislature, and their Right to Tax the Americans, Addressed to the Freemen and Liverymen of London, and Recommended to the serious Perusal of every Candid and Dispassionate Man.* London, 1775.

Anon., *Thoughts on Present War*
Anonymous, *Thoughts on the Present War, with an Impartial Review of Lord North's Administration, in Conducting the American, French, Spanish, and Dutch War; and in the Management of Contracts, Taxes, the Public Money, &c.* London, 1783.

Anon., *Thoughts on Quebec Act*
Anonymous, *Thoughts on the Act for making more Effectual Provision for the Government of the Province of Quebec.* London, 1774.

Anon., *Three Letters*
Anonymous, *Three Letters to a Member of Parliament, On the Subject of the Present Dispute With Our American Colonies.* London, 1775.

Anon., *To Freeholders of New York* (1768)
Anonymous, *To the Freeholders and Freemen of the City and County of New-York. This Vindication, of the Professors of the Law, in Answer to the Remarks on the 17 Queries, is humbly submitted by a sincere Friend to the Cause of Liberty, and this Colony.* [New York, 1768.]

Anon., *To Tax Themselves*
Anonymous, *An Argument in Defence of the Exclusive Right Claimed by the Colonies to Tax Themselves; With A Review of the Laws of England, Relative to Representation and Taxation. To which is Added, an Account of the Rise of the Colonies, and the Manner in which the Rights of the Subjects within the realm were communicated to those that went to America, with the Exercise of those Rights from the First Settlement to the Present Time.* London, 1774.

Anon., *Usurpations of England*
Anonymous, *The Usurpations of England the chief Sources of the Miseries of Ireland.* Dublin, 1780.

Anon., *View of North*
Anonymous, *A View of the History of Great-Britain, During the Administration of Lord North, to the Second Session of the Fifteenth Parliament.* London, 1782.

Authority of Rights
> John Phillip Reid, *Constitutional History of the American Revolution: The Authority of Rights*. Madison, Wisc., 1986.

Authority to Legislate
> John Phillip Reid, *Constitutional History of the American Revolution: The Authority to Legislate*. Madison, Wisc., 1991.

Authority to Tax
> John Phillip Reid, *Constitutional History of the American Revolution: The Authority to Tax*. Madison, Wisc., 1987.

Baillie, *Letter to Shebear*
> Hugh Baillie, *A Letter to Dr. Shebear: Containing a Refutation of his Arguments Concerning the Boston and Quebec Acts of Parliament: and his Aspersions upon the Memory of King William, and the Protestant Dissenters.* London, 1775.

[Baillie,] *Some Observations on a Pamphlet*
> [Hugh Baillie,] *Some Observations on a Pamphlet Lately Published, Entitled the Rights of Great-Britain Asserted against the Claims of America, Being an Answer to the Declaration of the General Congress.* London, 1766.

Bailyn, *Ideological Origins*
> Bernard Bailyn, *The Ideological Origins of the American Revolution*. Cambridge, Mass., 1967.

Bailyn, *Ordeal*
> Bernard Bailyn, *The Ordeal of Thomas Hutchinson*. Cambridge, Mass., 1974.

Bailyn, *Pamphlets*
> *Pamphlets of the American Revolution, 1750–1776.* Vol. 1. Edited by Bernard Bailyn. Cambridge, Mass., 1965.

[Bancroft,] *Remarks*
> [Edward Bancroft,] *Remarks on the Review of the Controversy Between Great Britain and her Colonies. In which the Errors of its Author are exposed, and the Claims of the Colonies vindicated, Upon the Evidence of Historical Facts and authentic Records.* London, 1769.

[Barrington,] *Revolution Principles*
> [John Shute Barrington, First Viscount Barrington,] *The Revolution and Anti-Revolution Principles Stated and Compar'd, the Constitution Explain'd and Vindicated, And the Justice and Necessity of Excluding the Pretender, Maintain'd against the Book Entituled, Hereditary Right of the Crown of England Asserted.* Second edition. London, 1714.

[Barron,] *History of Colonization*
> [William Barron,] *History of the Colonization of the Free States of Antiquity,*

Applied to the Present Contest between Great Britain and her American Colonies. With Reflections concerning the future Settlement of these Colonies. London, 1777.

[Basset,] *Equal Representation*
[Francis Basset, Baron Basset of Stratton,] *Thoughts on Equal Representation.* London, 1783.

Becker, *Declaration*
Carl Becker, *The Declaration of Independence: A Study in the History of Political Ideas.* Vintage Books ed. New York, 1958.

Bellot, *William Knox*
Leland J. Bellot, *William Knox: The Life & Thought of an Eighteenth-Century Imperialist.* Austin, Tex., 1977.

[Bernard,] *Appeal to the Public*
[Thomas Bernard,] *An Appeal to the Public; Stating and Considering the Objections to the Quebec Bill.* 2d ed. London, 1774.

Bernard, *Select Letters*
Francis Bernard, *Select Letters on the Trade and Government of America; and the Principles of Law and Polity, Applied to the American Colonies. Written by Governor Bernard at Boston.* London, 1774.

Bernard & Barrington, *Correspondence*
The Barrington-Bernard Correspondence and Illustrative Matter, 1760–1770. Edited by Edward Channing and Archibald Cary Coolidge. Cambridge, Mass., 1912.

[Blacklock,] *Remarks on Liberty*
[Thomas Blacklock,] *Remarks on the Nature and Extent of Liberty, as compatible with the Genius of Civil Societies; On the Principles of Government and the proper Limits of its Powers in Free States; And, on the Justice and Policy of the American War. Occasioned by Perusing the Observations of Dr. Price on these Subjects. In a Letter to a Friend.* Edinburgh, 1776.

Blackstone, *Commentaries*
William Blackstone, *Commentaries on the Laws of England.* 4 vols. Oxford, England, 1765–69.

[Bolingbroke,] *Dissertation*
[Henry Saint John, Viscount Bolingbroke,] *A Dissertation Upon Parties; In Several Letters to Caleb D'Anvers, Esq.* Second edition. London, 1735.

Bonwick, *English Radicals*
Colin Bonwick, *English Radicals and the American Revolution.* Chapel Hill, N.C., 1977.

Boston Chronicle
The Boston Chronicle (weekly newspaper).

Boston Evening-Post
   The Boston Evening-Post (weekly newspaper).

Boston Gazette
   The Boston Gazette and Country Journal (weekly newspaper).

Boston Post-Boy
   The Boston Post-Boy & Advertiser (weekly newspaper).

Boston Town Records
   A Report of the Record Commissioners of the City of Boston, Containing the Boston Town Records, 1758 to 1769. 16th Report. Boston, 1886.

Boyd, *Union*
   Julian P. Boyd, *Anglo-American Union: Joseph Galloway's Plans to Preserve the British Empire, 1774–1788.* Philadelphia, 1941.

Bradley, *Popular Politics*
   James E. Bradley, *Popular Politics and the American Revolution in England: Petitions, the Crown, and Public Opinion.* Mercer, Ga., 1986.

Brand, *Defence of Reeves*
   John Brand, *A Defence of the Pamphlet Ascribed to John Reeves, Esq. and Entitled "Thoughts on the English Government."* London, 1796.

Brennan, "James Otis"
   Ellen Elizabeth Brennan, "James Otis: Recreant and Patriot," *New England Quarterly* 12 (1939): 691–725.

Briefs of Revolution
   The Briefs of the American Revolution: Constitutional Arguments Between Thomas Hutchinson, Governor of Massachusetts Bay, and James Bowdoin for the Council and John Adams for the House of Representatives. Edited by John Phillip Reid. New York, 1981.

British in Boston
   The British in Boston; Being the Diary of Lieutenant John Barker of the King's own Regiment from November 15, 1774 to May 31, 1776. Edited by Elizabeth Ellery Dana. Cambridge, Mass., 1924.

[Burke,] *Letters of Valens*
   [William Burke,] *The Letters of Valens, (Which originally appeared in the London Evening Post) with Corrections, Explanatory Notes, and a Preface, by the Author.* London, 1777.

[Burke,] *Observations on Late State*
   [Edmund Burke,] *Observations on a Late State of the Nation.* Fourth edition. London, 1769.

Burke on American Revolution
   Edmund Burke on the American Revolution: Selected Speeches and Letters. Edited by Elliot Robert Barkan. New York, 1966.

Burke Writings
  The Writings and Speeches of Edmund Burke. Volume II. Party, Parliament, and the American Crisis. Edited by Paul Langford. Oxford, England, 1981.

Bushman, *King and People*
  Richard L. Bushman, *King and People in Provincial Massachusetts.* Chapel Hill, N.C., 1985.

Butler, *Sermon Preached in Dublin*
  Samuel Butler, *A Sermon Preached in the Parish Church of St. Michan's Dublin, On Friday the 13th Day of December, 1776, Being the Day appointed by His Majesty for holding a General Fast and Humiliation throughout this Kingdom.* Dublin, [1776].

Calhoon, "Smith's Alternative"
  Robert M. Calhoon, "William Smith Jr.'s Alternative to the American Revolution," *William and Mary Quarterly* 22 (1965): 105–18.

Caplan, "Ninth Amendment"
  Russell L. Caplan, "The History and Meaning of the Ninth Amendment," *Virginia Law Review* 69 (1983): 223–68.

[Cartwright,] *American Independence*
  [John Cartwright,] *American Independence the Interest and Glory of Great Britain; Containing Arguments which prove, that not only in Taxation, but in Trade, Manufactures, and Government, the Colonies are entitled to an entire Independency on the British Legislature; and that it can only be by a formal Declaration of these Rights, and forming thereupon a friendly League with them, that the true and lasting Welfare of both Countries can be promoted. In a Series of Letters to the Legislature.* London, 1774.

Cartwright, *Appeal on Constitution*
  John Cartwright, *An Appeal on the Subject of the English Constitution.* Boston, England, [1797].

Cartwright, *Constitutional Defence*
  John Cartwright, *The Constitutional Defence of England, Internal and External.* London, 1796.

Cartwright, *Constitution Produced*
  John Cartwright, *The English Constitution Produced and Illustrated.* London, 1823.

Cartwright, *Legislative Rights*
  John Cartwright, *The Legislative Rights of the Commonalty Vindicated; or, Take Your Choice! Representation and Respect: Imposition and Contempt. Annual Parliaments and Liberty: Long Parliaments and Slavery.* 2d ed. London, 1777.

[Cartwright,] *Letter to Burke*
  [John Cartwright,] *A Letter to Edmund Burke, Esq.; Controverting the Prin-*

ciples of American Government, Laid down in his lately published Speech on American Taxation, Delivered in the House of Commons, On the 19th of April, 1774. London, 1775.

Cartwright, *People's Barrier*
John Cartwright, *The People's Barrier Against Undue Influence and Corruption: Or the Commons' House of Parliament According to the Constitution.* London, 1780.

Carysfort, *Letter to Huntingdonshire*
John Joshua Proby, 1st earl of Carysfort, *Copy of a Letter from the Right Honourable Lord Carysfort, to the Huntingdonshire Committee.* London, 1780.

Celebrated Speeches of Flood
The Celebrated Speeches of Colonel Henry Flood, on the Repeal of the Declaratory Act of the 6th George 1st. As Delivered in the House of Commons of Ireland, On the 11th and 14th of June, 1782. Also, the Speech of Lord Abingdon, In the English House of Peers the 5th of July 1782, on Introducing his Bill for a Declaration of Right over every Part of the British Dependencies. Dublin, [1782].

Chambers, *Lectures*
Sir Robert Chambers, *A Course of Lectures on the English Law Delivered at the University of Oxford 1767–1773.* 2 vols. Edited by Thomas M. Curley. Madison, Wisc., 1986.

Chandler, *Appeal to Public*
Thomas Bradbury Chandler, *An Appeal to the Public in Behalf of the Church of England in America.* New York, 1767.

Chatham, *Speech 20 May*
Lord Chatham's Speech in the House of Lords on Friday the 20th of May 1777. (One-page broadside, Huntington Library Rare Book #87304.)

Christie, *Crisis*
I. R. Christie, *Crisis of Empire: Great Britain and the American Colonies 1754–1783.* New York, 1966.

Clarendon's History Compleated
The Lord Clarendon's History of the Grand Rebellion Compleated. London, 1717.

Clark, *British Opinion*
Dora Mae Clark, *British Opinion and the American Revolution.* New Haven, Conn., 1930.

Cobban, "Kings, Courts and Parliaments"
Alfred Cobban, "Kings, Courts and Parliaments from 1660 to the French Revolution," in *The Eighteenth Century: Europe in the Age of the Enlightenment.* Edited by Alfred Cobban. London, 1969, pp. 11–40.

Colbourn, *Lamp of Experience*
   H. Trevor Colbourn, *The Lamp of Experience: Whig History and the Intellectual Origins of the American Revolution*. Chapel Hill, N.C., 1965.

Collection of Irish Letters
   A Collection of the Letters which have been addressed to the Volunteers of Ireland, on the subject of a Parliamentary Reform. London, 1783.

Commemoration Ceremony
   Commemoration Ceremony in Honor of the Two Hundredth Anniversary of the First Continental Congress in the United States House of Representatives. House Document No. 93–413, 93d Congress, 2d Session. Washington, D.C., 1975.

Complete Account
   A Complete And Accurate Account of the Very Important Debate in the House of Commons, on Tuesday, July 9, 1782. London, 1782.

Concept of Liberty
   John Phillip Reid, *The Concept of Liberty in the Age of the American Revolution*. Chicago, 1988.

Concept of Representation
   John Phillip Reid, *The Concept of Representation in the Age of the American Revolution*. Chicago, 1989.

Conway, *Peace Speech*
   Henry Seymour Conway, *The Speech of General Conway, Member of Parliament for Saint Edmondsbury, on moving in the House of Commons, (On the 5th of May, 1780)*. London, 1781.

Coombe, *Sermon*
   Thomas Coombe, *A Sermon, Preached before the Congregation of Christ Church and St. Peter's, Philadelphia, On Thursday, July 20, 1775 Being the Day Recommended by the Honourable Continental Congress for a General Fast Throughout the Twelve United Colonies of North-America*. Philadelphia, 1775.

Correspondence George III
   The Correspondence of King George the Third From 1760 to December 1783. Vol. I 1760–1767. Vol. II 1768–June 1773. Vol. III July 1773–December 1777. Vol. IV 1778–1779. Edited by Sir John Fortescue. London, 1927–28.

Countryman, *Revolution*
   Edward Countryman, *The American Revolution*. New York, 1985.

Coupland, *Quebec Act*
   R. Coupland, *The Quebec Act: A Study in Statesmanship*. Oxford, England, 1925.

Crisis
> *The Crisis* (Newspaper "Printed and published for the Authors by T. W. Shaw," London, 20 January 1775 to 6 October 1776).

Critical Review
> *The Critical Review: Or Annals of Literature by a Society of Gentlemen* (monthly magazine, London).

[Crowley,] *Letters*
> [Thomas Crowley,] *Letters and Dissertations, on Various Subjects by the Author of the Letter Analysis A. P. on the Disputes between Great Britain and America.* London, 1782.

Dartmouth American Papers
> Historical Manuscripts Commission. *Fourteenth Report, Appendix, Part X. The Manuscripts of the Earl of Dartmouth. Vol. II. American Papers.* London, 1895.

Dartmouth Manuscripts
> *The Manuscripts of the Earl of Dartmouth.* Vol. 1. Historical Manuscripts Commission, 11th report, appendix, part 5. London, 1887.

Day, *Present State of England*
> Thomas Day, *Reflections Upon the Present State of England, and the Independence of America.* 3d ed. London, 1783.

Delaware House Minutes (1765–1770)
> *Votes and Proceedings of the House of Representatives of the Government of the Counties of New Castle, Kent and Sussex, upon Delaware. At Sessions held at New Castle in the Years 1765–1766–1767–1768–1769–1770.* Dover, Del., 1931.

De Lolme, *Constitution: New Edition*
> J. L. De Lolme, *The Constitution of England; or, an Account of the English Government; in which it is Compared Both with the Republican Form of Government, and the Other Monarchies in Europe.* New ed. London, 1807.

Dickinson, "Debate on Sovereignty"
> H. T. Dickinson, "The Eighteenth-Century Debate on the Sovereignty of Parliament," in *Transactions of the Royal Historical Society.* 5th series, 26 (1976): 189–210.

[Dickinson,] *New Essay*
> [John Dickinson,] *A New Essay [By the Pennsylvania Farmer] on the Constitutional Power of Great-Britain over the Colonies in America; with the Resolves of the Committee For the Province of Pennsylvania, and their Instructions to their Representatives in Assembly.* London, 1774.

Dobbs, *Letter to North*
> Francis Dobbs, *A Letter to the Right Honourable Lord North, on his Propositions in Favour of Ireland.* Dublin, 1780.

Donoughue, *British Politics*
　　Bernard Donoughue, *British Politics and the American Revolution: The Path to War, 1773–75.* London, 1964.

[Downer,] *Discourse in Providence*
　　[Silas Downer,] *A Discourse, Delivered in Providence, in the Colony of Rhode-Island, upon the 25th Day of July, 1768. At the Dedication of the Tree of Liberty, From the Summer House in the Tree.* Providence, 1768.

[Draper,] *Thoughts of a Traveller*
　　[Sir William Draper,] *The Thoughts of a Traveller Upon our American Disputes.* London, 1774.

[Drayton,] *Letter from Freeman*
　　[William Henry Drayton,] *A Letter From Freeman of South-Carolina, to the Deputies of North-America, Assembled in the High Court of Congress at Philadelphia.* Charles-Town, S. C., 1774.

[Dulany,] *Considerations on the Propriety*
　　[Daniel Dulany,] *Considerations on the Propriety of Imposing Taxes in the British Colonies, For the Purpose of raising a Revenue, by Act of Parliament.* 2d ed. Annapolis, Md., 1765.

Dunham, "Transatlantic View"
　　William Huse Dunham, Jr., "A Transatlantic View of the British Constitution, 1700–76," in *Legal History Studies 1972: Papers Presented to the Legal History Conference Aberystwyth, 18–21 July 1972.* Cardiff, Wales, 1972, pp. 50–64.

[Eardley-Wilmot,] *Short Defence*
　　[John Eardley-Wilmot,] *A Short Defence of the Opposition; in Answer to a Pamphlet Intitled "A Short History of the Opposition."* London, 1778.

Eighteenth-Century Constitution
　　E. Neville Williams, *The Eighteenth-Century Constitution 1688–1815: Documents and Commentary.* Cambridge, England, 1960.

Eliot, "Letters"
　　"Letters From Andrew Eliot to Thomas Hollis," *Collections of the Massachusetts Historical Society* 4 (1858): 398–461.

[Erskine,] *Reflections on the Rise*
　　[John Erskine,] *Reflections on the Rise, Progress, and Probable Consequences, of the Present Contentions with the Colonies. By a Freeholder.* Edinburgh, 1776.

[Erskine,] *Shall I go to War?*
　　[John Erskine,] *Shall I go to War with my American Brethren? A Discourse from Judges the XXth and 28th. Addressed to all Concerned in Determining that Important Question.* London, 1769.

Estwick, *Letter to Tucker*
> Samuel Estwick, *A Letter to the Reverend Josiah Tucker, D. D. Dean of Glocester, in Answer to His Humble Address and Earnest Appeal, &c. with a Postscript, in which the present War against America is shewn to be the Effect, not of the Causes assigned by Him and Others, But of a Fixed Plan of Administration Founded in System.* London, 1776.

[Evans,] *Letter to John Wesley*
> [Caleb Evans,] *A Letter to the Rev. Mr. John Wesley, Occasioned by his Calm Address to the American Colonies.* London, 1775.

Evans, *Reply to Fletcher*
> Caleb Evans, *A Reply to the Rev. Mr. Fletcher's Vindication of Mr. Wesley's Calm Address to Our American Colonies.* Bristol, England, [1776].

[Ferguson,] *Remarks on a Pamphlet*
> [Adam Ferguson,] *Remarks on a Pamphlet Lately Published by Dr. Price, Intitled, Observations on the Nature of Civil Liberty, the Principles of Government, and the Justice and Policy of the War with America, &c. In a Letter from a Gentleman in the Country to a Member of Parliament.* London, 1776.

[Ferguson,] *Remarks on Dr. Price*
> [Adam Ferguson,] *Remarks on a Pamphlet Lately Published by Dr. Price, Intitled, Observations on the Nature of Civil Liberty, the Principles of Government, and the Justice and Policy of the War with America, &c. in a Letter from a Gentleman in the Country to a Member of Parliament.* London, 1776.

Ferling, *Loyalist Mind*
> John E. Ferling, *The Loyalist Mind: Joseph Galloway and the American Revolution.* University Park, Pa., 1977.

[Fitch, et al.,] *Reasons Why*
> [Thomas Fitch, Jared Ingersoll, Ebenezer Silliman, and George Wyllys,] *Reasons Why the British Colonies, in America, Should not be Charged with Internal Taxes, by Authority of Parliament; Humbly offered, For Consideration, In Behalf of the Colony of Connecticut.* New Haven, Conn., 1764.

Fletcher, *American Patriotism*
> J. Fletcher, *American Patriotism Farther confronted with Reason, Scripture, and the Constitution: Being Observations on the Dangerous Politics Taught by the Rev. Mr. Evans, M. A. and the Rev. Dr. Price. With a Scriptual Plea for the Revolted Colonies.* 2d ed. London, 1777.

Fox, *Speeches*
> *The Speeches of the Right Honourable Charles James Fox, in the House of Commons.* Volumes 1 and 2. London, 1815.

Fox, *Speech of 2 July*
> Charles James Fox, *The Speech of the Right Honourable Charles James Fox, on American Independence: Spoken in the House of Commons, On Tuesday, July 2, 1782.* London, [1782].

Franklin, *Address to Ireland*
> Benjamin Franklin, *An Address to the Good People of Ireland, on behalf of America, October 4th, 1778.* Edited by Paul Leicester Ford. Brooklyn, N.Y.: Historical Printing Club, 1891.

Franklin, *Writings*
> *The Writings of Benjamin Franklin.* Vol. 5. Edited by Albert Henry Smyth. London, 1907.

Franklin-Jackson Letters
> *Letters and Papers of Benjamin Franklin and Richard Jackson 1753–1785.* Edited by Carl Van Doren. Memoirs of the American Philosophical Society, vol. 24. Philadelphia, 1947.

Franklin's Letters to the Press
> *Benjamin Franklin's Letters to the Press, 1758–1775.* Edited by Verner W. Crane. Chapel Hill, N.C., 1950.

Freeman Letters
> *The Letters of Freeman, Etc. Essays on the Nonimportation Movement in South Carolina Collected by William Henry Drayton.* Edited by Robert M. Weir. Columbia, S.C., 1977.

Gage, *Correspondence*
> *The Correspondence of General Thomas Gage With the Secretaries of State 1763–1775.* Vol. 1. Edited by Clarence Edwin Carter. New Haven, Conn., 1931.

Gage, *Papers*
> Military Papers of General Gage, Clements Library, University of Michigan.

[Galloway,] *Historical Reflections*
> [Joseph Galloway,] *Historical and Political Reflections on the Rise and Progress of the American Rebellion.* London, 1780.

[Galloway,] *Mutual Claims*
> [Joseph Galloway,] *A Candid Examination of the Mutual Claims of Great-Britain and the Colonies: With a Plan of Accommodation, on Constitutional Principles.* London, 1780.

Gazette & News-Letter
> *The Massachusetts Gazette and Boston News-Letter.*

Gazette & Post-Boy
> *The Massachusetts Gazette and Boston Post-Boy and the Advertiser.*

Gentleman's Magazine
> *The Gentleman's Magazine and Historical Chronicle* (monthly magazine, London).

Georgia Commons House Journal
> *The Colonial Records of the State of Georgia. Volume XIV. Journal of the*

Commons House of Assembly January 17, 1763, to December 24, 1768, Inclusive. Volume XV. Journal of the Commons House of Assembly October 30, 1769, to June 16, 1782, Inclusive. Atlanta, Ga., 1907.

Georgia Revolutionary Records
The Revolutionary Records of the State of Georgia. Three volumes. Compiled by Allen D. Candler. Atlanta, Ga., 1908.

Gibbes, *Documentary History*
R. W. Gibbes, *Documentary History of the American Revolution, Consisting of Letters and Papers Relating to the Contest for Liberty, Chiefly in South Carolina 1764–1776.* New York, 1855.

Gipson, "Revolution as Aftermath"
Lawrence Henry Gipson, "The American Revolution as an Aftermath of the Great War for the Empire, 1754–1763," *Political Science Quarterly* 65 (1950): 86–104.

Gipson, "Ripe for Revolt"
Lawrence Henry Gipson, "Colonies Ripe for Revolt: The Older British North American Colonies in 1768," in *The American Revolution: The Anglo-American Relation, 1763–1794.* Edited by Charles R. Ritcheson. Reading, Mass., 1969, pp. 13–29.

[Goodricke,] *Observations*
[Henry Goodricke,] *Observations on Dr. Price's Theory and Principles of Civil Liberty and Government, Preceded by a Letter to a Friend, on the Pretensions of the American Colonies, in respect of Right and Equity.* York, England, 1776.

[Goodricke,] *Speech*
[Henry Goodricke,] *A Speech on some Political Topics, the Substance of which was intended to have been Delivered in the House of Commons, on Monday the 14th of December, 1778, when the Estimates of the Army were agreed to in the Committee of Supply.* London, 1779.

Gordon, *Discourse Preached*
William Gordon, *A Discourse Preached December 15th 1774. Being the Day Recommended by the Provincial Congress; And Afterwards at the Boston Lecture.* London, 1775.

Grant, *Policy of Chatham*
W. L. Grant, *The Colonial Policy of Chatham.* Bulletin of the Department of History and of Political and Economic Science in Queen's University, Kingston, Ontario, Canada. No. 1, October, 1911.

[Gray,] *Right of the Legislature*
[John Gray,] *The Right of the British Legislature to Tax the American Colonies Vindicated; and the Means of Asserting that Right Proposed.* 2d ed. London, 1775.

[Green,] *Observations on Reconciliation*
> [Jacob Green,] *Observations: on the Reconciliation of Great-Britain, and the Colonies; In which are exhibited, Arguments for, and against, that Measure.* Philadelphia, 1776.

Greene, "Origins"
> Jack P. Greene, "Origins of the American Revolution: A Constitutional Interpretation," in *The Framing and Ratification of the Constitution.* Edited by Leonard W. Levy and Dennis J. Mahoney. New York, 1987, pp. 36–53.

Greene, *Peripheries and Center*
> Jack P. Greene, *Peripheries and Center: Constitutional Development in the Extended Polities of the British Empire and the United States, 1607–1788.* Athens, Ga., 1986.

Greene, "Plunge of Lemmings"
> Jack P. Greene, "The Plunge of Lemmings: A Consideration of Recent Writings on British Politics and the American Revolution," *South Atlantic Quarterly* 67 (1968): 141–75.

Greene, *Quest*
> Jack P. Greene, *The Quest for Power: The Lower Houses of Assembly in the Southern Royal Colonies, 1689–1776.* Norton Library ed. New York, 1972.

Grenville Letterbooks
> Letterbooks of George Grenville. ST 7, Huntington Library, San Marino, Calif.

Grenville, *Papers*
> *The Grenville Papers: Being the Correspondence of Richard Grenville Earl Temple, K.G., and The Hon: George Grenville their Friends and Contemporaries.* 4 vols. Edited by William James Smith. London, 1852–1853.

Grenville, "Present State"
> [Knox,] *Considerations on the Present State,* printed in *Boston Chronicle.*

Guttridge, *English Whiggism*
> G. H. Guttridge, *English Whiggism and the American Revolution.* Berkeley, Calif., 1966.

Hamilton, *Farmer Refuted*
> Alexander Hamilton, *The Farmer Refuted: or a more impartial and comprehensive View of the Dispute between Great-Britain and the Colonies, Intended as a Further Vindication of the Congress* (1775), reprinted in *The Papers of Alexander Hamilton.* Vol. 1. Edited by Harold C. Syrett. New York, 1961, pp. 81–165.

Hamilton, "Quebec Bill"
> Alexander Hamilton, "Remarks on the Quebec Bill," in *The Papers of Alexander Hamilton—Volume I. 1768–1778.* Edited by Harold C. Syrett. New York, 1961, "Part One," pp. 165–69, "Part Two," pp. 169–76.

Hartley, *Letters on the War*
David Hartley, *Letters on the American War. Addressed to the Right Worshipful the Mayor and Corporation, to the Worshipful the Wardens and Corporation of the Trinity-House, and to the Worthy Burgesses of the Town of Kingston-Upon-Hull.* 6th ed. London, 1779.

Headlam, "Constitutional Struggle"
Cecil Headlam, "The Constitutional Struggle With the American Colonies, 1765–1775," in *The Cambridge History of the British Empire: Volume I, The Old Empire From the Beginnings to 1783.* Edited by J. Holland Rose, A. P. Newton, and E. A. Benians. Cambridge, England, 1929, pp. 646–84.

Hibernian Magazine
The Hibernian Magazine or Compendium of Entertaining Knowledge Containing The greatest Variety of the most Curious & useful Subjects in every Branch of Polite Literature (monthly magazine, Dublin).

[Hicks,] *Nature of Parliamentary Power*
[William Hicks,] *The Nature and Extent of Parliamentary Power Considered; In some Remarks upon Mr. Pitt's Speech in the House of Commons, previous to the Repeal of the Stamp-Act: With an Introduction, Applicable to the present Situation of the Colonies.* Philadelphia, 1768.

Higginbotham, "Iredell and Origins"
Don Higginbotham, "James Iredell and the Origins of American Federalism," in *Perspectives on the American Revolution: A Bicentennial Contribution.* Edited by George G. Suggs, Jr. Carbondale, Ill., 1977, pp. 99–115.

Higginbotham, "James Iredell's Efforts"
Don Higginbotham, "James Iredell's Efforts to Preserve the First British Empire," *North Carolina Historical Review* 49 (1972): 127–45.

Hitchcock, *Sermon Preached before Gage*
Gad Hitchcock, *A Sermon Preached Before his Excellency Thomas Gage, Esq; Governor: The Honorable His Majesty's Council, and the Honorable House of Representatives, of the Province of the Massachusetts-Bay in New-England, May 25th, 1774. Being the Anniversary of the Election of His Majesty's Council for said Province.* Boston, 1774.

Hoffer & Hull, "Yates's Plan"
Peter C. Hoffer and N. E. H. Hull, "'To Determine on the Future Government': Robert Yates's Plan of Union, 1774–1775," *William and Mary Quarterly* 35 (1977): 298–306.

Holmberg, *British-American Whig Rhetoric*
Georgia McKee Holmberg, *British-American Whig Political Rhetoric 1765–1776: A Content Analysis of the "London Gazette," "London Chronicle," and "Boston Gazette."* Ph.D. dissertation, University of Pittsburgh, 1979.

[Home,] *Letter from Officer*
[M. J. Home,] *A Letter From an Officer Retired to his Son in Parliament.*
London, 1776.

Hopkins, *Rights*
Stephen Hopkins, *The Rights of Colonies Examined* (1765), reprinted in
Bailyn, *Pamphlets,* pp. 507–22.

[Howard,] *Halifax Letter*
[Martin Howard, Jr.,] *A Letter from a Gentleman at Halifax to his Friend in
Rhode-Island, Containing Remarks Upon a Pamphlet, Entitled, The Rights
of the Colonies Examined* (1765), reprinted in Bailyn, *Pamphlets,* pp. 532–
44.

Hutchinson, "Dialogue"
Thomas Hutchinson, "A Dialogue Between an American and a European
Englishman," edited by Bernard Bailyn, in *Perspectives in American History*
9 (1975): 369–410.

Hutchinson, *Letters*
*Copy of Letters Sent to Great-Britain, by His Excellency Thomas Hutchin-
son, the Hon. Andrew Oliver, and Several Other Persons, Born and Educated Among Us.* Boston, 1773.

[Hutchinson,] *Strictures Upon the Declaration*
[Thomas Hutchinson,] *Strictures Upon the Declaration of the Congress at
Philadelphia; In a Letter to a Noble Lord, &c.* London, 1776.

"In a Defensive Rage"
John Phillip Reid, "In a Defensive Rage: The Uses of the Mob, the Justi-
fication in Law, and the Coming of the American Revolution," *New York
University Law Review* 49 (1974): 1043–91.

In a Defiant Stance
John Phillip Reid, *In a Defiant Stance: The Conditions of Law in Mas-
sachusetts Bay, the Irish Comparison, and the Coming of the American
Revolution.* University Park, Pa., 1977.

In a Rebellious Spirit
John Phillip Reid, *In a Rebellious Spirit: The Argument of Facts, the Lib-
erty Riot, and the Coming of the American Revolution.* University Park,
Pa., 1979.

In Defiance of the Law
John Phillip Reid, *In Defiance of the Law: The Standing-Army Controversy,
the Two Constitutions, and the Coming of the American Revolution.* Chapel
Hill, N.C., 1981.

"Ingersoll Correspondence"
"A Selection from the Correspondence and Miscellaneous Papers of Jared

Ingersoll," edited by Franklin B. Dexter, *Papers of the New Haven Colony Historical Society* 9 (1918): 201–472.

"In Legitimate Stirps"
John Phillip Reid, "In Legitimate Stirps: The Concept of 'Arbitrary', the Supremacy of Parliament, and the Coming of the American Revolution," *Hofstra Law Review* 5 (1977): 459–99.

"In the Taught Tradition"
John Phillip Reid, "In the Taught Tradition: The Meaning of Law in Massachusetts-Bay Two Hundred Years Ago," *Suffolk University Law Review* 14 (1980): 931–74.

Jefferson, *Summary View*
Thomas Jefferson, *A Summary View of the Rights of British America Set Forth in some Resolutions Intended For the Inspection of the Present Delegates of the People of Virginia Now in Convention* (1774), reprinted in *The Papers of Thomas Jefferson*. Edited by Julian P. Boyd. Vol. 1. Princeton, N.J., 1950, pp. 121–35.

[Jenings,] *Considerations*
[Edmund Jenings,] *Considerations on the Mode and Terms of a Treaty of Peace with America*. London, 1778.

[Jenings,] *Plan*
[Edmund Jenings,] *A Plan for Settling the Unhappy Dispute Between Great Britain and her Colonies*. N.p., 1776.

Jenkins, *Lex Terrae*
David Jenkins, *Lex Terrae; or, Laws of the Land* (1647), in *Somers' Tracts*, vol. 5, pp. 98–114.

Johnson, "Parliamentary Egotisms"
Richard R. Johnson, "'Parliamentary Egotisms': The Clash of Legislatures in the Making of the American Revolution," *Journal of American History* 74 (1987): 338–62.

[Johnson,] *Political Tracts*
[Samuel Johnson,] *Political Tracts. Containing, The False Alarm. Falkland's Islands. The Patriot; and Taxation no Tyranny*. London, 1776.

[Johnson,] *Some Important Observations*
[Stephen Johnson,] *Some Important Observations, Occasioned by, and adapted to, the Publick Fast, Ordered by Authority, December 18th. A.D. 1765*. Newport, R.I., 1766.

Johnstone, "Speech of November 1775"
William [sic George] Johnstone, "Governor Johnstone's Speech to the House of Commons, November, 1775," in *The American Revolution: The Anglo-American Relation, 1763–1794*. Edited by Charles R. Ritcheson. Reading, Mass., 1969, pp. 85–91.

Journal of Burgesses
> *Journals of the House of Burgesses of Virginia [Vol. 10] 1761–1765, [Vol. 11] 1766–1769, [Vol. 12] 1770–1772, [Vol. 13] 1773–1776 Including the records of the Committee of Correspondence.* Edited by John Pendleton Kennedy. Richmond, Va., 1905, 1906, 1907.

Journals of Congress
> *Journals of the Continental Congress 1774–1789.* Edited by Worthington Chauncey Ford et al. 34 vols. Washington, D.C., 1904–37.

Judson, "Henry Parker"
> Margaret Atwood Judson, "Henry Parker and the Theory of Parliamentary Sovereignty," in *Essays in History and Political Theory in Honor of Charles Howard McIlwain.* Cambridge, Mass., 1936, pp. 138–67.

"Junius," *Junius*
> ["Junius,"] *Junius.* 2 vols. London, [1772].

Kammen, *Rope*
> Michael Kammen, *A Rope of Sand: The Colonial Agents, British Politics, and the American Revolution.* Ithaca, N.Y., 1968.

[Keld,] *Polity of England*
> [Christopher Keld,] *An Essay on the Polity of England.* London, 1785.

Kemp, *King and Commons*
> Betty Kemp, *King and Commons 1660–1832.* London, 1957.

Kemp, "Parliamentary Sovereignty"
> Betty Kemp, "Parliamentary Sovereignty," *London Review of Books* 5, no. 4 (18 January 1984): 12–14.

Kenyon, *Revolution Principles*
> J. P. Kenyon, *Revolution Principles: The Politics of Party 1689–1720.* Cambridge, England, 1977.

[Kippis,] *Considerations on Treaty*
> [Andrew Kippis,] *Considerations on the Provisional Treaty with America, and the Preliminary Articles of Peace with France and Spain.* London, 1783.

Knollenberg, *Growth of Revolution*
> Bernhard Knollenberg, *Growth of the American Revolution 1766–1775.* New York, 1975.

Knollenberg, *Origin*
> Bernhard Knollenberg, *Origin of the American Revolution. 1759–1766.* Revised ed. New York, 1965.

[Knox,] *Considerations on the Present State*
> [William Knox,] *Considerations on the Present State of the Nation. Addressed to the Right Hon. Lord Rawdon, and the Other Members of the Two*

Houses of Parliament, Associated for the Preservation of the Constitution, and Promoting the Prosperity of the British Empire. London, 1789.

[Knox,] *Extra Official Papers*
[William Knox,] *Extra Official State Papers. Addressed to the Right Hon. Lord Rawdon, and the Other Members of the Two Houses of Parliament, Associated for the Preservation of the Constitution and Promoting the Prosperity of the British Empire. Volume the Second.* London, 1789.

Koebner, *Empire*
Richard Koebner, *Empire.* New York, 1961.

Labaree, *Patriots and Partisans*
Benjamin W. Labaree, *Patriots and Partisans: The Merchants of Newburyport 1764–1815.* New York, 1975.

Lawson, "George Grenville"
Philip Lawson, "George Grenville and America: The Years of Opposition, 1765 to 1770," *William and Mary Quarterly* 37 (1980): 561–76.

"Lawyer Acquitted"
John Phillip Reid, "A Lawyer Acquitted: John Adams and the Boston Massacre Trials," *American Journal of Legal History* 18 (1974): 189–207.

Lee, *Answer*
Arthur Lee, *Answer to Considerations on Certain Political Transactions of the Province of South Carolina* (1774), reprinted in *The Nature of Colony Considerations: Two Pamphlets on the Wilkes Fund Controversy in South Carolina by Sir Egerton Leigh and Arthur Lee.* Edited by Jack P. Greene. Columbia, S.C., 1970, pp. 131–205.

Lee, *Appeal to Justice*
[Arthur] Lee, *An Appeal to the Justice and Interests of the People of Great Britain, in the Present Disputes with America.* 4th ed. London, 1774.

[Lee,] *Junius Americanus*
[Arthur Lee,] *The Political Detection; or, the Treachery and Tyranny of Administration, both at Home and Abroad; Displayed in a Series of Letters, signed Junius Americanus.* London, 1770.

Lee Letters
The Letters of Richard Henry Lee, 1762–1778. Edited by James Curtis Ballagh. 2 vols. New York, 1911–14.

Lee Papers
The Lee Papers. Vol. I. 1754–1776. Collections of the New-York Historical Society for the Year 1871, vol. 4, New York, 1872.

[Lee,] *Vindication of the Colonies*
[Arthur Lee,] *An Essay in Vindication of the Continental Colonies of Amer-*

ica, from a Censure of Mr. Adam Smith, in his Theory of Moral Sentiments. With some Reflections on Slavery in general. London, 1764.

Leonard, "Massachusettensis"
Daniel Leonard, "Massachusettensis Letters," reprinted in *The American Colonial Crisis: The Daniel Leonard–John Adams Letters to the Press 1774–1775.* Edited by Bernard Mason. New York, 1972.

Letters of Charles Carroll
Unpublished Letters of Charles Carroll of Carrollton, and of His Father, Charles Carroll of Doughoregan. Edited by Thomas Meagher Field. New York, 1902.

Letters of Delegates to Congress
Letters of Delegates to Congress: 1774–1789. 12 vols. Edited by Paul H. Smith. Washington, D.C., 1976–1985.

[Lind,] *Thirteenth Parliament*
[John Lind,] *Remarks on the Principal Acts of the Thirteenth Parliament of Great Britain. Vol. I. Containing Remarks on the Acts relating to the Colonies. With a Plan of Reconciliation.* London, 1775.

Locke, *Two Treatises*
John Locke, *Two Treatises of Government: A Critical Edition with an Introduction and Apparatus Criticus.* 2d ed. Edited by Peter Laslett. Cambridge, England, 1967.

[Lofft,] *View of Schemes*
[Capel Lofft,] *A View of the Several Schemes with Respect to America; and their Comparative Merit in Promoting the Dignity and Interest of Great Britain.* London, 1776.

London Evening Post
(newspaper, London.)

London Journal
(weekly newspaper, London.)

London Magazine
The London Magazine or Gentleman's Monthly Intelligencer (monthly magazine, London).

Lovejoy, *Rhode Island Politics*
David S. Lovejoy, *Rhode Island Politics and the American Revolution 1760–1776.* Providence, R.I., 1958.

Macaulay, *Address to the People*
Catharine Macaulay, *An Address to the People of England, Scotland, and Ireland, on the Present Important Crisis of Affairs.* Bath, England, 1775.

Maccoby, *English Radicalism*
S. Maccoby, *English Radicalism 1762–1785: The Origins.* London, 1955.

[Macfarlane,] *George Third*
[Robert Macfarlane,] *The History of the Reign of George the Third, King of Great-Britain, &c to the Conclusion of the Session of Parliament Ending in May 1770.* London, 1770.

[Macfarlane,] *Second Ten Years*
[Robert Macfarlane,] *The History of the Second Ten Years of the Reign of George the Third, King of Great-Britain, &c.* London, 1782.

Maier, "John Wilkes"
Pauline Maier, "John Wilkes and American Disillusionment with Britain," *William and Mary Quarterly* 20 (1963): 373–95.

Markham, *Sermon Preached*
William Markham, Archbishop of York, *A Sermon Preached before the Incorporated Society for the Propagation of the Gospel in Foreign Parts, at their Anniversary Meeting, in the Parish Church of St. Mary-le-Bow, on Friday, February 21, 1777.* London, 1777.

Marston, *King and Congress*
Jerrilyn Greene Marston, *King and Congress: The Transfer of Political Legitimacy, 1774–1776.* Princeton, N.J., 1987.

Maryland Gazette
The Maryland Gazette (weekly newspaper, Annapolis, Md.).

[Maseres,] *Canadian Freeholder*
[Francis Maseres,] *The Canadian Freeholder: In Two Dialogues Between an Englishman and a Frenchman, Settled in Canada.* 3 vols. London, 1777, 1779.

[Maseres,] *Considerations on Admitting Representatives*
[Francis Maseres,] *Considerations on the Expediency of Admitting Representatives From the American Colonies into the British House of Commons.* London, 1770.

[Maseres,] *To Obtain An Assembly*
[Francis Maseres,] *An Account of the Proceedings of the British, And other Protestant Inhabitants, of the Province of Quebeck, In North-America, In order to obtain An House of Assembly In that Province.* London, 1775.

Massachusetts Gazette
The Massachusetts Gazette (weekly newspaper, Boston).

Massachusetts Provincial Congresses
The Journals of Each Provincial Congress of Massachusetts in 1774 and 1775, and of the Committee of Safety, with an Appendix, Containing the Proceedings of the County Conventions—Narratives of the Events of the Nineteenth of April, 1775—Papers Relating to Ticonderoga and Crown Point,

and Other Documents, Illustrative of the Early History of the American Revolution. Boston, 1838.

Massachusetts Representatives Journal (1764)
Journal of the Honourable House of Representatives, Of His Majesty's Province of the Massachusetts-Bay, in New-England, Begun and held at Concord, in the County of Middlesex, on Wednesday the Thirtieth Day of May, Annoque Domini, 1764. Boston, 1764.

McIlwain, "Common Law"
C. H. McIlwain, "The English Common Law, Barrier Against Absolutism," American Historical Review 49 (1943): 23–31.

McIlwain, Constitutionalism
Charles Howard McIlwain, Constitutionalism: Ancient and Modern. Ithaca, N.Y., 1940.

McIlwain, Revolution
Charles Howard McIlwain, The American Revolution: A Constitutional Interpretation. Ithaca, N.Y., 1958.

Memoirs of William Smith
Historical Memoirs From 16 March 1763 to 9 July 1776 of William Smith Historian of the Province of New York Member of the Governor's Council and Last Chief Justice of that Province Under the Crown. Chief Justice of Quebec. In Two Volumes. Edited by William H. W. Sabine. New York, 1956.

[Meredith,] Question Stated
[Sir William Meredith,] The Question Stated, Whether the Freeholders of Middlesex lost their Right, by voting for Mr. Wilkes at the last Election? London, [1769].

Middlekauff Glorious Cause
Robert Middlekauff, The Glorious Cause: The American Revolution 1763–1789. New York, 1982.

Mitchell, "Sir James Wright"
Robert G. Mitchell, editor, "Sir James Wright Looks at the American Revolution," Georgia Historical Quarterly 53 (1969): 509–18.

Montgomery, Sermon at Christiana Bridge
Joseph Montgomery, A Sermon Preached at Christiana Bridge and Newcastle, the 10th of July, 1775. Being the Day appointed by the Continental Congress, as a Day of Fasting, Humiliation, and Prayer. Philadelphia, 1775.

Monthly Review
The Monthly Review; or, Literary Journal: by Several Hands (monthly magazine, London).

Morgan, *Birth*
　　Edmund S. Morgan, *The Birth of the Republic, 1763–89*. Chicago, 1956.

Morgan, *Inventing the People*
　　Edmund S. Morgan, *Inventing the People: The Rise of Popular Sovereignty in England and America*. New York, 1988.

Morgan, *Prologue*
　　Prologue to Revolution: Sources and Documents on the Stamp Act Crisis, 1764–1766. Edited by Edmund S. Morgan. Chapel Hill, N.C., 1959.

Morrill, *Revolt of the Provinces*
　　J. S. Morrill, *The Revolt of the Provinces: Conservatives and Radicals in the English Civil War 1630–1650*. London, 1976.

Mullett, "Tory Imperialism"
　　Charles F. Mullett, "Tory Imperialism on the Eve of the Declaration of Independence," *Canadian Historial Review* 12 (1931): 262–82.

North Carolina Colonial Records
　　The Colonial Records of North Carolina, Published Under the Supervision of the Trustees of the Public Libraries, By Order of the General Assembly. Vols. 7, 8, and 9. Edited by William L. Saunders, Raleigh, N.C., 1888, 1890.

Norton, "Loyalist Critique"
　　Mary Beth Norton, "The Loyalist Critique of the Revolution," in *The Development of a Revolutionary Mentality*. First Library of Congress Symposia on the American Revolution. Washington, D.C., 1972, pp. 127–48.

Olson, "Parliamentary Law"
　　Alison Gilbert Olson, "Parliament, Empire, and Parliamentary Law, 1776," in *Three British Revolutions*, pp. 289–322.

O'Sullivan, "Philosophy of Common Law"
　　Richard O'Sullivan, "The Philosophy of the Common Law," *Current Legal Problems* 2 (1949): 116–38.

Otis, *Rights*
　　James Otis, *The Rights of the British Colonies Asserted and Proved* (1764), reprinted in Bailyn, *Pamphlets*, pp. 419–82.

[Paine,] *Large Additions*
　　[Thomas Paine,] *Large Additions to Common Sense; Addressed to the Inhabitants of America, On the following Subjects. I. The American Patriot's Prayer. II. American Independency defended by Candidus. III. The Propriety of Independency, by Demophilus. IV. A Review of the American Contest, with some Strictures on the King's Speech. . . . V. Letter to Lord Dartmouth, by an English American. VI. Observations on Lord North's Conciliatory Plan, by Sincerus*. Philadelphia, 1776.

Papers of Franklin
The Papers of Benjamin Franklin. Edited by Leonard W. Labaree. 27 vols.
New Haven, Conn., 1959–1988.

Papers of Iredell
The Papers of James Iredell: Volume I. 1767–1777. Edited by Don Higginbotham. Raleigh, N.C., 1976.

Parliamentary History
The Parliamentary History of England, From the Earliest Period to the Year
1803. 36 vols. London, 1806–1820.

Peach, *Richard Price*
Bernard Peach, *Richard Price and the Ethical Foundations of the American
Revolution.* Durham, N.C., 1979.

Pemberton, *Lord North*
W. Baring Pemberton, *Lord North.* London, 1938.

Pitt, *Plan*
Plan Offered by the Earl of Chatham, to the House of Lords, Entitled, A
Provisional Act, for Settling the Troubles in America, and for Asserting the
Supreme Legislative Authority and Superintending Power of Great Britain
over the Colonies. Which was rejected, and suffered to lie upon the Table.
London, 1775.

Pocock, "Revolution Against Parliament"
J. G. A. Pocock, "1776: The Revolution Against Parliament," in *Three British
Revolutions,* pp. 265–88.

Pole, *Gift*
J. R. Pole, *The Gift of Government: Political Responsibility From the English
Restoration to American Independence.* Athens, Ga., 1983.

Pole, *Legislative Power*
J. R. Pole, *The Seventeenth Century: The Sources of Legislative Power.*
Jamestown Essays on Representation. Charlottesville, Va., 1969.

Political Register
The Political Register; and Impartial Review of New Books (monthly magazine, London).

Potter, *Liberty We Seek*
Janice Potter, *The Liberty We Seek: Loyalist Ideology in Colonial New York
and Massachusetts.* Cambridge, Mass., 1983.

Pownall, *Administration*
Thomas Pownall, *The Administration of the Colonies. Wherein their Rights
and Constitution are Discussed and Stated.* 4th ed. London, 1768.

Pownall, *Administration Fifth Edition*
Thomas Pownall, *The Administration of the British Colonies. The Fifth Edi-*

tion. Wherein their Rights and Constitution are discussed and stated. 2 vols. London, 1774.

Pownall, *Administration Sixth Edition*
> Thomas Pownall, *The Administration of the British Colonies. The Sixth Edition. Wherein their Constitutional Rights and Establishments as also those Disputed Points in the Constitutions and Administration of the Government of the Colonies, from whence the Present American War Sprung, and on which the Final Settlement of a Peace must Turn are discussed and stated.* 2 vols. London, 1777.

[Prescott,] *Calm Consideration*
> [Benjamin Prescott,] *A Free and Calm Consideration of the Unhappy Misunderstandings and Debates, which have of late Years arisen, and yet subsist, Between the Parliament of Great-Britain, and these American Colonies. Contained in Eight Letters, Six whereof, Directed to a Gentleman of Distinction in England, Formerly printed in the Essex Gazette. The other Two, directed to a Friend.* Salem, Mass., 1774.

Price, *Nature of Civil Liberty*
> Richard Price, *Observations on the Nature of Civil Liberty, the Principles of Government, and the Justice and Policy of the War with America.* London, 1776.

Price, *Two Tracts*
> Richard Price, *Two Tracts on Civil Liberty, the War with America, and the Debts and Finances of the Kingdom: with a General Introduction and Supplement.* London, 1778.

Price, *Two Tracts: Tract One*
> Richard Price, *Observations on the Nature of Civil Liberty, the Principles of Government, and the Justice and Policy of the War with America.* 8th ed. London, 1778, reprinted in Price, *Two Tracts*, pp. 1–112.

Price, *Two Tracts: Tract Two*
> Richard Price, *Additional Observations on the Nature and Value of Civil Liberty, and the War with America: Also Observations on Schemes for raising Money by Public Loans; An Historical Deduction and Analysis of the National Debt; And a brief Account of the Debts and Resources of France* [3d ed., 1778], reprinted in Price, *Two Tracts*, pp. vii–xiv, 1–216.

Proceedings and Debates
> *Proceedings and Debates of the British Parliaments Respecting North America 1754–1783.* Edited by R. C. Simmons and P. D. G. Thomas. 6 vols. White Plains, N.Y., 1982–1987.

Protests of the Peers
> *A Complete Collection of all the Protests of the Peers in Parliament, entered on their Journals, Since the Year 1774, on the Great Questions of the Cause*

and Issue of the War Between Great-Britain and America, &c. to the Present Time. London, 1782.

Providence Gazette
The Providence Gazette and Country Journal (weekly newspaper, Providence, R.I.).

Public Records of Connecticut
Charles J. Hoadly, *The Public Records of the Colony of Connecticut.* Vols. 12, 13, 14, 15. Hartford, Conn., 1881–1890.

Pulteney, *Considerations on Present State*
William Pulteney, *Considerations on the Present State of Public Affairs, and the Means of Raising the Necessary Supplies.* 2d ed. London, 1779.

Pulteney, *Plan of Reunion*
William Pulteney, *Plan of Re-Union Between Great Britain and Her Colonies.* London, 1778.

Pulteney, *Thoughts on Present State*
William Pulteney, *Thoughts on the Present State of Affairs with America, and the Means of Conciliation.* 5th ed. London, 1778.

Puritanism and Liberty
Puritanism and Liberty Being the Army Debates (1647–9) from the Clarke Manuscripts with Supplementary Documents. Edited by A. S. P. Woodhouse. Chicago, 1974.

Rakove, *Beginnings*
Jack N. Rakove, *The Beginnings of National Politics: An Interpretive History of the Continental Congress.* New York, 1979.

[Ramsay,] *Historical Essay*
[Allan Ramsay,] *An Historical Essay on the English Constitution: Or, An impartial Inquiry into the Elective Power of the People, from the first Establishment of the Saxons in this Kingdom. Wherein the Right of Parliament, to Tax our distant Provinces, is explained, and justified, upon such constitutional Principles as will afford an equal Security to the Colonists, as to their Brethren at Home.* London, 1771.

[Ramsay,] *Letters on Present Disturbances*
[Allan Ramsay,] *Letters on the Present Disturbances in Great Britain and her American Provinces.* London, 1777.

[Randolph,] *Present State of Virginia*
[John Randolph,] *Considerations on the Present State of Virginia* (1774), reprinted in *Revolutionary Virginia* 1: 206–18.

Raynal, *Revolution*
The Abbé Raynal, *The Revolution of America.* Philadelphia, 1775.

Remembrancer for 1775
  The Remembrancer, or Impartial Repository of Public Events, for the Year
  MDCCLXXV. London, [1776].

Remembrancer for 1776: Part I
  The Remembrancer; or, Impartial Respository of Public Events: Part I For
  the Year 1776. London, 1776.

Remembrancer for 1776: Part II
  The Remembrancer; or, Impartial Repository of Public Events: Part II. For
  the Year 1776. London, 1776.

Remembrancer for 1776: Part III
  The Remembrancer; or, Impartial Repository of Public Events. Part III. For
  the Year 1776. London, 1777.

Remonstrance of the Cities (1659)
  The Remonstrance and Protestation of the Well-affected People of the Cities
  of London, Westminster, and the other Cities, Counties and Places within
  the Common-wealth of England, against those Officers of the Army, who
  put force upon, and interrupted the Parliament; the 13th of Octob. 1659,
  and against all pretended Powers or Authoritys that they have or shall set
  up, to Rule or Govern, this Common-Wealth that is not Established by
  Parliament. London, 1659.

Report of Lords on Massachusetts
  The Report of the Lords Committees, Appointed by the House of Lords to
  Enquire into the several Proceedings in the Colony of Massachuset's Bay,
  in Opposition to the Sovereignty of His Majesty, in His Parliament of Great
  Britain, over that Province; and also what hath passed in this House relative
  thereto, from the First Day of January, 1764. London, 1774.

Revolution, Confederation, and Constitution
  Revolution, Confederation, and Constitution. Edited by Stuart Gerry
  Brown. New York, 1971.

Revolutionary Virginia
  Revolutionary Virginia The Road to Independence—Volume I: Forming
  Thunderclouds and the First Convention, 1763–1774. A Documentary
  Record. Compiled by William J. Van Schreeven, edited by Robert L. Scrib-
  ner. Volume II: The Committees and the Second Convention, 1773–1775. A
  Documentary Record. Compiled by William J. Van Schreeven and Robert L.
  Scribner. Volume III: The Breaking Storm and the Third Convention, 1775.
  A Documentary Record. Compiled and edited by Robert L. Scribner. Vol-
  ume IV: The Committee of Safety and the Balance of Forces, 1775. A Docu-
  mentary Record. Compiled and edited by Robert L. Scribner and Brent
  Tarter. Volume V: The Clash of Arms and the Fourth Convention, 1775–
  1776. A Documentary Record. Compiled and edited by Robert L. Scribner

and Brent Tarter. *Volume VI: The Time for Decision, 1776. A Documentary Record.* Compiled and edited by Robert L. Scribner and Brent Tarter. [Charlottesville, Va.,] 1973–1979.

Revolution Documents
Documents of the American Revolution 1770–1783. Edited by K. G. Davis. Vols. 1–16. Dublin, 1972–81.

Rhode Island Colony Records
Records of the Colony of Rhode Island and Providence Plantations in New England. Edited by John Russell Bartlett. 10 vols. Providence, R.I., 1856–1865.

Ritcheson, *British Politics*
Charles R. Ritcheson, *British Politics and the American Revolution.* Norman, Okla., 1954.

[Rivers,] *Letters*
[George Pitt, Baron Rivers of Stratfieldsaye,] *Letters to a Young Nobleman, upon Various Subjects, Particularly on Government and Civil Liberty.* London, 1784.

Robbins, *Absolute Liberty*
Absolute Liberty: A Selection from the Articles and Papers of Caroline Robbins. Edited by Barbara Taft. Wittenberg, Ohio, 1982.

Robson, *American Revolution*
Eric Robson, *The American Revolution in its Political and Military Aspects 1763–1783.* New York, 1966.

Roebuck, *Enquiry Whether the Guilt*
John Roebuck, *An Enquiry, Whether the Guilt of the Present Civil War in America, Ought to be Imputed to Great Britain or America.* New ed. London, 1776.

[Rokeby,] *Further Examination*
[Matthew Robinson-Morris, Second Baron Rokeby,] *A Further Examination of our Present American Measures and of the Reasons and the Principles on which they are founded.* Bath, England, 1776.

Rokeby, *Peace Best Policy*
Matthew Robinson-Morris, Second Baron Rokeby, *Peace the Best Policy Or Reflections upon the Appearance of a Foreign War, the Present State of Affairs at Home and the Commission for Granting Pardons in America.* 2d ed. London, 1777.

"Rule Of Law"
John Phillip Reid, "The Rule of Law," in *The Blackwell Encyclopedia of the American Revolution.* Edited by Jack P. Greene and J. R. Pole. Oxford, 1991, pp. 629–33.

Rusticus, *Remarks*

"Rusticus," *Remarks on A Late Pamphlet Entitled Plain Truth.* Philadelphia, 1776.

Ryder, "Parliamentary Diaries"

"Parliamentary Diaries of Nathaniel Ryder, 1764–7," edited by P. D. G. Thomas. *Camden Miscellany Vol. XXIII.* Camden Society Fourth Series, Vol. 7. London, [1969], pp. 229–351.

Ryerson, *Revolution Begun*

Richard Alan Ryerson, *The Revolution is Now Begun: The Radical Committees of Philadelphia, 1765–1776.* Philadelphia, 1978.

Sainsbury, *Disaffected Patriots*

John Sainsbury, *Disaffected Patriots: London Supporters of Revolutionary America 1769–1782.* Montreal, 1987.

Schutz, *Thomas Pownall*

John A. Schutz, *Thomas Pownall British Defender of American Liberty: A Study of Anglo-American Relations in the Eighteenth Century.* Glendale, Calif., 1951.

Scots Magazine

The Scots Magazine (monthly magazine, Edinburgh).

Sharp, *Declaration of Natural Right*

Grenville Sharp, *A Declaration of the People's Natural Right to a Share in the Legislature; which is the Fundamental Principle of the British Constitution of State.* London, 1774.

Shebbeare, *An Answer*

John Shebbeare, *An Answer to the Queries Contained in a Letter to Dr. Shebbeare, printed in the Public Ledger, August 10 . . .* London, [1775].

Shebbeare, *Essay on National Society*

J. Shebbeare, *An Essay on the Origin, Progress and Establishment of National Society; in which the Principles of Government, the Definitions of physical, moral, civil, and religious Liberty, contained in Dr. Price's Observations, &c. are fairly examined and fully refuted; Together with a Justification of the Legislature, in reducing America to Obedience by Force.* London, 1776.

[Shebbeare,] *Fifth Letter*

[John Shebbeare,] *A Fifth Letter to the People of England, on the Subversion of the Constitution: And, The Necessity of it's being restored.* 2d ed. London, 1757.

[Shebbeare,] *Second Letter*

[John Shebbeare,] *A Second Letter to the People of England on Foreign Subsidies, Subsidiary Armies, and Their Consequences to this Nation.* 4th ed. London, 1756.

[Sheridan,] *Observations on the Doctrine*
[Charles Francis Sheridan,] *Observations on the Doctrine laid down by Sir William Blackstone, Respecting the extent of the Power of the British Parliament, Particularly with relation to Ireland. In a letter to Sir William Blackstone, with a Postscript Addressed to Lord North, upon the Affairs of that Country.* Dublin, 1779.

[Sheridan,] *Review of Three Questions*
[Charles Francis Sheridan,] *A Review of the Three Great National Questions Relative to a Declaration of Right, Poynings' Law, and the Mutiny Bill.* Dublin, 1781.

Shy, "Thomas Pownall"
John Shy, "Thomas Pownall, Henry Ellis, and the Spectrum of Possibilities, 1763–1775," in *Anglo-American Political Relations*, pp. 155–86.

Smith, "Thoughts on Dispute"
William Smith, Jr., "Thoughts upon the Dispute between Great Britain and her Colonies," *William and Mary Quarterly* 22 (1965): 111–18.

Somers' Tracts
A Collection of Scarce and Valuable Tracts, on the Most Interesting and Entertaining Subjects: But Chiefly such as Relate to the History and Constitution of these Kingdoms. Selected from an Infinite Number in Print and Manuscript, in the Royal, Cotton, Sion, and other Public, as well as Private, Libraries; Particularly that of the Late Lord Somers. Edited by Walter Scott. Vols. 4 and 5. London, 1809–1815.

Sosin, "Massachusetts Acts"
Jack M. Sosin, "The Massachusetts Acts of 1774: Coercive or Preventive?" *Huntington Library Quarterly* 26 (1963): 235–52.

Sosin, *Revolution of 1688*
J. M. Sosin, *English America and the Revolution of 1688: Royal Administration and the Structure of Provincial Government.* Lincoln, Neb., 1982.

South Carolina Congress
Journal of the Provincial Congress of South Carolina, 1776. London, 1776.

Speeches
Speeches of the Governors of Massachusetts From 1765 to 1775; And the Answers of the House of Representatives to the Same; with their Resolutions and Addresses for that Period. Boston, 1818.

Speeches of Grattan
The Speeches of the Right Honourable Henry Grattan, in the Irish, and in the Imperial Parliament. Edited by Henry Grattan. Vol. 1. London, 1822.

Speeches of John Wilkes in Parliament
The Speeches of John Wilkes, One of the Knights of the Shire for the County of Middlesex, In the Parliament appointed to meet at Westminster the 29th

day of November 1774, to the Prorogation the 6th Day of June 1777. 2 vols. London, 1777.

[Spelman,] *View of a Printed Book*
[John Spelman,] *A View of a Printed Book Intituled Observations upon His Majesties Late Answers and Expresses [Expressions].* Oxford, England, [1642].

"Stamp Act Debates"
"Debates on the Declaratory Act and the Repeal of the Stamp Act, 1766," *American Historical Review* 17 (1912): 563–86.

Stearns, *View of the Controversy*
William Stearns, *A View of the Controversy subsisting between Great-Britain and the American Colonies. A Sermon, Preached at a Fast, in Marlborough in Massachusetts-Bay. On Thursday May 11, 1775. Agreeable to a Recommendation of the Provincial Congress.* Watertown, Massachusetts, 1775.

[Steuart,] *Jus Populi*
[Sir James Steuart,] *Jus Populi Vindicatum, or the Peoples Right, to defend themselves and their Covenanted Religion, vindicated.* N.p., [1669].

Steven's Facsimiles
B. F. Steven's Facsimiles of Manuscripts in European Archives Relating to America 1773–1783 with Descriptions, Editorial Notes, Collations, References and Translations.

Stewart, *Total Refutation*
James Stewart, *The Total Refutation and Political Overthrow of Doctor Price; or, Great Britain Successfully vindicated against all American Rebels, and their Advocates. In a Second Letter to that Gentleman.* London, 1776.

Stokes, *View of Constitution*
Anthony Stokes, *A View of the Constitution of the British Colonies, in North-America and the West Indies, at the Time the Civil War broke out on the Continent of America.* London, 1783.

Stout, *Perfect Crisis*
Neil R. Stout, *The Perfect Crisis: The Beginning of the Revolutionary War.* New York, 1976.

St. Patrick's Anti-Stamp Chronicle
St. Patrick's Anti-Stamp Chronicle: Or, Independent Magazine, of News, Politics, and Literary Entertainment. Dublin.

Taylor, *Western Massachusetts*
Robert J. Taylor, *Western Massachusetts in the Revolution.* Providence, R.I., 1954.

Thomas, *British Politics*
>P. D. G. Thomas, *British Politics and the Stamp Act Crisis: The First Phase of the American Revolution, 1763–1767.* Oxford, England, 1975.

Thomas, *Lord North*
>Peter D. G. Thomas, *Lord North.* London, 1976.

Thomas, *Townshend Duties*
>Peter D. G. Thomas, *The Townshend Duties Crisis: The Second Phase of the American Revolution, 1767–1773.* Oxford, England, 1987.

Three British Revolutions
>*Three British Revolutions: 1641, 1688, 1776.* Edited by J. G. A. Pocock. Princeton, N.J., 1980.

Toohey, *Liberty and Empire*
>Robert E. Toohey, *Liberty and Empire: British Radical Solutions to the American Problem 1774–1776.* Lexington, Ky., 1978.

Town and Country Magazine
>*The Town and Country Magazine; or Universal Repository of Knowledge, Instruction, and Entertainment* (monthly magazine, London).

Trevelyan, *Revolution Condensation*
>George Otto Trevelyan, *The American Revolution.* Edited by Richard B. Morris. London, 1964.

Trumbull Papers
>*The Trumbull Papers: Collections of the Massachusetts Historical Society.* Vol. 9, 5th series. Boston, 1885.

Tucker, *Letter to Burke*
>Josiah Tucker, *A Letter to Edmund Burke, Esq; Member of Parliament for the City of Bristol, and Agent for the Colony of New York, &c. In Answer to His Printed Speech, Said to be Spoken in the House of Commons on the Twenty-Second of March, 1775.* 2d ed. Gloucester, England, 1775.

Tucker, *True Interest of Britain*
>Jos[iah] Tucker, *The True Interest of Britain, Set Forth in Regard to the Colonies; and the only Means of Living in Peace and Harmony with Them.* Philadelphia, 1776.

Tucker & Hendrickson, *Fall*
>Robert W. Tucker and David C. Hendrickson, *The Fall of the First British Empire: Origins of the War of American Independence.* Baltimore, 1982.

Turner, *Election Sermon*
>Charles Turner, *A Sermon Preached Before His Excellency Thomas Hutchinson, Esq; Governor: The Honorable His Majesty's Council, and the Honorable House of Representatives, of the Province of the Massachusetts-Bay*

in New-England, May 26th. 1773. Being the Anniversary of the Election of His Majesty's Council for said Province. Boston, 1773.

Valentine, *Lord North*
Alan Valentine, *Lord North*. Two volumes. Norman, Okla., 1967.

Van Alstyne, "Parliamentary Supremacy"
Richard W. Van Alstyne, "Parliamentary Supremacy versus Independence: Notes and Documents," *Huntington Library Quarterly* 26 (1964): 201–33.

Van Tyne, *Causes of War*
Claude H. Van Tyne, *The Causes of the War of Independence: Being the First Volume of a History of the Founding of the American Republic*. Boston, 1922.

Virginia Gazette
Rival newspapers published in Williamsburg, Virginia, and identified by their owners or printers: "Dixon and Hunter" (John Dixon and William Hunter), "Pinkney" (John Pinkney), "Purdie and Dixon" (Alexander Purdie and John Dixon), "Purdie" (Alexander Prudie), and "Rind" (William Rind or Clememtina Rind).

Wade, *Junius*
John Wade, *Junius: Including Letters by the Same Writer Under Other Signatures; to Which are Added his Confidential Correspondence with Mr. Wilkes, and his Private Letters to Mr. H. S. Woodfall*. 2 vols. Philadelphia, 1836.

Wagner, "Judicial Review"
D. O. Wagner, "Some Antecedents of the American Doctrine of Judicial Review," *Political Science Quarterly* 40 (1925): 561–93.

[Watson,] *Cursory Remarks on Price*
[Jonathan Watson,] *Cursory Remarks on Dr. Price's Observations on the Nature of Civil Liberty. In a Letter to a Friend. By a Merchant*. London, 1776.

Watson, *Principles of the Revolution*
Richard Watson, *The Principles of the Revolution vindicated in a Sermon Preached Before the University of Cambridge, on Wednesday, May 29, 1776*. Cambridge, England, 1776.

Weir, "Introduction to Freeman"
Robert M. Weir, "Introduction" to *Freeman Letters*.

Weir, *Most Important Epocha*
Robert M. Weir, "A *Most Important Epocha": The Coming of the Revolution in South Carolina*. Columbia, S.C., 1970.

West, *Election Sermon*
Samuel West, *A Sermon Preached Before the Honorable Council, and the*

Honorable House of Representatives, of the Colony of the Massachusetts-Bay, in New-England. May 29th, 1776. Being the Anniversary for the Election of the Honorable Council for the Colony. Boston, 1776.

Wheeler, "Calvin's Case"
Harvey Wheeler, "Calvin's Case (1608) and the McIlwain-Schuyler Debate," *American Historical Review* 61 (1956): 587–97.

[Wheelock,] *Reflections*
[Matthew Wheelock,] *Reflections Moral and Political on Great Britain and her Colonies.* London, 1770.

Willcox, *Age of Aristocracy*
William B. Willcox, *The Age of Aristocracy 1688 to 1830.* Lexington, Mass., 1966.

Williams, "Chatham and Representation"
Basil Williams, "Chatham and the Representation of the Colonies in the Imperial Parliament," *English Historical Review* 22 (1907): 756–58.

[Williams,] *Letters on Liberty*
[David Williams,] *Letters on Political Liberty, and the Principles of the English and Irish Projects of Reform. Addressed to a Member of the English House of Commons.* 3d ed. London, 1789.

[Williamson,] *Plea of the Colonies*
[Hugh Williamson,] *The Plea of the Colonies On the Charges brought against them by Lord Mansfield, and Others, in a letter to His Lordship.* Philadelphia, 1777.

Witherspoon, *Sermon Preached at Princeton*
John Witherspoon, *The Dominion of Providence over the Passions of Men. A Sermon Preached at Princeton, on the 17th of May, 1776. Being the General Fast appointed by the Congress through the United Colonies. To which is added, an Address to the Natives of Scotland, residing in America.* Philadelphia, 1777.

Works of Edmund Burke
The Works of Right Honorable Edmund Burke. 6th ed. 12 vols. Boston, 1880.

Wright, *Fabric of Freedom*
Esmond Wright, *Fabric of Freedom, 1763–1800.* New York, 1961.

Zubly, *Law of Liberty*
John J. Zubly, *The Law of Liberty. A Sermon on American Affairs, Preached at the Opening of the Provincial Congress of Georgia. Addressed to the Right Honourable the Earl of Dartmouth.* Philadelphia, 1775.

NOTES

INTRODUCTION

1 Anon., *Political Reflections*, p. 3.
2 Although taxation still seemed to be the main issue in 1774, it is reasonable to suggest that, had it been the only constitutional point in controversy, uncomplicated by the question of parliamentary sovereignty, a solution avoiding armed rebellion could more easily have been devised. *Authority to Tax*, pp. 234–84. After all, in 1778, when the war was three years old and the Declaration of Independence long promulgated, Parliament renounced any pretension to authority to tax "for the Purpose of raising a Revenue in any of the Colonies, Provinces, or Plantations." Ibid., pp. 260–61.
3 *Authority to Legislate*, pp. 79–221.
4 Potter, *Liberty We Seek*, p. 106.
5 "In the Taught Tradition," pp. 931–74.
6 For the concept of "rule of law" in the era of the American Revolution, see "Rule of Law," pp. 629–33.
7 *Authority to Legislate*, pp. 9–10, 294–98, 306–9; "In a Defensive Rage," pp. 1050–52, 1062–69.
8 For the significance of the vocabulary of "the right" in the revolutionary controversy, see *Authority to Legislate*, pp. 289–90, 298.
9 "To the People of America," Boston, September 1774, *American Archives* 1:756.

NOTES TO PAGES 6–10

10 For Galloway's address, see below, pp. 112–18.
11 [Galloway,] *Historical Reflections*, pp. 75–76.
12 Discussed in chap. 1.
13 Speeches of Edmund Burke and Lord North, Commons Debates, 2 May 1774, *Parliamentary History* 17:1315.
14 Petition of the Aldermen, Sheriff, et al., of Nottingham to the House of Commons, 22 February 1775, *American Archives* 1:1632.
15 Speech of Lord Hillsborough, Lords Debates, 14 March 1776, *Proceedings and Debates* 6:478.
16 Speech of Lord North, Commons Debates, 2 May 1774, *Parliamentary History* 17:1315–16.
17 An obvious example is the New York Suspending Act. *Authority to Legislate*, pp. 276–81.
18 Ibid., pp. 289–90.
19 Letter from William Samuel Johnson to William Pitkin, 2 May 1769, *Trumbull Papers*, p. 350.
20 *Authority to Legislate*, pp. 290–99.
21 Speech of Henry Seymour Conway, Commons Debates, 5 May 1780, Conway, *Peace Speech*, p. 9.
22 *Authority to Legislate*, pp. 296–97.

CHAPTER ONE: THE COERCIVE ACTS

1 *Gazette & Post-Boy* (Supplement), 2 May 1774, p. 1, col. 2 (quoting London newspaper of 12 March 1774).
2 [Eardley-Wilmot,] *Short Defence*, pp. 9, 11, 15–16; Anon., *Letter to Mansfield*, pp. 3–4; *Annual Register 1774*, p. [61]; Anon., *Address to People of Britain*, p. 59; Ritcheson, *British Politics*, p. 157 (quoting Lord Rockingham); Thomas, *Lord North*, pp. 77–78 (quoting North).
3 14 George III, cap. 19; Speech of Lord North, Commons Debates, 14 March 1774, *Proceedings and Debates* 4:60.
4 Speech of Lord North, Commons Debates, 23 March 1774, *London Magazine* 43 (1774): 173; Speeches of Lord North, Commons Debates, 14 March 1774 and 18 March 1774, *Proceedings and Debates* 4:56–57, 84. For discussion of the purpose, see Sosin, "Massachusetts Acts," pp. 245–46.
5 Speech of Lord North, Commons Debates, 25 March 1774, *Proceedings and Debates* 4:143. Also, see Thomas, *Lord North*, pp. 76–78.
6 Speech of Lord North, Commons Debates, 14 March 1774, *London Magazine* 43 (1774): 169; Instructions from Lord Dartmouth to Governor Thomas Gage, 9 April 1774, *American Archives* 1:245–46. Also, see Speech of John Sawbridge, Commons Debates, 25 March 1774, *London Magazine* 43 (1774): 179; Speeches of Lord North and Charles James Fox, Commons Debates, 14 March 1774, and Welbore Ellis, Commons Debates, 25 March 1774, *Proceedings and Debates* 4:63–64, 72, 135–36.
7 Speeches of Henry Seymour Conway, George Byng, Hans Stanley, and Lord

North, Commons Debates, 23 March 1774, *Proceedings and Debates* 4:99, 105, 106, 108; Speech of Grey Cooper, Commons Debates, 25 March 1774, ibid., pp. 136–37; [Randolph,] *Present State of Virginia*, pp. 211–12; [Galloway,] *Historical Reflections*, p. 18; Allen, *American Crisis*, pp. 59–60; Anon., *Examination into the Conduct*, p. 2; Donoughue, *British Politics*, p. 79 (quoting Isaac Barré).

8 Speech of Lord North, Commons Debates, 23 March 1774, *London Magazine* 43 (1774): 171. It was claimed that this assurance muted opposition in both houses. Speech of the duke of Richmond, Lords Debates, 15 November 1775, *Proceedings and Debates* 6:256 (speaking of Lords); Anon., *Characters*, p. 45 (quoting Isaac Barré on Commons). Also, see Anon., *Experience preferable to Theory*, p. 65; Anon., *Review of Present Administration*, p. 39. Contrary, see Speeches of Edmund Burke and John Sawbridge, Commons Debates, *London Magazine* 43 (1774): 177, 179.

9 Speech of Lord North, Commons Debates, 23 March 1774, *Proceedings and Debates* 4:108–9. Also, see Letter from Arthur Lee to Richard Henry Lee, 18 March 1774, *American Archives* 1:229; Ritcheson, *British Politics*, p. 158. Again the claim would be made that this assurance silenced opposition. Speech of Charles James Fox, Commons Debates, 12 June 1782, Fox, *Speeches* 1:390. Contrary, see Speech of George Johnstone, Commons Debates, 25 March 1774, and Petition of several Natives of North America to the House of Commons, 25 March 1774, *Proceedings and Debates* 4:138, 115–16; *Annual Register 1774*, p. [67].

10 New York City Resolves, 19 July 1774, *Boston Evening-Post*, 1 August 1774, p. 2, col. 2; Resolves of Charles Town, South Carolina, July 1774, *American Archives* 1:316. Similarly, see Resolves of Connecticut House of Representatives, May 1774, *Public Records of Connecticut* 14:348–49; Northampton County, Pennsylvania, Resolves, 21 June 1774, Fauquier County, Virginia, Resolves, 9 July 1774, Rye, New York, Resolves, 10 August 1774, Resolves of the Massachusetts Provincial Congress, 6 December 1774, *American Archives* 1:435, 529, 703, 999.

11 Diary entry for 18 May 1774, *Memoirs of William Smith* 1:186; Ammerman, *Common Cause*, p. 6 (quoting Thomas Whaton, Sr.). Similarly, see Letter from Daniel Dulany, Jr., to Arthur Lee, May 1774, *American Archives* 1:355; Stout, *Perfect Crisis*, pp. 89–90 (quoting John Andrews); Letter from Governor John Penn to Lord Dartmouth, 5 July 1774, *Revolution Documents* 8:142.

12 "To All the English Colonies of North America," Philadelphia, 1 July 1774, *American Archives* 1:378. Similarly, see Resolutions of Queen Anne's County, Maryland, 30 May 1774, and Letter from John Scollay to Arthur Lee, 31 May 1774, ibid., pp. 366, 369.

13 Letter from Richard Henry Lee to Arthur Lee, 26 June 1774, Lee, *Letters*, p. 114. Contrary, see [Randolph,] *Present State of Virginia*, p. 212.

14 Letter from Governor John Penn to Lord Dartmouth, 5 July 1774, *Revolution Documents* 8:142. The most commonly enacted resolution was: "That the

act of parliament shutting up the port of Boston is unconstitutional, oppressive to the inhabitants of that town, dangerous to the liberties of the British colonies; and, therefore, that we consider our brethren in Boston suffering in the common cause of these colonies." Philadelphia Resolves, 15 July 1774, *Gentleman's Magazine* 44 (1774): 438.

15 Speech of Edmund Burke, Commons Debates, 20 February 1775, *Proceedings and Debates* 5:450.

16 Resolves of the House of Representatives, May 1774, *Public Records of Connecticut* 14:348; Address from the Continental Congress to the People of Great Britain, 21 October 1774, *Journals of Congress* 1:86.

17 *Gazette & Post-Boy* (Supplement), 2 May 1774, p. 1, col. 1 (printing despatch from London, 10 March 1774).

18 Speech of Lord North, Commons Debates, 22 April 1774, *Proceedings and Debates* 4:276.

19 *In a Defiant Stance*, pp. 17–99.

20 Speech of Lord North, Commons Debates, 25 March 1774, *London Magazine* 43 (1774): 179; Anon., *View of North*, p. 138; *Annual Register 1774*, p. [69].

21 Speech of Richard Rigby, Commons Debates, 2 May 1774, *Proceedings and Debates* 4:380. See also Speeches of Lord North, Commons Debates, 23 March 1774, and John St. John, Commons Debates, 2 May 1774, ibid., 108, 352–53.

22 Speech of Charles Townshend, Commons Debates, 7 February 1766, Ryder, "Parliamentary Diaries," p. 283; Book Review, *Political Register* 5 (1769): 300 (criticizing Bernard's plan); Letter from Thomas Hutchinson to Lord Hillsborough, October 1770, *Remembrancer for 1776: Part I*, p. 158; Anon., *History of Lord North*, p. 162 (attributing all of North's reforms to Hutchinson).

23 "Measures Proposed by Lord Hillsborough to the Cabinet," 15 February 1769, *Correspondence George III* 2:82–83; Thomas, *Townshend Duties*, pp. 126–27; Tucker & Hendrickson, *Fall*, p. 265. The idea may have been raised earlier. Letter from William Samuel Johnson to Governor William Pitkin, 11 April 1767, *Trumbull Papers*, p. 226.

24 "Memorandum by the King," February 1769, *Correspondence George III* 2:84. Also, see Thomas, *Townshend Duties*, p. 129; Christie, *Crisis*, p. 74; Ritcheson, *British Politics*, pp. 124–25.

25 Speech of Lord Barrington, Commons Debates, 26 April 1770, *Proceedings and Debates* 3:261; Letters from William Samuel Johnson to Governor Jonathan Trumbull, 28 June 1770, 15 November 1770, 2 January 1771, *Trumbull Papers*, pp. 442–43, 466–67, 471; Thomas, *Townshend Duties*, pp. 193, 195.

26 De Lolme, *Constitution: New Edition*, p. 202; Letter from Governor Thomas Hutchinson to Lord Hillsborough, December 1770, *Remembrancer for 1776: Part I*, p. 160.

27 *In a Defiant Stance*, pp. 27–134; *In Defiance of the Law*, pp. 206–11; *In a Rebellious Spirit*, pp. 30–35.

28 Anon., *Letter to Lord Camden*, p. 20; Anon., *Review of Present Administra-*

tion, p. 39. Also, see Speech of Hans Stanley, Commons Debates, 8 November 1768, *Proceedings and Debates* 3:4; [Lind,] *Thirteenth Parliament*, p. 411.

29 Anon., *Letter to Lord Camden*, p. 20; Answer of the Massachusetts House, 26 January 1773, *Briefs of Revolution*, p. 73.

30 Speech of Lord North, Commons Debates, 2 May 1774, *Proceedings and Debates* 4:372, 383.

31 Anon., *View of North*, p. 138; *Boston Evening-Post*, 3 September 1770, p. 3, col. 1 (reprinting a letter from London to Philadelphia quoting Hillsborough); *Annual Register 1774*, p. [69].

32 Speech of Lord North, Commons Debates, 28 March 1774, *Proceedings and Debates* 4:148.

33 Speech of Lord North, Commons Debates, 22 April 1774, ibid., p. 276.

34 Commons Debates, 28 March 1774, ibid., p. 148.

35 Dissent of the Lords, 11 May 1774, ibid., p. 418. Also, see [Lind,] *Thirteenth Parliament*, p. 412.

36 Speech of Lord North, Commons Debates, 2 May 1774, *Proceedings and Debates* 4:383; Protest of 11 May 1774, *Protests of the Peers*, p. 7.

37 14 George III, cap. 39.

38 Ibid. For the concept, likelihood of execution, and force of whig law, see *In a Defiant Stance*, pp. 65–99.

39 [Hutchinson,] *Strictures Upon the Declaration*, p. 21. The statute clearly intended every person, including private citizens, to support imperial law enforcement, but the idea for the bill seems to have developed from discussions about why the military was reluctant to act and what could be done to make military law enforcement more effective. Ritcheson, *British Politics*, p. 161; Donoughue, *British Politics*, p. 92; Sosin, "Massachusetts Acts," p. 248. Also, see Speeches of Lord Beauchamp, Commons Debates, 21 April 1774 and Constantine Phipps, Commons Debates, 29 April 1774, *Proceedings and Debates* 4:261, 320.

40 14 George III, cap. 39. The word "inquisition" means a inquest conducted, in those days, by a coroner.

41 For the Act of Henry and the Dockyards Act, see *Authority to Legislate*, pp. 281–86.

42 [Williamson,] *Plea of the Colonies*, p. 11; Petition of the Lord Mayor, Aldermen, and Livery of London to the King, 10 April 1775, *American Archives* 1:1853.

43 Countryman, *Revolution*, p. 3; Weir, *Most Important Epocha*, p. 53; Becker, *Declaration*, p. 114; Holmberg, *British-American Whig Rhetoric*, p. 156.

44 Trevelyan, *Revolution Condensation*, p. 119. For the charge of "exemption," see Petition to the King from Natives of America, 19 May 1774, *American Archives* 1:96; Address of the Congress to "the People in general, and particularly to the Inhabitants of Pennsylvania and the adjacent States," 10 December 1776, *Journals of Congress* 6:1018.

45 See generally, "Lawyer Acquitted."

46 *Crisis,* 6 April 1776, p. 410 ("they cannot have *their peers*"); Speech of Constantine Phipps, Commons Debates, 15 April 1774, *Proceedings and Debates* 4:167 ("obnoxious"); Speech of John Sawbridge, Commons Debates, 21 April 1774, *Proceedings and Debates* 4:261 ("mockery of justice"). Also, see Speeches of George Byng, Commons Debates, 21 April 1774, Constatine Phipps, Commons Debates, 29 April 1774, and George Dempster, Commons Debates, 6 May 1774, *Proceedings and Debates* 4:261, 320, 402; Speech of Lord Camden, Lords Debates, 16 March 1775, *Proceedings and Debates* 5:542–43; Olson, "Parliamentary Law," p. 312.

47 Protest of the Lords reprinted in [Macfarlane,] *Second Ten Years,* p. 154.

48 Speech of George Dempster, Commons Debates, 6 May 1774, *Proceedings and Debates* 4:402–3. Also, see Speech of John Sawbridge, Commons Debates, 6 May 1774, ibid., p. 401. The administration's answer was that "trial of persons in England will seldom take place." Speech of Thomas De Grey, Jr., Commons Debates, 6 May 1774, ibid., p. 403.

49 Petition of American Natives to the House of Commons, 2 May 1774, ibid., p. 327; Speech of Colonel Issac Barré, Commons Debates, 13 April 1774, *Scots Magazine* 36 (1774): 341. Similarly, see Speech of Henry Seymour Conway, Commons Debates, 2 May 1774, *Proceedings and Debates* 4:380.

50 Speeches of Philip Jennings, Lord North, Constantine Phipps, and Alexander Wedderburn, Commons Debates, 29 April 1774, *Proceedings and Debates* 4:320–21. Similarly, see Speeches of Constantine Phipps, Commons Debates, 29 April 1774, Colonel Isaac Barré, Commons Debates, 2 May 1774, and John Sawbridge, Commons Debates, 6 May 1774, ibid., pp. 319, 378, 401.

51 For the restraints the Mutiny Act had permitted local Massachusetts law to place on the military's authority, see *In a Defiant Stance,* pp. 107–11.

52 Valentine, *Lord North* 1:325; Becker, *Declaration,* p. 114.

53 14 George III, cap. 54, sec. 2; Speech of Lord Barrington, Commons Debates, 29 April 1774, *Proceedings and Debates* 4:318; Stout, *Perfect Crisis,* p. 61; Knollenberg, *Growth of Revolution,* p. 379 n. 26.

54 Supremacy issues raised by the Quartering Act were more analogous to statutes which altered civil procedure in the colonies, such as the 1732 "Act for the more easy Recovery of Debts." See *Authority to Legislate,* pp. 256–59.

55 Speech of Stephen Fox, Commons Debates, 2 May 1774, *Proceedings and Debates* 4:378.

56 Speech of John Sawbridge, 21 April 1774, ibid., p. 260.

57 *Concept of Liberty,* pp. 38–54.

58 Speech of Lord North, Commons Debates, 21 April 1774, *Proceedings and Debates* 4:261.

59 Speech of Lord Camden, Lords Debates, 17 May 1775, *Scots Magazine* 37 (1775): 240; Argument of Mr. Mansfield, House of Commons, 31 May 1774, *Proceedings and Debates* 4:498–500; Anon., *Thoughts on Quebec Act,* pp. 5–13; Robbins, *Absolute Liberty,* p. 318.

60 14 George III, cap. 83, sec. 12; Coupland, *Quebec Act,* p. 92; [Lind,] *Thirteenth Parliament,* pp. 446, 479–81; Stokes, *View of Constitution,* p. 31.

61 Speech of John Dunning, Commons Debates, 26 May 1774, *Scots Magazine* 36 (1774): 299; Hamilton, "Quebec Bill," p. 167.

62 Speech of Lord North, Commons Debates, 26 May 1774, *Proceedings and Debates* 4:447; [Bernard,] *Appeal to the Public*, p. 15.

63 For a historian's defense of the Bill, see Coupland, *Quebec Act*, pp. 109–10. Also, see Speech of Lord North, Commons Debates, 8 June 1774, *Proceedings and Debates* 5:163.

64 Petition of Lord Mayor, et al., to the House of Commons, 3 June 1774, *American Archives* 1:194; Abingdon, *Thoughts on Burke's Letter*, p. lxix. Also, see Petition of Lord Mayor, Aldermen, and Commons of London to the King, 23 June 1774, *Scots Magazine* 36 (1774): 307–8.

65 "Political Character of Mr. Dunning," *London Magazine* 45 (1776): 689; Hamilton, "Quebec Bill," p. 168 (also, see p. 167); Speech of Lord Chatham, Lords Debates, 17 June 1774, *Scots Magazine* 36 (1774): 304; Answer of Baron Maseres, 10 February 1775, and Letter from the New York General Committee to the Mayor, Aldermen, and Common Council of London, 5 May 1775, *Addresses and Petitions of Common Council*, pp. 62, 87; *Annual Register 1774*, p. [76] (summarizing "arbitrary" arguments of parliamentary opposition).

66 Petition of the Lord Mayor, et al., to the King, 23 May 1774, *London Magazine* 43 (1774): 302.

67 *Authority of Rights*, pp. 139–45 (the original colonial contract), pp. 153–55 (the proclamation contract), pp. 155–58 (*Campbell* v. *Hall*).

68 Speech of Lord Camden, Lords Debates, 17 May 1775, *Scots Magazine* 37 (1775): 242.

69 Speech of Constantine Phipps, Commons Debates, 31 May 1774, *Proceedings and Debates* 4:485–86; Proceedings of 31 May 1774, ibid., p. 500 (reprinting *St. James's Chronicle*, 31 May–2 June 1774: "As soon as Mr. *Mansfield* [appearing as counsel against the Quebec Bill] had finished his argument, he called a Mr. *Watts*, a person who had been a resident merchant at Quebec for nine years, to prove . . . that numbers went to settle in that country on the faith of the King's Proclamation").

70 *Authority to Tax*, pp. 53–62.

71 Ibid., pp. 55–60 (the original contract), pp. 60–63 (the settlement contract); *Authority of Rights*, pp. 124–31 (the migration purchase), pp. 155–58 (Lord Mansfield, C. J.).

72 Speech of John Dunning, Commons Debates, 26 May 1774, *Proceedings and Debates* 4:449, 452 (similarly, see pp. 459–60). Also, see Speech of Serjeant John Glynn, Commons Debates, 26 May 1774, ibid., p. 464 (saying that Britons in Quebec had "rights secured to them, by the laws of this country, secured to them by the Royal Proclamation"). Contrary, see Thomas, *Townshend Duties*, p. 10.

73 Speech of John Dunning, Commons Debates, 26 May 1774, *American Archives* 1:182. Those settlers would be "deprived of some of the most valuable parts of the law of their own country." Speech of Thomas Townshend, Jr., Commons Debates, 26 May 1774, *Proceedings and Debates* 4:443. Also, see

Speech of George Johnstone, Commons Debates, 6 June 1774, *Proceedings and Debates* 5:100; Protest of 9 March 1778, *Protests of the Peers*, p. 83; Anon., *History of Lord North*, p. 162.

74 Anon., *Observations on Quebec*, pp. 24–25; Drayton, "A Letter from 'Freeman,'" 10 August 1774, Gibbes, *Documentary History*, p. 14.

Chapter Two: The Coercive Grievance

1 Speech of Edmund Burke, Commons Debates, 13 November 1770, *Burke Writings* 2:336; "To the People of Pennsylvania," July 1774, *American Archives* 1:655; Speech of George Johnstone, Commons Debates, 23 January 1775, *Parliamentary History* 18:178 (recalling North's argument). Although the constitutional strategy of precedent creation and precedent avoidance is not known today, it appears to have been quite familiar in the eighteenth century, even in small American towns. For example, the voters of one town resolved that the Tea Act "is undoubtedly designed to make a precedent for establishing taxes in America." Resolves of Richmond Town Meeting, 28 February 1774, *Rhode Island Colony Records* 7:276. Also part of the legal mentality of the eighteenth century was the theory of provocation, sometimes confused with conspiracy. It would be said that an action was intended to provoke a response: "It is expected that the province of Massachusetts-Bay will be irritated into some violent action, that may displease the rest of the continent, or that may induce the people of Great-Britain to approve the medicated vengeance of an imprudent and exasperated ministry." Continental Congress Memorial to the Inhabitants of the Colonies, 21 October 1774, *Journals of Congress* 1:98. Provocation justified response. For example, the East India Company knew that "the intention" of sending tea to Boston "was generally understood to be expressly to enforce the Tea Act, as the duty was payable when the tea was landed." The tea was "an instrument for affecting that purpose," and Boston had "no alternative but to destroy it, or suffer it to be entered for duty." "To the Inhabitants of New-York," 6 October 1774, *American Archives* 1:825. As a matter of law, the Company's tea was no longer "property," and Bostonians had a "legal" right to destroy it. *In a Defiant Stance*, pp. 98–99.

2 Stout, *Perfect Crisis*, p. 42 (quoting Letter from Walpole to Sir Horace Mann, 1 May 1774).

3 Anon., *Honor of Parliament*, p. 35; Leonard, "Massachusettensis," p. 63. Historians' arguments that the Acts were lenient are often based on imperial legal assumptions. Tucker & Hendrickson, *Fall*, p. 320. Also, see Sosin, "Massachusetts Acts," p. 250. One necessity, often overlooked, was that had Parliament not acted it would have been consigning the colonies to the prerogative. Speech of Lord Hillsborough, Lords Debates, 14 March 1776, *Proceedings and Debates* 6:478–79.

4 Speech of Lord North, Commons Debates, 2 May 1774, *American Archives* 1:91.

5 Day, *Present State of England*, p. 6. Historians have also depicted the Coercive

Acts as harsh. "The Massachusetts Government Act . . . revised the charter beyond recognition." Taylor, *Western Massachusetts*, p. 63; "The act in effect abrogated the charter of 1691 by legislative fiat." Bushman, *King and People*, p. 187.

6 Worcester County Resolves, 10 August 1774, *Massachusetts Provincial Congresses*, p. 630; Bushman, *King and People*, p. 189 (quoting instructions of 4 October 1774).

7 Hampshire County Resolves, 23 September 1774, *Massachusetts Provincial Congresses*, p. 619.

8 Letter from Benjamin Franklin to William Franklin, 22 March 1775, *Papers of Franklin* 21:560.

9 Speeches of Charles James Fox, Commons Debates, 2 May 1774 and Earl Camden, Lords Debates, 11 May 1774, *Proceedings and Debates* 4:381, 421. Similarly, see argument attributed to the duke of Richmond, ibid., pp. 420–21 (quoting *London Evening Post*, 26–28 May 1774).

10 Speech of Edmund Burke, Commons Debates, 19 March 1773, *London Magazine* 43 (1774): 221. Similarly, see Petition of East India Company to House of Commons, 14 December 1772, and "Proceedings and Debates in Parliament," *Scots Magazine* 35 (1773): 123, 126.

11 Georgia Committee to Virginia Committee, 10 August 1774, *Revolutionary Virginia* 2:158.

12 Argument of counsel, 18 December 1772, *Parliamentary History* 17:651; Argument of Mr. Adair, 18 December 1772, "Proceedings and Debates in Parliament," *Scots Magazine* 35 (1773): 126.

13 For the concept of arbitrary in eighteenth-century constitutional law, see "In Legitimate Stirps," *passim*.

14 2 William & Mary, Sess. 1, cap. 8; Protest of the Lords, 23 December 1772, *Parliamentary History* 17:682–83.

15 For the Stamp Act, see *Authority to Tax*, pp. 12–24, 208–16.

16 For the Hat Act, see *Authority to Legislate*, pp. 267–71.

17 For the right to lawful government in eighteenth-century constitutional law, see *Authority of Rights*, pp. 39–46.

18 Chatham, *Speech 20 May*, p. 1, col. 1; Speech of John St. John, Commons Debates, 2 May 1774, *Proceedings and Debates* 4:379.

19 Petition of American Natives to the House of Commons, 2 May 1774, and Speech of Colonel Isaac Barré, Commons Debates, 2 May 1774, *Proceedings and Debates* 4:327, 377; Turner, *Election Sermon*, p. 25.

20 [Drayton,] *Letter from Freeman*, p. 7. For "absolutism" of the Quebec Act, see Speech of Lord George Cavendish, Commons Debates, 31 May 1774, *Proceedings and Debates* 4:497; Hartley, *Letters on the War*, pp. 65–66; Hamilton, "Quebec Bill," p. 167.

21 Price, *Two Tracts: Tract One*, p. 46; Price, *Nature of Civil Liberty*, p. 46. Similarly, see Speech of Serjeant John Glynn, Commons Debates, 26 May 1774, *Proceedings and Debates* 4:465; [Erskine,] *Reflections on the Rise*, p. 40; Bushman, *King and People*, p. 187.

22 Address to the People of Great Britain, 21 October 1774, *Journals of Congress*

1:88; Baillie, *Letter to Shebear*, p. 24. Chatham described the Quebec Bill as "the worst of despotism," putting "the whole people under arbitrary power." Speech of Lord Chatham, Lords Debates, 17 June 1774, *Proceedings and Debates* 5:229.

23 Letter from the Continental Congress to the People of Great Britain, *London Magazine* 43 (1774): 628.

24 Countryman, *Revolution*, p. 50; Hartley, *Letters on the War*, p. 66; *St. Patrick's Anti-Stamp Chronicle* 2 (1774): 54. Similarly, see Macaulay, *Address to the People*, pp. 6–7, 16; Ammerman, *Common Cause*, pp. 12, 147 (quoting a loyalist, Thomas Wharton, Sr.).

25 Anon., *View of North*, pp. 160–61; [Macfarlane,] *Second Ten Years*, pp. 155–56. Similarly, see "Extract of a Letter. . . . June 22, 1774," *American Archives* 1:437. The attorney general of Quebec advised those who wanted an elected assembly in that province to acknowledge Parliament's sovereignty and to promise that representatives would take an oath to that effect. Letter from Francis Maseres to the Committee of the Petitioners, 19 March 1774, [Maseres,] *To Obtain an Assembly*, pp. 37–38. The charge was being repeated as late as 1783. [Kippis,] *Considerations on Treaty*, p. 36.

26 See, for example, Address to the People of Great Britain, 21 October 1774, *Journals of Congress* 1:87–88; "Richard Henry Lee's Draft Address to the People of Great Britain," 27? June 1775, *Letters of Delegates to Congress* 1:549.

27 Speech of Lord Camden, Lords Debates, 17 May 1775, *Scots Magazine* 37 (1775): 240; Anon., *View of North*, p. 158 (paraphrasing Dunning). "[W]e have converted the province of Canada . . . as a terror upon all our ancient and protestant colonies." Speech of David Hartley, Commons Debates, 27 March 1775, *Proceedings and Debates* 5:643. Similarly, see Address, Remonstrance, and Petition of the Lord Mayor, Aldermen, and Livery of London to the King, 11 April 1775, *London Magazine* 44 (1775): 209.

28 Knollenberg, *Origin*, p. 23. It easily could have been introduced at Georgia where there was no charter right to an assembly. Message from Governor James Wright to Commons House of Assembly, 1 February 1768, *Georgia Commons House Journal* 14:518.

29 Constitution, Minutes of 26 March 1776, *South Carolina Congress*, pp. 108–9.

30 See *Authority to Legislate*, pp. 142–50; *Concept of Liberty*, pp. 55–59.

31 *Concept of Liberty*, pp. 32–59.

32 Resolves of the Delaware Convention, 2 August 1774, *American Archives* 1:668.

33 Price, *Two Tracts: Tract Two*, p. 5.

34 Anon., *View of North*, p. 160.

35 Speech of John Dunning, Commons Debates, 7 June 1774, *Proceedings and Debates* 5:141; Address and Petition of the Corporation of London to the King, *Gentleman's Magazine* 44 (1774): 248. Similarly, see Letter to the Inhabitants of Quebec, 26 October 1774, *Journals of Congress* 1:110–11.

36 *Concept of Liberty*, pp. 98–107.

37 Message from the Massachusetts Congress to General Thomas Gage, 13 Octo-

ber 1774, *Massachusetts Provincial Congresses*, p. 18 (also *American Archives* 1:835).

38 *Concept of Liberty*, pp. 38–59.

39 Ibid., p. 49 (quoting John Cartwright). For consent as a test for liberty, see ibid., 79–83, 110–11.

40 Georgia Resolves, January 1775 and Middlesex County Resolves, 31 August 1774, *American Archives* 1:1157, 751.

41 Greene, *Quest*, pp. 443–44 (quoting Iredell). Also, see "The Principles of an American Whig," *Papers of Iredell* 1:336; Ammerman, *Common Cause*, p. 8.

42 Gordon, *Discourse Preached*, p. 23; Ebenezer Baldwin, "A Settled Fix'd Plan for Inslaving the Colonies," 31 August 1774, *Commemoration Ceremony*, p. 50. For a Briton sounding the same warning, see Price, *Two Tracts: Tract One*, p. 47.

43 *Authority of Rights*, pp. 34–38; *Concept of Liberty*, pp. 68–73, 87–88.

44 [Williamson,] *Plea of the Colonies*, p. 11; Knollenberg, *Growth of Revolution*, p. 118; Greene, *Quest*, p. 443. For right to government, see *Authority of Rights*, pp. 39–46.

45 South Carolina Resolutions, 6, 7, 8 July 1774, *Scots Magazine* 36 (1774): 412. Similarly, see Speech of the Duke of Grafton, Lords Debates, 5 March 1776, *Proceedings and Debates* 6:446; Memorial from New York General Assembly to the House of Lords, 25 March 1775, *American Archives* 1:1317. A different argument was that the specific terms of the Massachusetts Government Act made "life and property" in that colony insecure. *Monthly Review* 52 (1775): 177.

46 Christie, *Crisis*, p. 84. The grievance was occasionally stated that the colonists "had no security in the permanency of their government, but that it was liable to be altered or subverted at our pleasure." Speech of Charles James Fox, Commons Debates, 2 February 1778, *Parliamentary History* 19:676.

47 For the distinction between "power" and "right," see "In the Taught Tradition," pp. 947–61. The House of Commons had had this definition in mind in 1689 when it voted that judgments ordering the surrender of borough, university, and colonial charters were "illegal." Anon., *To Tax Themselves*, p. 52. See also Resolves of Albemarle County, 4 August 1774, *Revolutionary Virginia* 1:112–13.

48 Suffolk Resolves, 9 September 1774 and Bristol County Resolves, 29 September 1774, *Massachusetts Provincial Congresses*, pp. 602, 627.

49 Resolutions of London Court of Common Council, 21 February 1775, *American Archives* 1:1253 (also published in *Addresses and Petitions of Common Council*, pp. 67–68). Also, see Spottsylvania County, Virginia, Resolutions, 24 June 1774, *American Archives* 1:449.

50 Thomson Mason, "British American, No. IX," 28 July 1774, *Revolutionary Virginia* 1:200. Also, see Coombe, *Sermon*, p. 25 (a future loyalist saying "security consisted in *a spirited resistance*"); *St. Patrick's Anti-Stamp Chronicle* 2 (1774): 56 (Irish magazine reprinting London press).

51 [Johnson,] *Some Important Observations*, p. 18 footnote (the writer was sug-

gesting that the Stamp Act or any other attempt to tax for purposes of revenue annuled the charters). Similarly, see the Worcester County Resolves quoted *supra*, text to note 6. A special aspect of the breach-of-contract theory, unrelated to the authority to legislate, was that the Coercive Acts were to be "enforced by military power." Resolves of Scituate, 26 September 1774, *Rhode Island Colony Records* 7:283.

52 Draft letter undated and unsigned, *Dartmouth Manuscripts* 1:355 (also reprinted in Bellot, *William Knox*, p. 125). The date of letter is said to be 11 July 1774. Stout, *Perfect Crisis*, p. 63.

Chapter Three: The Supremacy Issue

1 As a governance grievance, these statutes are associated with the prerogative proclamations declaring the colonies in rebellion. They included acts restraining and prohibiting trades and fishing, authorizing the taking of American ships as prizes and the impressing of American sailors serving on prizes. 15 George III, cap. 10; 15 George III, cap. 18; 16 George III, cap. 5.

2 See, for example, Speech of Charles James Fox, Commons Debates, 9 July 1782, *Complete Account*, p. 18; Conway, *Peace Speech*, pp. 7–8 (Commons Debates, 5 May 1780); Speech of Charles James Fox, Commons Debates, 2 February 1778, Fox, *Speeches* 1:108; Speech of Sir Grey Cooper, Commons Debates, 2 March 1778, *Parliamentary History* 19:790; Speech of George Johnstone, Commons Debates, 18 May 1775, *Scots Magazine* 37 (1775): 249; General Committee of Association for New York County to the Lord Mayor and Corporation of London, 5 May 1775, *American Archives* 2:511–12; [Burke,] *Letters of Valens*, p. 80; Butler, *Sermon Preached in Dublin*, pp. 5–9; [Rokeby,] *Further Examination*, p. 58; [Lofft,] *View of Schemes*, pp. 1–12; [Evans,] *Letter to John Wesley*, p. 3.

3 Address of Governor William Franklin to New Jersey Legislators, 16 May 1775, *American Archives* 2:595.

4 "[I]f the claim of taxation was fairly relinquished, without reservation, I am confident the supremacy of the British Parliament would be acknowledged and acquiesced in by America, and peace between both countries be once more happily restored." Speech of the Earl of Shelburne, Lords Debates, 15 November 1775, *Proceedings and Debates* 6:255. Similarly, see Anon., "Introduction" to *Lords Report*, p. vi; [Ferguson,] *Remarks on a Pamphlet*, p. 28.

5 Anon., *Thoughts on Present War*, p. 12.

6 [Macfarlane,] *Second Ten Years*, p. 198 (summarizing the opposition's arguments against North peace plan of February 1775).

7 North gave up most claims by February 1775. *Authority to Tax*, pp. 247–61. Taxation was given up entirely in 1778. Instructions to Carlisle Commission, 12 April 1778, *Revolution Documents* 15:87.

8 Speech of the Duke of Manchester, Lords Debates, 15 December 1775, *Proceedings and Debates* 6:356.

9 Speech of Lord North, Commons Debates, 13 November 1775, ibid., pp. 242–

43. Similarly, see Speech of Lord North, Commons Debates, 17 February 1778, *Gentleman's Magazine* 48 (1778): 53.

10 [Sir John Dalrymple,] "The Address," *Scots Magazine* 37 (1775): 381–83 (one of four causes).

11 Anon., *History of North and South America* 2:243; [Anderson,] *Free Thoughts*, p. 2, col. 2.

12 Speech of Hans Stanley, Commons Debates, 26 January 1775, *Parliamentary History* 18:186; Speech of Lord Camden, Lords Debates, 16 March 1775, *Proceedings and Debates* 5:542. The same was sometimes said by British citizens. See Petition of the Aldermen, Sheriff, et al., of Nottingham to the House of Commons, 22 February 1775, *American Archives* 1:1632.

13 Except for those believing that taxation for purposes of revenue was the sole issue. Then it could be argued that if Britain gave up the authority to tax, Americans would willingly acknowledge the authority to legislate. Anon., *Serious and Impartial Observations*, p. 36.

14 *Boston Post-Boy*, 8 April 1765, p. 3, col. 2; Rakove, *Beginnings*, pp. 54, 60 (discussing Galloway); Middlekauff, *Glorious Cause*, p. 244 (disbelieving Galloway); Speech of Lord Mansfield, Lords Debates, 6 February 1775, *Gentleman's Magazine* 45 (1775): 107 (also printed in *Scots Magazine* 37 [1775]: 129). Also, see Anon., *Some Fugitive Thoughts*, p. 3.

15 Speech of Lord Suffolk, Lords Debates, 20 January 1775, *Parliamentary History* 18:161. Also, see Speech of Welbore Ellis, Commons Debates, 7 March 1774, *Proceedings and Debates* 4:39; Letter from King George to Lord North, 11 September 1774, *Correspondence George III* 3:131.

16 Speech of Earl Gower, Lords Debates, 14 March 1776, *Proceedings and Debates* 6:484. Also, see Speech of Lord Ongley, Commons Debates, 11 February 1778, *Parliamentary History* 19:724; Speech of Captain Harvey, Commons Debates, 18 May 1775, *Scots Magazine* 37 (1775): 246; Speech of Lord Suffolk, Lords Debates, 20 January 1775, *Parliamentary History* 18:161–62.

17 Speech of Lord George Germain, Commons Debates, 26 January 1775, *Proceedings and Debates* 5:314; Speech of Isaac Wilkins, General Assembly Debates, 23 February 1775, *American Archives* 1:1294.

18 Thomas, *Lord North*, p. 76 (quoting Matthew Brickdale's account of North's speech against Boston); Speech of Lord Rochford, Lords Debates, 22 December 1774, *American Archives* 1:1502. Also, see Speech of R_____se, Commons Debates, 6 November 1776, *Gentleman's Magazine* 47 (1777): 7; *Proceedings and Debates* 5:434 (reprinting *London Chronicle*, 25 February 1775, report of Speech of Lord North, Commons Debates, 20 February 1775); Speech of Charles Wolfran Cornwall, Commons Debates, 19 April 1774, *Proceedings and Debates* 4:235–36; "Book Review," *Critical Review* 22 (1766): 442–44.

19 Letter from Thomas Hutchinson to John Pownall, January 1773, *Remembrancer for 1776: Part II*, p. 60.

20 Letter from Thomas Hutchinson, February 1770, *Remembrancer for 1775*, p. 49.

21 Letter from Thomas Hutchinson to Lord Hillsborough, 22 January 1771, *Remembrancer for 1776: Part I*, p. 162.

22 Ibid. For letters detailing the program, see Letter from Thomas Hutchinson to unknown, 27 August 1772, *Remembrancer for 1776: Part II*, p. 59; Letter from Thomas Hutchinson to Thomas Gage, 13 May 1773, Gage, *Papers;* Letter from Thomas Hutchinson, February 1770, *Remembrancer for 1775*, pp. 48–49. Also, see Potter, *Liberty We Seek*, p. 143 (quoting letter of July 1774).

23 Letter from Thomas Hutchinson to unknown, 27 August 1772, *Remembrancer for 1776: Part II*, p. 59.

24 Speech of John Burgoyne, Commons Debates, 27 February 1775, *Proceedings and Debates* 5:477; Stearns, *View of the Controversy*, p. 18.

25 Abingdon, *Dedication*, pp. lxviii–lxix (also, see p. lxiv). Similarly, see Letter from Thomas Cushing [Massachusetts Speaker] to Speaker of Rhode Island House of Representatives, 3 June 1773, *Rhode Island Colony Records* 7:230; Anon., *Appeal to Reason and Justice*, p. 99; "Candidus," Portsmouth, New Hampshire, 14 April 1775, *American Archives* 2:335; Anon., *Summary of Important Arguments*, at "introduction" (no pagination).

26 Protest of 15 December 1775, *Protests of the Peers*, p. 57. Also, see Pitt, *Plan*, pp. 4–5 (Chatham's Provisional Bill which has as a preamble the duty of the colonies to obey "the Supreme Legislative Authority and Superintending Power of the Parliament of Great Britain"); Speech of Lord Chatham, Lords Debates, 18 November 1777, *Parliamentary History* 19:365 footnote; [Home,] *Letter from Officer*, pp. 3–4; [Cartwright,] *American Independence*, pp. 26–27 (says sovereignty and taxation are the issues); Cartwright, *Legislative Rights*, p. 108 footnote.

27 Protest of 31 October 1776, *Protests of the Peers*, p. 69.

28 "Petition of Nova Scotia Assembly, 24 June 1775," *Gentleman's Magazine* 46 (1776): 5 (also reprinted in *Proceedings and Debates* 6:91–94). Similarly, see Address of Inhabitants of Anson County, North Carolina, to Governor Josiah Martin, March 1775, *American Archives* 2:116; Letter from Governor Patrick Tonyn to Lord George Germain, 30 July 1781, *Revolution Documents* 20:204.

29 [Galloway,] *Historical Reflections*, p. 75; Galloway's Statement on his Plan of Union, 28 September 1774, *Letters of Delegates to Congress* 1:124.

30 Declaration and Resolves, 14 October 1774, *Journals of Congress*, pp. 71–73; Speech of Lord Camden, Lords Debates, 30 May 1777, *Gentleman's Magazine* 47 (1777): 511.

31 Speech of Henry Cruger, Commons Debates, 10 December 1777, *Parliamentary History* 19:587. Similarly, see Speech of Isaac Wilkins, New York Assembly Debates, 23 February 1775, *American Archives* 1:1296.

32 Speech of Charles James Fox, Commons Debates, 15 May 1775, *American Archives* 1:1822 (also printed in Fox, *Speeches* 1:42). Similarly, see Speech of Edmund Burke, Commons Debates, 19 April 1774, *Burke on American Revolution*, pp. 26–27; Resolution of the North Carolina House of Assembly, 6 April 1775, *American Archives* 2:262; Anon., *Answer to Sheridan*, pp. 36–38. For similar appraisals that seem to give more weight to the exercise

of the power but which also say that the claim to the power was a grievance, see Speech of Henry Seymour Conway, Commons Debates, 22 April 1774, *Proceedings and Debates* 4:276; Message from the House of Burgesses to Governor Lord Dunmore, 10 June 1775, *American Archives* 2:1201.

33 [Rivers,] *Letters*, p. 148. Also, see Proceedings of the Deputies of Pennsylvania, 15 July 1774, *London Magazine* 43 (1774): 584; Speech of Charles Jenkinson, Commons Debates, 15 May 1775, *American Archives* 1:1821; "Brutus," An Address to a Virginia County, 14 July 1775, *Revolutionary Virginia* 3:131; [Maseres,] *Canadian Freeholder* 1:337; Price, *Two Tracts: Tract One*, p. 43; Anon., *Some Seasonable Observations*, p. 8.

34 Lee, *Answer*, p. 176 (quoting Blackstone, *Commentaries* 3:135).

35 Gage, *Correspondence* 1:69–70. Similarly, see Letter from William Samuel Johnson to Governor William Pitkin, 15 December 1768, *Proceedings and Debates* 3:48 (quoting Lord Hillsborough in Parliament).

36 Speech of Earl Gower, Lords Debates, 30 May 1777, *Parliamentary History* 19:320–21.

37 Gordon, *Discourse Preached*, p. 11 footnote.

38 Montgomery, *Sermon at Christiana Bridge*, p. 9; Address to the People of Great Britain, 21 October 1774, *Journals of Congress* 1:83. Also, see [Goodricke,] *Speech*, p. 33.

39 "Extract of a Letter from a Gentleman of Philadelphia, to a Member of the British Parliament, Dated December 26, 1774," *American Archives* 1:1067. Similarly, see, An American, "To the Inhabitants of New-York," 28 April 1775, *American Archives* 2:429.

40 Speech of Sir William Meredith, Commons Debates, 10 December 1777, *Parliamentary History* 19:588.

41 Speech of George Johnstone, Commons Debates, 18 May 1775, *Scots Magazine* 37 (1775): 249 (also printed in *Gentleman's Magazine* 45 [1775]: 211).

CHAPTER FOUR: THE GLORIOUS REVOLUTION ISSUE

1 Speech of George Johnstone, Commons Debates, 16 December 1774, *Parliamentary History* 18:60. Also printed in *Gentleman's Magazine* 44 (1774): 595; *Hibernian Magazine* 5 (1775): 4.

2 A Scots advocate, for example, said Americans were "rebels in the same way, and for the same reasons that the people of Britain were rebels, for supporting the Revolution, and establishing the succession in the present royal family." [Baillie,] *Some Observations on a Pamphlet*, pp. 2–3. The comparison was also made to disparage, as when colonial whigs were likened to "fierce frantic spirits, that, inflamed with the same zeal which animated the Roundheads in England, directed their zeal to the same purposes, to the demolition of regal authority, and to the subversion of all power which they did not themselves possess." Speech of Lord Lyttleton, Lords Debates, 17 June 1774, *Scots Magazine* 36 (1774): 306.

3 Argument of James Otis, Massachusetts Superior Court, April 1761, Adams,

Legal Papers 2:140–41. Similarly, see Speech of Lord Chatham, Lords Debates, 20 January 1775, *American Archives* 1:1496; Bonwick, *English Radicals*, pp. 63–64 (quoting Arthur Lee).

4 Petition of the Mayor, Aldermen, and Livery of London to the King, 10 April 1775, *American Archives* 1:1854. Similar references to Charles I and James II were made when arguing for British reform. For example, Address of the Mayor, Aldermen, and Livery of London to the King, 14 March 1770, *Town and Country Magazine* 2 (1770): 127 (also reprinted in *Eighteenth-Century Constitution*, pp. 311–12).

5 "Lucius," Boston, 17 March 1775, *American Archives* 2:159. Also, see Hitchcock, *Sermon Preached Before Gage*, p. 33.

6 "A Short View of the ancient and present State of our American Colonies," *Remembrancer for 1776: Part II*, p. 12. Also, see Address of the New Jersey Council to Governor William Livingston, 28 September 1776, *Remembrancer for 1776: Part III*, p. 226.

7 For ship money of Charles I and the American Revolution, see *Authority to Tax*, pp. 22, 25–27, 117–18, 139–40, 220, 278–79.

8 *Remonstrance of the Cities* (1659), p. 1. For comment, see Wheeler, "Calvin's Case," p. 597; Letter 39, 28 May 1770, "Junius," *Junius* 2:101–2; Speech of George Dempster, Commons Debates, 11 December 1775, *Proceedings and Debates* 6:348.

9 William Henry Drayton, Charge to Charlestown District Grand Jury, 23 April 1776, Gibbes, *Documentary History*, pp. 281–82.

10 Ibid., p. 282; "An Appeal from the New to the Old Whigs," 1791, *Works of Right Honorable Edmund Burke* 4:101; McIlwain, *Constitutionalism*, p. 7; Guttridge, *English Whiggism*, p. 142. Also see McIlwain, "Common Law," p. 24; Speech of 6 February 1775, *Speeches of John Wilkes in Parliament* 1:27.

11 Kemp, *King and Commons*, p. 30. Also, see [Bolingbroke,] *Dissertation*, p. 96; Willcox, *Age of Aristocracy*, p. 3; Cobban, "Kings, Courts and Parliaments," p. 39.

12 Answer of the House, 26 January 1773, *Briefs of Revolution*, p. 72. Also, see Message from North Carolina House of Assembly to Governor Josiah Martin, 7 April 1775, *American Archives* 2:264.

13 Worcester County Resolves, 10 August 1774, *Massachusetts Provincial Congresses*, p. 630. Also, see Speech of Lord Chatham, Lords Debates, 22 December 1774, *American Archives* 1:1494–95; Franklin, *Address to Ireland;* [Paine,] *Large Additions*, p. 83; Letter from F. B., 27 August 1774, *Scots Magazine* 36 (1774): 418–19; Anon., *Reflections on Critical Situation*, p. 22; Wagner, "Judicial Review," p. 581; Morgan, *Birth*, pp. 16–17.

14 *Concept of Liberty*, pp. 32–83, 108–22.

15 Charge of High Treason and other High Crimes Exhibited against Charles I, *Clarendon's History Compleated*, p. 95.

16 [Spelman,] *View of a Printed Book*, pp. 34–38.

17 A. S. P. W. Woodhouse, "Introduction" to *Puritanism and Liberty*, p. 17; Pole, *Legislative Power*, p. 13.
18 *The Hunting the Foxes* . . . (1649), reprinted in *Somers' Tracts* 6:52. A Somerset Association defended the right to resist violation of rights saying, "for it is possible that a Parliament may erre (and that foully) as well as a general Councell." Morrill, *Revolt of the Provinces*, p. 10.
19 Anon., *Prospect of the Consequences*, p. 17; *Franklin's Letters to the Press*, p. 173 (reprinting *Public Advertiser*, 8 January 1770).
20 Letter from the Massachusetts House to Lord Shelburne, 15 January 1768, *Speeches*, pp. 139–40; Adams, *Writings* 1:158.
21 Locke, *Two Treatises*, Book 2, sec. 201; [Steuart,] *Jus Populi*, pp. 39, 337–39 (a future Scots Lord Advocate, whose argument reflects the time, 1669, as he is primarily concerned that Parliament will betray its trust by failing to keep the king to the original contract).
22 Kenyon, *Revolution Principles*, p. 58 (quoting Daniel Defoe in his *Legion Memorial*, 14 May 1701); [Barrington,] *Revolution Principles*, pp. 48–49; McIlwain, "Common Law," pp. 29–30 (quoting Bishop Atterbury and Viscount Bolingbroke); Letter 37, 19 March 1770, "Junius," *Junius* 2:74–75.
23 [Daniel Defoe,] Legion Memorial to the House of Commons, 8 May 1701, *Parliamentary History* 5:1256; *Crisis*, 20 January 1775, p. 5.
24 *London Journal* (#726), 26 May 1733, p. 1., col. 1. Also, see *London Journal* (#765), 23 February 1733/34, p. 1., cols. 1–2.
25 *Crisis*, 1 April 1775, p. 62 (plagiarizing [Shebbeare,] *Fifth Letter*, p. 11).
26 *Crisis*, 1 April 1775, p. 64.
27 *London Magazine* 42 (1773): 219.
28 It might be thought that the Wilkes expulsion case was the leading incident of parliamentary arbitrariness in the two decades before the American Revolution. But that event involved only one of the two houses of Parliament. The lord mayor's case also involved one house, but it was exercising a power the other house also exercised.
29 Guttridge, *English Whiggism*, pp. 29–30.
30 Address of the Inhabitants of the Ward of Broad-Street to Lord Mayor Brass Crosby, 2 May 1771, Anon., *Magna Charta Opposed to Privilege*, p. 213; Answer of Alderman Richard Oliver to the Inhabitants of Aldgate Ward, 29 April 1771, ibid., pp. 178–79.
31 This idea was relatively new. *Concept of Liberty*, pp. 76, 109–12.
32 Speech of Alderman Townshend in Defense of the Lord Mayor, Commons Debates, *Hibernian Magazine* 1 (1771): 124.
33 Speech of Lord Camden, Lords Debates, 20 January 1775, *Scots Magazine* 37 (1775): 82. Also, see Kemp, "Parliamentary Sovereignty," p. 12 (especially argument of the earl of Abingdon); Watson, *Principles of the Revolution*, p. 10. For a good summary of the theory in 1770, see [Macfarlane,] *George Third*, pp. 338–39.
34 Carysfort, *Letter to Huntingdonshire*, p. 5.

35 Anon., *Considerations on National Independence*, pp. 69–70. The kingliness of Parliament theory is well summarized in [Shebbeare,] *Second Letter*, p. 18. Also, see Cartwright, *Constitution Produced*, pp. 350–51; Anon., *Speech in Behalf*, p. 88; Colbourn, *Lamp of Experience*, p. 81 (quoting Josiah Quincy, Jr., who quotes Camden); Toohey, *Liberty and Empire*, pp. 84–85 (quoting Catharine Macaulay); Anon., *Inquiry into the Nature*, p. 26; [Rokeby,] *Further Examination*, p. 74.

36 Fletcher, *American Patriotism*, pp. 6–7; Price, *Nature of Civil Liberty*, p. 50; Stewart, *Total Refutation*, p. 14; Roebuck, *Enquiry Whether the Guilt*, pp. 20–21; Speech of Edward Thurlow, Commons Debates, 1 December 1775, *Gentleman's Magazine* 46 (1776): 196. Also, see Shebbeare, *Essay on National Society*, p. 136; Shebbeare, *An Answer*, p. 56; Howard, *Halifax Letter*, p. 532.

37 Anon., *Common Sense Conferences*, p. 9 (also, see p. 13); Anon., *Remarks on the New Essay*, p. 43. Also, see, Abingdon, *Thoughts on Burke's Letter*, p. lii; Anon., *Remarks upon a Discourse*, p. 4.

38 [Gray,] *Right of the Legislature*, p. 37; Speech of John St. John, Commons Debates, 2 May 1774, *Proceedings and Debates* 4:352. Also, see Pownall, *Administration Fifth Edition* 1:44; Anon., *Remarks upon a Discourse*, p. 4.

39 Instructions from the Massachusetts House to Agent de Berdt, 1768, *Scots Magazine* 30 (1769): 463; Instructions to the Pennsylvania Representatives, 16 July 1774, *American Archives* 1:577–78; Anon., *Prospect of the Consequences*, p. 18; "F.S.," to the *London Chronicle*, *Scots Magazine* 30 (1768): 28; Colbourne, *Lamp of Experience*, p. 165 (quoting Jefferson, *Summary View*); Camilus, "To the Printers of the Pennsylvania Gazette," 1 March 1775, *American Archives* 2:11; J. Boerhadem, "A Few Thoughts on American Affairs," *Gentleman's Magazine* 45 (1775): 70.

40 [Dickinson,] *New Essay*, pp. 73–79; *American Archives* 1:576–77.

41 Speech of Richard Pennant, Commons Debates, 19 April 1774, *Proceedings and Debates* 4:228. Similarly, see Speech of John Wilkes, Commons Debates, 27 November 1780, *Parliamentary History* 21:892–93; "Junius Americanus," *Boston Evening-Post*, 28 January 1771, p. 1., col. 3; Camillus, "To the Printers of the Philadelphia Gazette," 22 February 1775, *American Archives* 2:10; Anon., *Defence of Resolutions*, pp. 33–34. The analogy was also drawn to Charles I's claim to the authority to legislate. Anon., *Prospect of the Consequences*, p. 139.

42 [Lee,] *Junius Americanus*, p. 73; *Boston Evening-Post*, 3 December 1770, p. 1., col. 2. The argument may have been best presented in a little noticed pamphlet. [Barron,] *History of Colonization*, p. 139.

43 *Crisis*, 20 July 1775, p. 498.

44 McIlwain, *Constitutionalism*, p. 9; Lee, *Appeal to Justice*, p. 26; Gordon, *Discourse Preached*, pp. 4–5; Roebuck, *Enquiry Whether the Guilt*, p. 18; Anon., *Letter to Rev. Cooper*, p. 32; Pulteney, *Thoughts on Present State*, p. 33.

45 Judson, "Henry Parker," p. 139; Anon., *Prospect of the Consequences*, pp.

17–18. Similarly, see Letter from the Massachusetts House to Lord Shelburne, 15 January 1768, Adams, *Writings* 1:158; [Burke,] *Letters of Valens*, p. 33; "Sobrius," *Boston Evening-Post*, 14 September 1767, p. 1, col. 1; Anon., *Defence of Resolutions*, p. 29; *St. Patrick's Anti-Stamp Chronicle* 2 (1774): 56.

46 [Erskine,] *Reflections on the Rise*, p. 17. Also, see [Lee,] *Junius Americanus*, p. 74. There was also the related argument that an unrepresentative Parliament not subject to annual elections was not an improvement over royal tyranny. Speech of John Sawbridge, Commons Debates, 26 January 1773, *London Magazine* 43 (1773): 373.

47 *Crisis*, 20 July 1775, p. 498; Johnson, "Parliamentary Egotisms," p. 348.

48 [Watson,] *Cursory Remarks on Price*, p. 2.

49 Bradley, *Popular Politics*, p. 71.

50 Bonwick, *English Radicals*, p. xv.

51 Brand, *Defence of Reeves*, p. 63.

52 Dickinson, "Debate on Sovereignty," p. 189. Similarly, see Bailyn, *Pamphlets*, p. 117. Contrary, see Pole, *Gift*, p. 86.

53 As late as 1778, Benjamin Franklin was still asserting that the issue in conflict was whether sovereignty was subject to law. Franklin, *Address to Ireland*, pp. 7–8.

54 Anon., *Address to People of Britain*, p. 28. Contrary, see Olson, "Parliamentary Law," p. 289.

55 Anon., *Letter to North on Re-election*, p. 16 (quoting but disagreeing with Bolingbroke).

56 Barrington, *Revolution Principles*, p. 48.

57 Speech of Charles James Fox, Commons Debates, 25 March 1771, *Parliamentary History* 17:149.

58 "Speech of Serjeant Glynn in defence of the City of London," *Hibernian Magazine* 1 (1771): 129, 128. Also, see "Junius on the Privileges of the House of Commons," ibid., pp. 182–84.

59 Speech of Charles James Fox, Commons Debates, 2 February 1778, *Parliamentary History* 19:679. "Although almost every other Colony on the Continent has transferred the business of petitioning from their own proper Legislature to a General Congress, the Province of *New-York* has ventured to be singular in reverence and obedience to her Colonial Constitution, and has resolutely adhered to her duty, uninfluenced by the example of her neighbours." Speech of Henry Cruger, Commons Debates, 15 May 1775, *American Archives* 1:1820.

60 Valentine, *Lord North* 1:365.

61 Speech of Lord North, Commons Debates, 15 May 1775, *American Archives* 1:1819.

62 Thomas, *Lord North*, pp. 86–87.

63 Speech of Charles Wolfran Cornwall, Commons Debates, 15 May 1775, *American Archives* 1:1821.

64 Dartmouth's words reveal another complaint. The New York General Assembly

"petitioned" the crown. But to avoid conceding any authority to Parliament, the documents sent the two houses avoided the title "petition." Speech of Charles Jenkinson, Commons Debates, 15 May 1775, *American Archives* 1:1821; Speeches of Lord Gower, Lords Debates, 18 May 1775, *Proceedings and Debates* 6:60.

65 Letter from Lord Dartmouth to Governor William Tryon, 23 May 1775, *Revolution Documents* 9:141.

66 Letter from Alexander Elmsly to Samuel Johnston, 17 May 1774, *North Carolina Colonial Records* 9:1001.

67 Anon., *Review of Present Administration*, pp. 30-31.

CHAPTER FIVE: THE LIBERTY ISSUE

1 Bonwick, *English Radicals*, pp. 62-63. Also, see Holmberg, *British-American Whig Rhetoric*, pp. 197-200.

2 *Boston Evening-Post*, 22 October 1770, p. 1, col. 2 (Arthur Lee was *Junius Americanus*); "Serious Truth" to the Editor, *Political Register* 4 (1769): 176. Also, see Speech of Edmund Burke, Commons Debates, 22 March 1775, *Burke on American Revolution*, pp. 88-89; *Boston Evening-Post*, 21 October 1765, p. 1, col. 2.

3 Jack P. Greene, "Review," in *Revolution, Confederation, and Constitution*, pp. 20-21.

4 Clark, *British Opinion*, pp. 155-56; Van Tyne, *Causes of War*, p. 233.

5 Speech of Frederick Bull to the Livery of London, 8 October 1772, *Gentleman's Magazine* 42 (1772): 491; "engagement" of 26 September 1774, *Gentleman's Magazine* 44 (1774): 444.

6 Resolves of the Freeholders of Middlesex, 30 April 1773, *Gentleman's Magazine* 43 (1773): 246; Resolutions of the Supporters of the Bill of Rights, n.d., *Political Register* 9 (1771): 292.

7 John Dickinson's Notes for a Speech in Congress, [8-10? June 1776], *Letters of Delegates to Congress* 4:168; Letter from Thomas Johnson, Jr., to Horatio Gates, 18 August 1775, *Letters of Delegates to Congress* 1:703.

8 *Authority to Legislate*, pp. 142-50 (where the theory of the constraints of liberty was outlined); *Concept of Liberty*, passim.

9 [Lind,] *Thirteenth Parliament*, p. 499.

10 "Constitution," Minutes of 26 March 1776, *South Carolina Congress*, pp. 107-8.

11 Speech of Colonel Bland, First Continental Congress, 6 September 1774, *Commemoration Ceremony*, p. 89. Similarly, see James Wilson, "Parliamentary Authority," 17 August 1774, reprinted in ibid., p. 58.

12 Anon., *Inquiry into the Nature*, p. 39.

13 Zubly, *Law of Liberty*, p. 7. Also, see Address of the Essex Grand Jury to Frederick Smyth, chief justice of New Jersey, November 1774, *American Archives* 1:967-68 ("tyranny"); Cartwright, *Appeal on Constitution*, p. 11 footnote ("despotism"); [Dulany,] *Considerations on the Propriety*, p. 29.

14 Letter from Thomas Cushing to Speaker of Rhode Island House of Represen-
    tatives, 3 June 1773, *Rhode Island Colony Records* 7:231. Also, see [Hicks,]
    Nature of Parliamentary Power, p. 10; Norton, "Loyalist Critique," p. 133
    (quoting a loyalist, Peter Van Schaack).
15 Anon., *Usurpations of England*, p. 28.
16 [Fitch, et al.,] *Reasons Why*, p. 11. Also, see Fox, *Speech of 2 July*, p. 23;
    Rokeby, *Peace Best Policy*, p. 32.
17 Letter from the General Committee of Charlestown to the New York Com-
    mittee, 1 March 1775, *American Archives* 2:2. Also, see [Joseph Hawley,]
    "To the Inhabitants of Massachusetts-Bay," 6 April 1775, ibid., p. 290; "The
    Crisis, No. I," reprinted ibid., p. 58; Anon., *Reflections on Critical Situation*,
    pp. 19–20.
18 Resolves of the Delaware Convention, 2 August 1774, *American Archives* 1:668
    (Also, see Resolves of Woodstock, Virginia, 6 June 1774, ibid., p. 417);
    Letter from John Winthrop to Richard Price, 20 September 1774, Peach,
    Richard Price, p. 288; "An Anti-Despot," Address to New York, [2 June
    1775], *American Archives* 2:883.
19 Letter from Charles Carroll of Carrolton to Henry Graves, 15 September 1766,
    Letters of Charles Carroll, p. 90.
20 Talk to Stockbridge Indians, 1 April 1775, *Massachusetts Provincial Con-
    gresses*, p. 115. Also, see Talk to the "sachem" of Mohawk Nation, 4 April
    1775, ibid., p. 119.
21 "Cassandra," *Maryland Gazette*, 2 May 1775, p. 2, col. 1.
22 Speech of Lord Hillsborough, Lords Debates, 18 May 1770, *Parliamentary
    History* 16:1018–19.
23 *Massachusetts Gazette* [probably *Gazette & Post-Boy*], 28 November 1768,
    p. 2, col. 1 (quoting *Public Ledger*); Hopkins, *Rights*, p. 518.
24 *Boston Gazette*, 2 January 1769, p. 4, col. 1; Anon., *Power and Grandeur*, p. 8;
    "Letter . . . supposed to be written by Mr. Edmund Burke" to Lord North,
    published Williamsburg, Virginia, 19 May 1774, *American Archives* 1:338.
    It is possible that the New Jersey Stamp Act resolves intended to make the
    same point: "That the giving unlimited Power to any Subject or Subjects,
    to impose what Taxes they please in the Colonies, under the Mode of regu-
    lating the Prices of stamped Vellum, Parchment and Paper, appears to us
    unconstitutional. . . ." New Jersey Resolves, 30 November 1765, Morgan,
    Prologue, p. 60.
25 *London Magazine* 43 (1774): 574. Also, see Thomson Mason, "British Ameri-
    can, No. IX," 28 July 1774, *Revolutionary Virginia* 1:200; Anon., *Defence
    of Resolutions*, p. 69.
26 "Brutus," An Address to a Virginia County, 14 July 1775, *Revolutionary Vir-
    ginia* 3:128–29.
27 Anon., *Inquiry into the Nature*, p. 25; Price, *Two Tracts: Tract Two*, p. 5.
    Also, see Price, *Two Tracts: Tract One*, p. 19; Resolution of Newburyport,
    Massachusetts, October 1765, Labaree, *Patriots and Partisans*, p. 18; Weir,
    "Introduction to Freeman," pp. xxvii–xxviii (quoting from Henry Laurens).

28 Resolutions of Rye, 10 August 1774, *American Archives* 1:703; James Iredell, "To the Inhabitants of Great Britain," September 1774, *Papers of Iredell* 1:253–54.

29 General Committee of Association of New York County to the Lord Mayor and Corporation of London, 5 May 1775, *American Archives* 2:511; David Griffith, *Passive Obedience* (31 December 1775), reprinted in *Revolutionary Virginia* 5:302.

30 Anon., *Considerations Upon Rights of Colonists*, p. 20. For contractarian argument, see Petition of the Assembly of Jamaica to the King, 23 March 1775, *Revolutionary Virginia* 2:364. For "discussion elsewhere," see *Authority to Legislate*, pp. 97–125.

31 Thomas Jefferson, "Summary View," reprinted in *Commemoration Ceremony*, p. 68.

32 Knollenberg, *Origin*, p. 190 (quoting a New York petition of 1764). A variation was to argue that it was no better to be taxed "by an Hundred instead of One." Letter to Agent Mauduit, 13 June 1764, *Massachusetts Representatives Journal* (1764), p. 74.

33 Anon., *Observations of Consequence*, p. 68. Also, see Raynal, *Revolution*, p. 24; Anon., *Reflections on the Contest*, p. 24. But, see [Meredith,] *Question Stated*, p. 64.

34 Anderson, *Interest of Britain*, p. 6; [Blacklock,] *Remarks on Liberty*, p. 36 ("America may, perhaps, be regarded by the English as subjected to the individuals of that nation; but, in Scotland, no such arrogant pretenses are indulged"); Anon., *Letter to Lord Camden*, p. 16 (refers to Americans as "our subjects"); Raynal, *Revolution*, p. 24.

35 Price, *Two Tracts: Tract One*, p. 32 (also Price, *Nature of Civil Liberty*, p. 32). Similarly, see [Cartwright,] *American Independence*, p. 37; Headlam, "Constitutional Struggle," p. 650 (quoting Franklin).

36 [Downer,] *Discourse in Providence*, p. 8. Also, see New York Resolves, 18 December 1765, Morgan, *Prologue*, p. 62. Americans who were students of the extant constitution were more concerned about being the subjects of the ministry than of the people ("To the Inhabitants of the Province of South Carolina," 20 June 1774, *American Archives* 1:431) or through the House of Commons the subjects of British merchants ([Lee,] *Vindication of the Colonies*, p. 20).

37 James Wilson, "Parliamentary Authority," 17 August 1774, reprinted in *Commemoration Ceremony*, p. 56.

38 [Williams,] *Letters on Liberty*, pp. 24, 82.

39 Price, *Two Tracts: Tract One*, p. 99. Most of Price's critics missed his point and contended that Price's conclusion that Americans were the fellow subjects of the British was the same as saying they were subjects of Parliament. Anon., *Remarks on Price's Observations*, pp. 66–67; [Ferguson,] *Remarks on Dr. Price*, p. 46; [Rivers,] *Letters*, pp. 143–44.

40 Lovejoy, *Rhode Island Politics*, p. 172. James Burgh saw it from still a third perspective: "What could be more absurd than the commons giving and

granting what was neither their own property, nor that of their own constituents, what they had no more right to give and grant than they had to give and grant the property of the people of Holland and France." Toohey, *Liberty and Empire*, p. 72.

41 [Downer,] *Discourse in Providence*, p. 11.

42 Town Meeting of Leicester, 22 January 1770, *Boston Evening-Post*, 5 February 1770, p. 2, col. 2; "To the Inhabitants of the Province of South Carolina," 20 June 1774, *American Archives* 1:431; [Hicks,] *Nature of Parliamentary Power*, p. iv. Also, see Letter from the Massachusetts House of Representatives to Lord Hillsborough, 30 June 1768, *American Gazette*, p. 9; [Prescott,] *Calm Consideration*, p. 70; Adams, "Novanglus," p. 211.

43 Anon., *Summary of Important Arguments*, p. 16. Similarly, see, Anon., *American Resistance Indefensible*, p. 13.

44 *An English American*, "Part of an Address to the British Soldiery, dated at New York, May 1," *Gentleman's Magazine* 45 (1775): 330.

45 *Boston Evening-Post*, 17 September 1764, p. 1, col. 1 (reprinting "A New Englander," *Providence Gazette*, 18 August 1764).

46 *Boston Post-Boy*, 15 July 1765, p. 1, col. 2 (quoting the *Providence Gazette*).

47 "Phocion, Letter to the King," *Virginia Gazette* (Rind), 15 September 1774, p. 1, col. 1.

48 *Virginia Gazette* (Rind), 19 May 1774, p. 3, col. 3 (supposed Letter from Edmund Burke to Lord North, copied from London's *Morning Chronicle*) (also reprinted in *American Archives* 1:338).

CHAPTER SIX: THE REPRESENTATION ISSUE

1 Memorial to the Inhabitants of the Colonies, 21 October 1774, *Journals of Congress* 1:94. For liberty and representation, see *Concept of Liberty*, pp. 88–90, 109–12; *Concept of Representation*, pp. 11, 119–20.

2 For the theory developed, see *Concept of Representation*, pp. 50–62.

3 [Cartwright,] "Declaration of Rights," Cartwright, *People's Barrier*, p. 20.

4 Anon., *Prospect of the Consequences*, pp. 14–15.

5 *Concept of Representation*, pp. 142–44 (discussing especially reports from South Carolina); Intelligence of Massachusetts Military Preparations sent General Gage, 4 March 1775, *Revolution Documents* 9:64.

6 Speech of Sir William Blackstone, Commons Debates, 1766, "Stamp Act Debates," pp. 568–69; Grant, *Policy of Chatham*, p. 12 (quotes Lord Mansfield as saying American representation in Parliament was set by the constitution); Cartwright, *Constitutional Defence*, p. 94; [Galloway,] *Historical Reflections*, p. 78.

7 [Galloway,] *Historical Reflections*, pp. 117–18. For Galloway's constitutional analysis, see Letter from Joseph Galloway to Richard Jackson, 10 August 1774, *Commemoration Ceremony*, p. 76. For the thoughts of other important loyalists, see Letter from Governor William Franklin to Lord Dartmouth, 28 June 1774, *Revolution Documents* 8:138; Letter from Thomas Hutchin-

son, February 1770, *Remembrancer for 1775*, p. 48. For similar theory of an imperial official, see Letter from Governor Sir James Wright to Lord George Germain, 13 February 1777, Mitchell, "Sir James Wright," p. 512. For the constitutional theory of a "statesman in Britain" referred to by Galloway, see Stokes, *View of Constitution*, p. 10.

8 Petition from the Assembly of Jamaica to the King, 28 December 1774, *Revolutionary Virginia* 2:363; Barrington, *Revolution Principles*, p. 49.

9 Fox, *Speech of 2 July*, pp. 23–24. For the theory of local interests and local knowledge, see *Concept of Representation*, pp. 130–36.

10 James Wilson, "Parliamentary Authority," 17 August 1774, reprinted in *Commemoration Ceremony*, p. 57. For the doctrine of shared interests, see *Concept of Representation*, pp. 2, 23, 45–50, 130–33.

11 Price, *Two Tracts: Tract One*, p. 48; James Wilson, "Parliamentary Authority," 17 August 1774, reprinted in *Commemoration Ceremony*, p. 57; "A Freeholder in the county of Worcester," *Gazette & News-Letter*, 9 March 1775, p. 2, col. 1. For extended discussion of the doctrine of shared burdens and the American Revolution, see *Concept of Representation*, pp. 48–50, 60–62, 132–33.

12 [Galloway,] *Historical Reflections*, p. 62.

13 Speech of Lord Shelburne, Commons Debates, 10 July 1782, *Parliamentary History* 23:196; *Complete Account*, p. 54.

14 *Authority to Tax*, pp. 22–24, 59–60, 86–89, 106–21, 135–57, 167–68, 244–46, 272–76; *Concept of Representation*, pp. 8–28, 130–31, 138–44.

15 See, for example, speech of Temple Luttrell, Commons Debates, 27 November 1775, *Proceedings and Debates* 6:297; Letter from Jared Ingersoll to William Livingston, 1 October 1765, "Ingersoll Correspondence," pp. 349–50.

16 "[T]he Americans are the people, at present, that are preserving the constitution, by defending *the principle* on which it is founded, the right of assent and consent in taxation." Anon., *Case Stated*, p. 25.

17 For whigs tieing consent to liberty, see Presentment of the Grand Jury, Camden District, South Carolina, 5 November 1774, *London Magazine* 44 (1775): 128. For loyalists joining consent to liberty, see Chandler, *Appeal to Public*, p. 69; Tucker & Hendrickson, *Fall*, p. 335 n. 13 (John Adams quoting Joseph Galloway).

18 Sharp, *Declaration of Natural Right*, p. 9; *Concept of Representation*, pp. 25–28, 55–56, 79–80, 130–31, 134–35.

19 For the various migration theories, see *Authority of Rights*, pp. 114–45.

20 Phileirene, "My Worthy Friends," *Gazette & News-Letter*, 30 March 1775, p. 1, col. 2.

21 Message to the Inhabitants of Great Britain, 8 July 1775, *Journals of Congress* 2:168.

22 Proclamation of the Great and General Court of Massachusetts, 23 January 1776, *Remembrancer for 1776: Part II*, p. 53.

23 Speech of Lord North, Commons Debates, 15 May 1775, *American Archives*

1:1819; Memorial from New York General Assembly to the House of Lords, 25 March 1775, ibid., p. 1316.

24 Letter from Thomas Hutchinson to unknown, 27 August 1772, *Remembrancer for 1776: Part II*, p. 59.

25 For example, Sosin, *Revolution of 1688*, pp. 64–65.

26 Resolutions as Recalled by Patrick Henry, and Maryland Resolves, Morgan, *Prologue*, pp. 48, 53.

27 Resolution of the North Carolina House of Assembly, October 1769, *Boston Evening-Post*, 22 January 1770, p. 4, col. 1; Resolves of 16 May 1769, *Journal of Burgesses* 11:214; Resolution of the South Carolina Commons House, 19 August 1769, *Boston Chronicle*, 1 October 1769, p. 316, col. 1; Resolution of the Maryland Lower House, 28 December 1769, *Boston Chronicle*, 18 January 1770, p. 22, col. 2; Petition from the New Jersey House to the King, n.d., *Boston Evening-Post*, 25 July 1768, p. 2, col. 2.

28 Resolves of the First Provincial Congress, 27 August 1774, *North Carolina Colonial Records* 9:1044. Also, see "Proceedings of the Freeholders in Rowan County," 8 August 1774, and "Proceedings of Freeholders in Granville County," 15 August 1774, ibid., at 1025, 1035; Speech of Isaac Wilkins, New York Assembly Debates, 23 February 1775, and Resolutions of the New York General Assembly, 8 March 1775, *American Archives* 1:1293–94, 1302.

29 It was argued that the Virginia Stamp Act resolves had gone too far and had claimed exclusive internal legislative autonomy. Anon., *To Freeholders of New York* (1768), p. 2.

30 For example, Letter from Governor Francis Bernard to Lord Barrington, 23 November 1765, Ritcheson, *British Politics*, p. 43.

31 Instructions of Ipswich, 21 October 1765, *Boston Post-Boy*, 4 November 1765, p. 2, col. 2. Also, see Instructions of Boston, 18 September 1765, *Boston Evening-Post*, 23 September 1765, p. 1, col. 2.

32 Letter from Thomas Hutchinson to Thomas Whately, 3 October 1770, Bailyn, *Ordeal*, p. 228 n. 14. For the debate of 1773, see ibid., pp. 206–11 and *Briefs of Revolution*.

33 Letter from Thomas Hutchinson to Lord Dartmouth, 23 October 1772, *Revolution Documents* 5:205; Speech of Governor Thomas Hutchinson, 6 January 1773, *Briefs of Revolution*, pp. 17–18.

34 *Authority to Legislate*, pp. 162–71; *Briefs of Revolution*, pp. 103–7, 111.

35 Answer of the House, 26 January 1773, *Briefs of Revolution*, p. 63.

36 Speech of Lord North, Commons Debates, 14 March 1774, *Proceedings and Debates* 4:79–80, 63. The quotes come from two different reports of the same speech. The first is from the *London Evening Post*, 15 and 17 March 1774 and the *London Magazine* 43 (1774): 169. The second is from the Cavendish diary. Similarly, see *Report of Lords on Massachusetts*, p. 3.

37 [Joseph Hawley,] "To the Inhabitants of Massachusetts," 2 March 1775, *American Archives* 2:18. Also, see Resolutions of York County, Virginia, 18 July 1774, and "Extract of a Letter from a Gentleman in Massachusetts to his

Friend in London, Dated January 21, 1775," *American Archives* 1:596, 1168.

38 Memorial from the New York General Assembly to the House of Lords, 25 March 1775, *American Archives* 1:1318. Also, see Representation from the New York General Assembly to the House of Commons, 25 March 1775, ibid., pp. 1319, 1320; Instructions of the Pennsylvania Convention to the Pennsylvania Assembly, 25 July 1774, *Revolutionary Virginia* 2:151–52.

39 Resolves of the First Provincial Congress, 27 August 1774, *North Carolina Colonial Records* 9:1048.

40 "Proceeding of Freeholders in Granville, County," 15 August 1774, ibid., p. 1035; Rakove, *Beginnings*, p. 32.

41 For example, Resolutions of Newtown, Connecticut, 6 February 1775, *American Archives* 1:1215.

42 Petition from the Assembly of Jamaica to the King, 28 December 1774, *Revolutionary Virginia* 2:365.

43 See especially, West, *Election Sermon*, p. 279.

44 Resolutions of Albemarle County, Virginia, 26 July 1774, *American Archives* 1:637–38; Greene, *Quest*, pp. 444–45. Similarly, see James Wilson, "Parliamentary Authority," 17 August 1774, reprinted in *Commemoration Ceremony*, p. 60; Greene, *Peripheries and Center*, pp. 139–40 (Assembly of Jamaica).

45 Spottsylvania County Resolutions, 24 June 1774, *American Archives* 1:448, 449. An argument was also made that Parliament could not legislate for the colonies because parliamentary legislation rendered "Assemblies useless." Address from the Continental Congress to the Inhabitants of the Colonies, 21 October 1774, *Journals of Congress* 1:93. "If America may be bound by the Parliament of England; of what use are Parliaments in America?" *Political Register* 2 (1768): 97 (quoting *Boston Gazette*, 24 August 1767).

46 Resolutions of Chesterfield County, Virginia, 14 July 1774, *American Archives* 1:537.

47 Worcester County Resolves, 10 August 1774, *Massachusetts Provincial Congresses*, p. 630.

48 Address from the House of Assembly of the Counties upon Delaware to the King, 27 October 1768, *Delaware House Minutes* (1765–1770), p. 168. In the House of Commons it was even argued that the right of legislative autonomy had vested in the colonists by the second original contract, and that neither the king could grant the right to Parliament nor could Parliament usurp the right, "unless America had consented to such a cession." Speech of Sir Cecil Wray, Commons Debates, 6 April 1778, *Parliamentary History* 19:1011.

49 Resolves of Dunmore County, 16 June 1774, and of Frederick County, 8 June 1774, *Revolutionary Virginia* 1:122, 135.

50 It is sometimes said that Congress rejected the resolution offered by John Sullivan. If so, the doctrine was not rejected for Congress adopted Sullivan's elements of autonomy. Sullivan, however, did not base his doctrine on liberty

or even on the right of representation. See, Caplan, "Ninth Amendment," pp. 233–34.

51 Declaration and Resolves, 14 October 1774, *Journals of Congress* 1:68. It is said there was no debate. Rakove, *Beginnings*, p. 58. This resolution was adopted by some of the revolutionary assemblies. For example, House of Assembly Resolves, January 1775, *Georgia Revolutionary Records* 1:50 (also reprinted in *American Archives* 1:1157).

52 After reciting other rights, the Congress, in Resolution Ten voted: "All and each of which the aforesaid deputies, in behalf of themselves and their constituents, do claim, demand, and insist on, as their indubitable rights and liberties; which cannot be legally taken from them, altered or abridged by any power whatever, without their own consent, by their representatives in their several provincial legislatures." Declaration and Resolves, 14 October 1774, *Journals of Congress* 1:70–71.

CHAPTER SEVEN: REPRESENTATION SOLUTIONS

1 Presentments of the Grand Jury of Cheraws District, South Carolina, [5 November 1774], *American Archives* 1:962.

2 Anon., *Constitutional Advocate*, p. 30; Anon., *Summary of Important Arguments*, pp. 30–31. For the British theory of representation, see *Concept of Representation*, pp. 31–62.

3 Anon., *Summary of Important Arguments*, pp. 31–32. For the theory of vicarious consent, which should not be confused with a legal fiction, see *Concept of Representation*, pp. 11–30.

4 Anon., *Constitutional Advocate*, p. 30; [Maseres,] *Canadian Freeholder* 1:139–40 (resident attorney general of Quebec, probably wrong about American standard for voting, and probably right about American disinterest in a universal franchise). For American theory of representation, see *Concept of Representation*, pp. 128–36.

5 Anon., *Observations of Consequence*, p. 36.

6 Letter of 14 December 1765, Bernard, *Select Letters*, p. 39.

7 But also see *Massachusetts Gazette [News-Letter]*, 16 January 1766, p. 2, col. 2; *Boston Chronicle*, 20 February 1769, p. 58, col. 3; *Boston Evening-Post*, 17 April 1769, p. 4, col. 1; ibid., 11 March 1771, p. 1, col. 1.

8 Pownall, *Administration Fifth Edition* 2:xi, 82, 131–80; Bailyn, *Ordeal*, p. 231; Extract of a letter from Governor William Franklin to James [*sic*] Galloway, 12 March 1775, *Revolution Documents* 9:78.

9 Lawson, "George Grenville," pp. 571–72. William Knox followed Grenville's lead and was criticized by Burke. There were rumors that Lord Chatham would introduce legislation for American representation. *Boston Evening-Post*, 11 March 1771, p. 1, col. 1.

10 A fact that Bernard reluctantly admitted. Letter from Governor Francis Bernard

to Lord Barrington, 28 January 1768, Bernard & Barrington, *Correspondence*, pp. 136–37.

11 Otis, *Rights*, p. 445; Letter from Governor Francis Bernard to Lord Barrington, 28 January 1768, Bernard & Barrington, *Correspondence*, pp. 138–39, 250–51; Brennan, "James Otis," pp. 699–700. At one time Benjamin Franklin also urged American representation. Letter from Benjamin Franklin to Governor William Shirley, 22 December 1754, *Remembrancer of 1776: Part I*, p. 190; Greene, *Peripheries and Center*, p. 123.

12 Letter from Governor Francis Bernard to Lord Barrington, 28 January 1768, Bernard & Barrington, *Correspondence*, pp. 246–47. Similarly, see ibid., pp. 136, 249; Samuel Clay Harvey, "To Lord North," London *Publick Ledger*, January 1775, *American Archives* 1:1205; [Crowley,] *Letters*, p. 87. Even the king of Poland thought the solution obvious. Letter from the king of Poland to Charles Lee, 20 March 1768, *Lee Papers*, p. 65.

13 Letter from Governor Francis Bernard to Lord Barrington, 28 January 1768, Bernard & Barrington, *Correspondence*, p. 251; "Joseph Galloway's Statement on his Plan of Union," *Letters of Delegates to Congress* 1:126; Anon., *Considerations on Expediency*, pp. 8–9; Anon., *Inquiry into the Nature*, p. 25.

14 Letter from Governor Francis Bernard to Lord Barrington, 28 January 1768, Bernard & Barrington, *Correspondence*, p. 137. Similarly, see Letter of 23 November 1765, Bernard, *Select Letters*, pp. 32–33; *Critical Review* 37 (1774): 381; Anon., *General Opposition*, pp. 32–35.

15 *Burke Writings* 2:178; [Burke,] *Observations on Late State*, p. 98; Grenville, "Present State," 23 January 1769, p. 29, col. 3; *London Magazine* 45 (1776): 322 (quoting Adam Smith).

16 Letter from Governor Francis Bernard to Lord Barrington, 28 January 1768, Bernard & Barrington, *Correspondence*, pp. 138, 139. Also, see Letter same to same, 20 October 1768, ibid., p. 180; Letter of 23 November 1765, Bernard, *Select Letters*, pp. 33–34; Letter from Andrew Oliver of 13 February 1769, Hutchinson, *Letters*, p. 32; [Barron,] *History of Colonization*, p. 146; Anon., *Inquiry into the Nature*, p. 23.

17 [Burke,] *Observations on Late State*, p. 99; *Works of Edmund Burke* 1:373; *Burke Writings* 2:178–79.

18 [Barron,] *History of Colonization*, pp. 148–49. Chatham is said to have had a list of twenty-nine colonies that would be represented. Williams, "Chatham and Representation," p. 757.

19 Governor Franklin thought Ireland not only would have to be given British representation but "also establish a more equal representation for itself than at present subsists in that kingdom." Extract of a letter from William Franklin to James [*sic*] Galloway, 12 March 1775, *Revolution Documents* 9:78.

20 Letter from Governor Francis Bernard to Lord Barrington, 23 November 1765, Bernard & Barrington, *Correspondence*, p. 98; [Maseres,] *Considerations on Admitting Representatives*, p. 10; Dunham, "Transatlantic View," p. 61 (discussing Adams). Chatham may have been willing to admit forty-five to

fifty-two members. Williams, "Chatham and Representation," p. 757. For other figures, with a colony by colony breakdown, see Samuel Clay Harvey, "To Lord North," London *Publick Ledger*, January 1775, *American Archives* 1:1205; Anon., *Considerations on Expediency*, p. 10; Gipson, "Ripe for Revolt," pp. 25–26. All plans assumed existing colonies, not new districts would be represented. For exception, see Anon., *Serious and Impartial Observations*, p. 31.

21 [Lind,] *Thirteenth Parliament*, p. 492; *Concept of Representation*, pp. 31–62. The difficulties British theorists would have encountered with American notions of population representation is illustrated by disagreements as to whether Scotland, with one-fourth the land of Great Britain, one-sixth of the population, and paying one-fortieth part of the land tax, was "represented" by one-thirteenth part of the House of Commons and sixteen peers in the House of Lords. [Maseres,] *Considerations on Admitting Representatives*, pp. 34–35; Letter from Alexander Elmsly to Samuel Johnston, 22 December 1774, *North Carolina Colonial Records* 9:1094; Anon., *Some Candid Suggestions*, p. 28; Anon., *Three Letters*, p. 47; Anon., *Considerations on Expediency*, pp. 34–36; Robson, *American Revolution*, p. 202.

22 Letter from Benjamin Franklin to Governor William Shirley, 22 December 1754, *Remembrancer for 1776: Part I*, pp. 189–90. However, many in Great Britain argued that the West Indies were effectively represented in Parliament because a few wealthy planters who lived in Britain were elected from British constituencies. They proved that the colonies could be protected by a small number of representatives. Anon., *Considerations on Expediency*, pp. 37–38.

23 Pownall, *Administration Fifth Edition* 1:174; [Burke,] *Observations on Late State*, pp. 99–100; *Burke Writings* 2:179–80. Also, see Koebner, *Empire*, p. 189.

24 Anon., *Considerations on Expediency*, pp. 11, 18–19; [Maseres,] *Considerations on Admitting Representatives*, pp. 11, 18. Also, see [Maseres,] *Canadian Freeholder* 1:180–243.

25 Anon., *Letter to Doctor Tucker*, p. 13. Some suggestions may have been impractical, for example, that writs for American elections be issued "a session, or twelve-month, before those for Great Britain." Anon., *Reflexions on Representation*, p. 24.

26 Pownall, *Administration Fifth Edition* 1:174–75 (Pownall, *Administration*, pp. 171–72). Also, see Williams, "Chatham and Representation," pp. 757–58; Anon., *Inquiry into the Nature*, p. 44.

27 There were also very serious problems of how to resolve contested elections. *Burke Writings* 2:180; [Burke,] *Observations on Late State*, p. 100; Anon., *Inquiry into the Nature*, p. 44.

28 [Crowley,] *Letters*, p. 31. But exceptions to the pecuniary qualifications were then "allowed with respect to Scottish Members and those of the two universities of Oxford and Cambridge." Anon., *Considerations on Expediency*, pp. 10–11.

29 *Burke Writings* 2:180; [Burke,] *Observations on Late State*, p. 101; Anon., *Considerations on Expediency*, pp. 20–21; Gipson, "Ripe for Revolt," pp. 25–26.

30 *Pennsylvania Journal*, 13 March 1766, reprinted in Morgan, *Prologue*, p. 89.

31 Burke, *Writings* 2:180; [Burke,] *Observations on Late State*, p. 101.

32 [Maseres,] *Considerations on Admitting Representatives*, pp. 22–26; Letter from Alexander Elmsly to Samuel Johnston, 22 December 1774, *North Carolina Colonial Records* 9:1094.

33 Anon., *Considerations on Expediency*, pp. 22–25. Also, see Evans, *Reply to Fletcher*, p. 41; Anon., *Some Candid Suggestions*, p. 27. It was even suggested that the colonies could select as representatives members already elected to Parliament. "Such County Members, on business appertaining to the Colonies, to have each a double vote, one as an *English*, the other as an *American Member.*" Samuel Clay Harvey, "To Lord North," London *Publick Ledger*, January 1775, *American Archives* 1:1206.

34 [Knox,] *Extra Official Papers*, p. 31. Also, see Letter from George Grenville to Thomas Pownall, 17 July 1768, *Grenville Papers* 4:317; Thomas, *British Politics*, p. 366; Gipson, "Revolution as Aftermath," p. 99.

35 Shy, "Thomas Pownall," p. 174; Pownall, *Administration Fifth Edition* 2:11.

36 Pownall, *Administration Fifth Edition* 2:83. For the assertion that American representation was "Utopia," see [Lofft,] *View of Schemes*, p. 5.

37 Speech of Edmund Burke, Commons Debates, 22 March 1775, *Burke on American Revolution*, p. 106; [Burke,] *Observations on Late State*, p. 102. Even as late as 1782 American representation in Parliament was called "ridiculous." Anon., *Plan of Reconciliation with America*, p. 28.

38 Letter from Lord Barrington to Francis Bernard, 12 March 1768, Bernard & Barrington, *Correspondence*, p. 140.

39 [Barron,] *History of Colonization*, p. 139; Abercromby, "De Jure," p. 128; [Wheelock,] *Reflections*, p. 31; [Macfarlane,] *Second Ten Years*, p. 205.

40 Koebner, *Empire*, p. 156.

41 Anon., *Plain Question*, p. 19.

42 Pulteney, *Thoughts on Present State*, p. 43. Also, see Williams, "Chatham and Representation," p. 758.

43 Anon., *Three Letters*, pp. 40–41. For other problems caused by distance, see Leonard, "Massachusettensis," pp. 36–37; [Bancroft,] *Remarks*, p. 117; Anon., *Argument in Defence*, p. 80.

44 Anon., *To Tax Themselves*, p. 116; Anon., *Reflexions on Representation*, p. 23. Contrary, see Anon., *Letter to People of America*, pp. 48–49.

45 Tucker, *True Interest of Great Britain*, pp. 25–26. For the practice of consultation and instructions, see *Concept of Representation*, pp. 85–109.

46 [Barron,] *History of Colonization*, p. 149.

47 Anon., *Constitutional Right*, p. 50. There was also comment about what kind of representatives America would send. "Would our Morals be safe under Virginian Legislatures, or would our Church be in no Danger from Pumkin Senators?" A London newspaper reprinted in Morgan, *Prologue*, p. 102 (also see p. 103, reprinting *London Chronicle*, 20 February 1766).

48 *Critical Review* 21 (1766): 68.

49 [Ramsay,] *Letters on Present Disturbances*, p. 25 (reprinting *Public Advertiser*, 25 January 1775).

50 Pownall, *Administration Fifth Edition* 1:173.

51 Speech of Isaac Barré, Commons Debates, 3 February 1766, *Proceedings and Debates* 2:144. The reverse argument was also made: that the certain growth of America's population made it imperative to settle on a scheme of representation immediately. Smith, "Thoughts on Dispute," p. 116; Shy, "Thomas Pownall," p. 172.

52 Anon., *Constitutional Right*, pp. 50–51.

53 Morgan, *Prologue*, pp. 89–90 (reprinting *Pennsylvania Journal*, 13 March 1766). America "must preponderate, and Britain become the appurtenance." Anon., *Reflections on the Contest*, p. 23. Americans could "become the masters of Europe." Anon., *Constitutional Considerations*, p. 9.

54 Connecticut: [Fitch, et al.,] *Reasons Why*, reprinted in Bailyn, *Pamphlets*, p. 391; South Carolina and Virginia: Gipson, "Revolution as Aftermath," p. 99.

55 Resolutions of the Massachusetts House, 25 October 1765, Petition of the House to the King, 20 January 1768, and Letter from the House to Lord Rockingham, 22 January 1768, *Speeches*, pp. 50, 123, 143.

56 Adams, "Novanglus," p. 108; Leonard, "Massachusettensis," p. 36.

57 *Pennsylvania Journal*, 13 March 1766, reprinted in Morgan, *Prologue*, p. 90.

58 [Bancroft,] *Remarks*, pp. 116–17.

59 Adams, "Novanglus," p. 232. Also, see Howard, *Halifax Letter*, p. 538 (a loyalist); Allen, *American Crisis*, pp. 29–30. Governor Pownall considered the problems of distance and thought they all could be solved. Pownall, *Administration Fifth Edition* 1:172.

60 Instructions of 22 December 1767, *Boston Town Records* 16:228–29. Also, see West, *Election Sermon*, p. 305; Morgan, *Inventing the People*, p. 242.

61 Pownall, *Administration*, p. 165. Also, see *Pennsylvania Journal*, 13 March 1766, reprinted in Morgan, *Prologue*, p. 91; Letter from Andrew Eliot to Thomas Hollis, 29 January 1769, Eliot, "Letters," p. 440.

62 West, *Election Sermon*, p. 279. There is, however, no evidence to support the claim that representation "would have run counter to a growing sense of American separateness." Tucker & Hendrickson, *Fall*, p. 151.

63 *Pennsylvania Journal*, 13 March 1766, reprinted in Morgan, *Prologue*, p. 90; Gipson, "Ripe for Revolt," p. 26.

64 Letter from House Committee to Dennys de Berdt, 20 December 1765, Adams, *Writings* 1:67. Also, see Letter from Samuel Adams to G.W., 13 November 1765, and Letter from Samuel Adams to Dennys de Berdt, 30 January 1768, ibid., pp. 39, 178; Letter from Massachusetts House to Lord Camden, 29 January 1768, *Boston Evening-Post*, 4 April 1768, p. 1, col. 1; Adams, "Novanglus," p. 232.

65 *Pennsylvania Journal*, 13 March 1766, reprinted in Morgan, *Prologue*, p. 89 (also, see p. 90).

66 *Concept of Representation*, pp. 31–39.

67 Instructions to Carlisle Commissioners, 12 April 1778, *Revolution Documents* 15:91.
68 Pownall, *Administration Fifth Edition* 1:173; Pownall, *Administration*, p. 171.
69 *Pennsylvania Journal*, 13 March 1766, reprinted in Morgan, *Prologue*, p. 92; Adams, "Novanglus," p. 232.

Chapter Eight: Intermediate Solutions

1 [Hicks,] *Nature of Parliamentary Power*, p. xiv; Letter from John Willday to Lord Dartmouth, 19 March 1774, *Dartmouth American Papers* 2:204; Wagner, "Judicial Review," pp. 575, 592; Gipson, "Ripe for Revolt."
2 Suspend for year: [Maseres,] *Considerations on Admitting Representatives*, p. 13; Anon., *Considerations on Expediency*, pp. 12–13; enroll British statutes: Speech of Sir George Savile, Commons Debates, 7 December 1775, *Proceedings and Debates* 6:336.
3 Bill proposed by Edmund Burke, House of Commons, 16 November 1775, *Parliamentary History* 18:978–82; Speech of Edmund Burke, Commons Debates, 9 May 1770, *Burke on American Revolution*, p. 9; *Gentlemen's Magazine* 47 (1777): 235–36 (discussing Burke's theories).
4 Pownall, *Administration Sixth Edition* 2:77 (also, see pp. 41–76). Also, see Shy, "Thomas Pownall," pp. 165, 168; Schutz, *Thomas Pownall*, pp. 241–42.
5 Conway, *Peace Speech*, p. 49.
6 A related principle was that two independent legislatures could not exist in the same community. Although it may be doubted if anyone listened, this theory was effectively refuted by Governor Johnstone. Speech of George Johnstone, Commons Debates, 26 October 1775, *Parliamentary History* 18:748. For a brief discussion of Johnstone's "brilliant speech," see Ritcheson, *British Politics*, pp. 225–26.
7 Abingdon, "Speech on Right," pp. 36–37; Resolutions of the Continental Congress, 14 October 1774, *Journals of Congress*, p. 69. The American consitutional proposal is discussed in *Authority to Legislate*, pp. 233–45.
8 Speech of Lord Abingdon, 5 July 1782, *Parliamentary History* 23:150. A similar plan was published by Christopher Keld in 1785. [Keld,] *Polity of England*, pp. 422–23, 425–26. Earlier proposals for dividing legislative authority generally contemplated continued parliamentary supremacy. [Maseres,] *Considerations on Admitting Representatives*, pp. 14–15.
9 Pownall, *Administration Sixth Edition* 2:82 (for Pownall's rule see p. 77). There was another solution infrequently mentioned. It was to have an imperial parliament with representatives from Great Britain, Ireland, and the American colonies, again dividing sovereignty with the British and Irish parliaments and the American assemblies exercising local, police jurisdiction. Anon., *Plan of Reconciliation with America*, pp. 40–43; Anon., *Plan for Conciliating*, pp. viii–x; Greene, *Peripheries and Center*, p. 123.
10 Rusticus, *Remarks*, p. 30; Speech of Temple Luttrell, Commons Debates, 7 November 1775, *Proceedings and Debates* 6:194.

11 Anon., *Observations of Consequence*, p. 35.
12 Anon., *Inquiry into the Nature*, p. 67.
13 Speech of Edmund Burke, Commons Debates, 25 March 1774, *Proceedings and Debates* 4:141; [Macfarlane,] *Second Ten Years*, p. 271.
14 *Pennsylvania Journal*, 13 March 1766, reprinted in Morgan, *Prologue*, pp. 91–92.
15 Letter from Samuel Chase to James Duane, 5 February 1775, *Letters of Delegates to Congress* 1:306; Anon., *America Vindicated*, pp. 40–41.
16 Potter, *Liberty We Seek*, p. 159 (discussing Bladen); Pownall, *Administration Sixth Edition* 2:86. An alternate proposal was for an American board of trade. Proposals of Stephen Sayre, *Dartmouth American Papers* 2:252.
17 "A Plan of an American Compact with Great Britain," first published in New York and reprinted in [Green,] *Observations on Reconciliation*, p. 37. Some British proposals, too, gave the crown an active role. Tucker, *Letter to Burke*, p. 58; Anon., *Plan for Conciliating*, pp. viii–ix.
18 Smith, "Thoughts on Dispute," p. 114; Calhoon, "Smith's Alternative," p. 108.
19 Anon., *Proposals for Union*; Anon., *Plan for Conciliating*.
20 These plans are printed and discussed in Boyd, *Union*. They are discussed as a single plan in Ferling, *Loyalist Mind*, pp. 95–100.
21 Letter from Joseph Galloway and Samuel Rhodes to the Virginia Committee, 1 July 1774, *Revolutionary Virginia* 2:137–38. For the doctrine of "right" against "power," see "In the Taught Tradition," pp. 947–61.
22 Speech of Joseph Galloway, Continental Congress, 28 September 1774, [Galloway,] *Historical Reflections*, p. 79.
23 John Adams's Notes of Debates, 8 September 1774, *Letters of Delegates to Congress* 1:48. For a brief appraisal of Galloway's theory of consent, see *Concept of Representation*, p. 142.
24 Mullett, "Tory Imperialism," p. 269.
25 Norton, "Loyalist Critique," p. 134.
26 *Concept of Representation*, p. 141.
27 [Ramsay,] *Historical Essay*, pp. 195–96. The argument was more widely discussed after Galloway spoke due to its restatement by Samuel Johnson. [Johnson,] *Political Tracts*, pp. 209–10; Anon., *Resistance No Rebellion*, pp. 27–28 (answering Johnson); Book Review, *Monthly Review* 52 (1775): 258 (answering Johnson); Pulteney, *Plan of Reunion*, pp. 54–55. For a related argument, see [Draper,] *Thoughts of a Traveler*, pp. 24–25.
28 John Adams's Notes of Debates, 8 September 1774, *Letters of Delegates to Congress* 1:48.
29 Ibid., pp. 47–48.
30 Anon., *Letter*, pp. 271–72. For the eighteenth-century theory of the authority for rights, see *Authority of Rights*, pp. 65–145.
31 See above, p. 85.
32 [Galloway,] *Historical Reflections*, p. 118.
33 Extract of a letter from James [sic] Galloway to Governor William Franklin, 26 March 1775, *Revolution Documents* 9:87.

34 Speech of Joseph Galloway, Continental Congress, 28 September 1774, *Letters of Delegates to Congress*, pp. 125–26. Galloway wrote this version of the speech several years after it was delivered, so we cannot be certain the delegates heard exactly what is said here. Also, see *Concept of Representation*, p. 138.

35 "Proposed Union between Great Britain and the Colonies," 6 December 1774, *Revolution Documents* 8:236.

36 John Adams's Notes of Debates, 28 September 1774, *Letters of Delegates to Congress* 1:110.

37 Ferling, *Loyalist Mind*, p. 95.

38 "Proposed Union between Great Britain and the Colonies," 6 December 1774, *Revolution Documents* 8:237.

39 Ibid., p. 236.

40 [Galloway,] *Historical Reflections*, p. 81.

41 Ibid., p. 125.

42 Letter from Joseph Galloway to Richard Jackson, 10 August 1774, *Commemoration Ceremony*, p. 77.

43 Section 2, "Proposed Union between Great Britain and the Colonies," *Revolution Documents* 8:236. It is not clear, however, whether Galloway's plan incorporated the doctrine of equal assessments. It may have for taxes levied on the colonies, but not for taxes apportioned between Great Britain and the colonies. For the doctrine, see *Concept of Representation*, p. 61.

44 [Galloway,] *Historical Reflections*, p. 79. Also, see [Galloway,] *Mutual Claims*, p. 86.

45 Section 9, "Proposed Union between Great Britain and the Colonies," *Revolution Documents* 8:237.

46 Ibid., p. 237.

47 [Galloway,] *Historical Reflections*, p. 82.

48 For an excellent defense of the plan, see C.E., "To the Public," Philadelphia, April 1775, *American Archives* 2:398. Governor Franklin felt it should have included an upper house or a privy council. Letter from William Franklin to James [sic] Galloway, 12 March 1775, *Revolution Documents* 9:78. Galloway's later plans included an upper house. Potter, *Liberty We Seek*, p. 175. So did some other plans. Hoffer & Hull, "Yates's Plan," pp. 398–406.

49 *Journals of Congress* 1:51 n. 1; Letter from Lieutenant Governor Cadwallader Colden to Lord Dartmouth, 7 December 1774, *Revolution Documents* 8:238.

50 Mullett, "Tory Imperialism," p. 268.

51 Speech of Patrick Henry, Continental Congress, 28 September 1774, *Commemoration Ceremony*, p. 95.

52 Section 9, "Proposed Union between Great Britain and the Colonies," *Revolution Documents* 8:237.

53 Rakove, *Beginnings*, p. 61; Stout, *Perfect Crisis*, p. 140.

CHAPTER NINE: PARLIAMENTARY SOLUTIONS

1 Guttridge, *English Whiggism*, pp. 142–43. For Chatham's theory why American taxes were unconstitutional, see *Authority to Tax*, pp. 85–86, 91–93.
2 Letter from Arthur Lee to Richard Henry Lee, 26 December 1774, *American Archives* 1:1059.
3 Lords Debates, 1 February 1775, *Parliamentary History* 18:198. Earlier he had proposed his more famous motion to withdraw the troops from Boston. Lords Debates, 20 January 1775, ibid., p. 149.
4 Ritcheson, *British Politics*, p. 231; Lords Debates, 30 May 1777, *Parliamentary History* 19:316–52.
5 Speech of Lord Gower, Lords Debates, 30 May 1777, *Gentleman's Magazine* 47 (1777): 254.
6 Chatham also had plans for an American representation in Parliament. Grant, *Policy of Chatham*, p. 11; Williams, "Chatham and Representation," pp. 756–58.
7 Chatham's Provisional Act, 1 February 1775, *Parliamentary History* 18:199. The bill was extensively printed. See, for example, Pitt, *Plan; London Magazine* 44 (1776): 71–73. It is summarized in Ritcheson, *British Politics*, pp. 183–85. It is discussed in Grant, *Policy of Chatham*, pp. 6–10.
8 *Authority of Rights*, pp. 223–24.
9 Resolutions, 14 October 1774, *Journals of Congress*, p. 69.
10 Ibid., p. 68; Chatham's Provisional Act, 1 February 1775, *Parliamentary History* 18:202–3.
11 *Authority of Rights*, p. 224.
12 Resolutions, 14 October 1774, *Journals of Congress*, pp. 68–69; Chatham's Provisional Act, 1 February 1775, *Parliamentary History* 18:199.
13 Chatham's Provisional Act, 1 February 1775, *Parliamentary History* 18:200.
14 Ibid., pp. 201, 200, 202.
15 Ibid., p. 202.
16 Middlekauff, *Glorious Cause*, pp. 263–64.
17 Stout, *Perfect Crisis*, p. 173.
18 [Blacklock,] *Remarks on Liberty*, p. 68.
19 Witherspoon, *Sermon Preached at Princeton*, p. 41.
20 Donoughue, *British Politics*, p. 237.
21 Higginbotham, "Iredell and Origins," p. 109; Higginbotham, "James Iredell's Efforts," p. 143.
22 Message from the House of Burgesses to Governor Lord Dunmore, 12 June 1775, *American Archives* 2:1206.
23 Letter from Thomas Jefferson to William Small, 7 May 1775, ibid., p. 523; Higginbotham, "Iredell and Origins," p. 109. It was also said that Chatham's plan resembled Franklin's "hints." Stout, *Perfect Crisis*, p. 173; Letter from Benjamin Franklin to William Franklin, 22 March 1775, *Papers of Franklin* 21:581.
24 Chatham's Provisional Act, 1 February 1775, *Parliamentary History* 18:202;

Speech of Lord Chatham, Lords Debates, 30 May 1777, *Parliamentary History* 19:344.

25 Speech of Lord Chatham, Lords Debates, 20 January 1775, *Parliamentary History* 18:155 footnote. The Continental Congress also spoke of obtaining "relief from fears" by repeal of the offensive acts. Petition to the King, 26 October 1774, *Journals of Congress* 1:120.

26 Speeches of John Wilkes, Henry Cruger, Commons Debates, 10 December 1777, *Parliamentary History* 19:569, 587. Another member urged repeal to divide the colonies. "While your Acts stand unrepealed, it is their interest to be united; remove the cause of that union, and the effect will cease." Speech of William Jolliffe, Commons Debates, 23 February 1778, ibid., pp. 782–83.

27 Speech of William Jolliffe, Commons Debates, 23 February 1778, ibid., p. 782.

28 Declaration of Richard Viscount Howe and General William Howe, 19 September 1776, *Parliamentary History* 18:1432; Speech of Lord John Cavendish, Commons Debates, 6 November 1776, ibid., p. 1434; Letter from Lord North to the King, 6 November 1775, *Correspondence George III* 3:276; Speech of Charles James Fox, Commons Debates, 2 February 1778, *Parliamentary History* 19:681.

29 One variation was a blanket repeal without naming the statutes: "That all and every of such acts of parliament . . . intended to declare or maintain a supreme legislative power and authority over the people of the British American colonies . . . are . . . repealed." "A draught for a bill," Cartwright, *Letter to Burke*, p. 39.

30 *Journals of Congress* 1:71. As late as 1780, Henry Seymour Conway named the same acts as did Chatham, with the addition of one enacted after Chatham wrote his plan. "General Conway's Bill for Conciliation with Colonies, 5 May 1780," Conway, *Peace Speech*, p. 48.

31 For example, Resolves of the Georgia Commons House of Assembly, January 1775, *American Archives* 1:1157–58.

32 [Dickinson,] *New Essay*, pp. 17–18; *London Magazine* 43 (1774): 586. Governor Pownall thought these instructions important enough to discuss. Pownall, *Administration Fifth Edition* 1:102–3.

33 Instructions of the Pennsylvania Convention, 21 July 1774, *Revolutionary Virginia* 2:150–51. For the vice-admiralty grievance, see *Authority of Rights*, pp. 177–83.

34 Declaration of 14 October 1774, *Journals of Congress* 1:72.

35 James Duane's Notes of Debates, 15–17 October 1774, *Letters of Delegates to Congress* 1:198. Some members of Parliament moved repeal of the Quebec Act as a necessary concession for peace. Speech of Sir George Savile, Commons Debates, 14 April 1778, *Parliamentary History* 19:1127–28.

36 Speeches of Earl Gower and Lord Chatham, Lords Debates, 30 May 1777, *Parliamentary History* 19:320, 343.

37 Speech of Lord North, Commons Debates, 27 October 1775, *Proceedings and Debates* 6:133; Speech of Sir George Savile, Commons Debates, 7 Decem-

ber 1775, *Parliamentary History* 18:1053; Price, *Two Tracts: Tract Two,* p. 76; Speech of John Wilkes, Commons Debates, 10 December 1777, *Parliamentary History* 19:572.

38 [Macfarlane,] *Second Ten Years,* pp. 147–48.

39 "To the Author . . . ," Philadelphia, 8 March 1775, *American Archives* 2:90; Speech of James Adair, Commons Debates, 27 October 1775, *Proceedings and Debates* 6:138. Similarly, see [Macfarlane,] *Second Ten Years,* pp. 265–66 (arguments made in House of Lords).

40 "[T]he Navigation, and every other restrictive Act, must first give way to their unreasonable demands; and, with them, the sovereignty of this country." He was addressing Wilkes, who had said: "I fix on that period [1763], because the Congress complain of nothing prior to that era. They have never hinted at the repeal of the Navigation Act, nor any other Acts before that year." Speeches of Lord North and John Wilkes, Commons Debates, 10 December 1777, *Parliamentary History* 19:577, 572. Similarly, see Speech of Lord North, Commons Debates, 19 February 1778, ibid., p. 764.

41 Speech of Lord North, Commons Debates, 1 November 1775, *Proceedings and Debates* 6:158; [Galloway,] *Historical Reflections,* pp. 71–72.

42 Extract of a letter from James [*sic*] Galloway to Governor William Franklin, 26 March 1775, *Revolution Documents* 9:84; Speech of George Rice, Commons Debates, 19 April 1774, *Proceedings and Debates* 4:182.

43 Speech of Lord Mansfield, Lords Debates, 7 February 1775, *Parliamentary History* 18:270; Speech of Attorney General Edward Thurlow, Commons Debates, 10 December 1777, *Parliamentary History* 19:587; Speech of Solicitor General Alexander Wedderburn, Commons Debates, 19 April 1774, *Proceedings and Debates* 4:190. See also Speech of Lord Mansfield, Lords Debates, 30 May 1777, *Parliamentary History* 19:351.

44 Speech of Constantine John Phipps, Commons Debates, 19 April 1774, *Proceedings and Debates* 4:184.

45 Speech of Lord North, Commons Debates, 6 November 1776, *Gentleman's Magazine* 47 (1777): 4. Similarly, see Speech of Lord Hillsborough, Lords Debates, 14 March 1776, *Proceedings and Debates* 6:478.

46 Speech of Solicitor General Alexander Wedderburn, Commons Debates, 19 April 1774, *Proceedings and Debates* 4:189.

47 Letter from Lord North to Lord Dartmouth, 10 February 1778, *Stevens Facsimiles* 24:2089. Also, see Anon., *Conciliatory Bills Considered,* p. 23; Ritcheson, *British Politics,* pp. 260–61.

48 18 George III, cap. 11.

49 18 George III, cap. 12; *Authority to Tax,* pp. 260–61.

50 18 George III, cap. 13.

51 Speech of Lord North, Commons Debates, 17 February 1778, *Gentleman's Magazine* 48 (1778): 52. For another version of this speech, see *Parliamentary History* 19:764.

52 18 George III, cap. 13. The date, 10 February 1763, marked the signing of the Treaty of Paris, ending the French and Indian War.

53 Even the militant Lord George Germain described the Declaratory Act as "but waste paper." Letter from George III to Lord North, February 1778, *Correspondence George III* 4:35.

54 The legislation did not make an exception of the Declaratory Act, but Governor Johnstone, one of the peace commissioners, complained that he should have authority to suspend the Act, which he called "downright nonsense"; after passage of the Peace Act Sir William Meredith moved that the Declaratory Act be repealed, but was opposed by both Lord North and Edmund Burke (who said "the House had already formally renounced the obnoxious power"). Speech of George Johnstone, Commons Debates, 10 April 1778, and Speech of Lord North and Edmund Burke, Commons Debates, 6 April 1778, *Parliamentary History* 19:1086, 1011–12, 1012.

55 Governor Johnstone also complained that he should be authorized to promise the Quebec Act would be repealed.

56 Instructions to the Carlisle Commission, 12 April 1778, *Revolution Documents* 15:87–88.

57 Ibid., p. 83. See also p. 87.

58 Ibid., pp. 91–92.

59 Letter from the Carlisle Commissioners to the Continental Congress, 9 June 1778, *Revolution Documents* 15:136.

60 Instructions of the Pennsylvania Provincial Congress to the Deputies to the Continental Congress, 15 July 1774, *London Magazine* 43 (1774): 586.

61 Proclamation of the Peace Commission, 29 December 1780, *Revolution Documents* 18:261. Also see Instructions to General Sir Henry Clinton, 22 July 1779, *Revolution Documents* 17:167. The peace commissioners were Clinton and Admiral Marriott Arbuthnot.

62 Speech of Lord Osborne, Lords Debates, 5 March 1778, *Parliamentary History* 19:850.

CHAPTER TEN: "RIGHT," "ACKNOWLEDGMENT,"
AND "RENUNCIATION" SOLUTIONS

1 Speech of Edmund Burke, Commons Debates, 23 February 1778, *Parliamentary History* 19:778–79.

2 "To the Author . . . ," Philadelphia, 8 March 1775, *American Archives* 2:90; Anon., *Reflections on the Contest*, p. 48. "[N]o British politician—certainly not Burke—had ever envisaged a solution of the colonial problem which did not involve the ultimate sovereignty of Parliament; Burke had only said that Parliament should refrain from exercising it." Pocock, "Revolution Against Parliament," p. 283. For Hat Act, see *Authority to Legislate*, pp. 267–71. For the White Pine Act, see ibid., p. 270.

3 Letter from Thomas Cushing to Benjamin Franklin, 6 May 1773, quoted in Thomas, *Townshend Duties*, p. 240. Also, see Letter from Thomas Cushing to Lord Dartmouth, 22 August 1773 and Letter from Thomas Cushing to Arthur Lee, September 1773, quoted in *Briefs of Revolution*, pp. 26 n. 5,

159 n. 18; Memorial from the Continental Congress to the Inhabitants of the Colonies, 21 October 1774, *Journals of Congress* 1:92.

4 Speech of Earl Gower, Lords Debates, 30 May 1777, Speech of George Johnstone, Commons Debates, 10 April 1778, and Speech of Edmund Burke, Commons Debates, 6 April 1778, *Parliamentary History* 19:321, 1086, 1012. For other opposition to the repeal of the Declaratory Act, see Speech of Lord North, Commons Debates, 6 April 1778, ibid., pp. 1011–12; Letter from George III to Lord North, February 1778, *Correspondence George III* 4:35 (quoting Lord George Germain).

5 Speech of Edmund Burke, Commons Debates, 16 November 1775, *Proceedings and Debates* 6:266.

6 [Goodricke,] *Observations*, p. 30; Letter from Governor Thomas Gage to Lord Dartmouth, 30 October 1774, *Revolution Documents* 8:223.

7 Speech of Lord Lyttelton, Lords Debates, 3 February 1766, *Proceedings and Debates* 2:127. Just ten days later Franklin was asked: "If the Stamp Act should be repealed would not the Americans think they could oblige the Parliament to repeal every external law now in force?" Franklin answered in part: "It is hard to answer." Testimony of Benjamin Franklin, House of Commons, 13 February 1766, ibid., p. 231.

8 Which could be the authority to tax as well as the authority to legislate. Speech of Charles Wolfran Cornwall, Commons Debates, 19 April 1774, *Proceedings and Debates* 4:236. Also, see Speech of George Rice, Commons Debates, 19 April 1774, and Speech of Thomas Townshend, Jr., Commons Debates, 2 May 1774, ibid., pp. 234–35, 343.

9 Speech of Lord North, Commons Debates, 20 November 1775, *Gentleman's Magazine* 46 (1776): 99.

10 [Hutchinson,] *Strictures Upon the Declaration*, pp. 29–30.

11 Speech of Lord North, Commons Debates, 6 November 1776, *Parliamentary History* 18:1435–36; Speech of Lord Suffolk, Lords Debates, 20 January 1775, *Proceedings and Debates* 5:271.

12 *Authority to Tax*, pp. 247–53.

13 Speeches of Welbore Ellis and Henry Dundas, Commons Debates, 20 February 1775, *Parliamentary History* 18:331, 332.

14 Speech of Lord George Germain, Commons Debates, 2 May 1774, *American Archives* 1:89.

15 Speech of Lord North, Commons Debates, 2 February 1775, *Proceedings and Debates* 5:352–53.

16 Christie, *Crisis*, p. 95 (quoting North in early February 1775). Also, see Speech of Lord North, Commons Debates, 6 November 1776, *Gentleman's Magazine* 47 (1777): 4.

17 Speech of George Johnstone, Commons Debates, 6 February 1775, *Proceedings and Debates* 5:376.

18 Van Alstyne, "Parliamentary Supremacy," p. 209.

19 [Jenings,] *Plan*, p. 12. However, there may have been members of Parliament who intended more than a mere acknowledgment. Later, when finally

giving up all hope of acknowledgment, one member of Parliament admitted that had Americans acknowledged the right, he had wanted Parliament to exercise it. Speech of Lord Suffolk, Lords Debates, 5 March 1778, *Parliamentary History* 19:844–45. Also, there were American whigs who thought the acknowledgment solution could be a constitutional trick. Letter from Samuel Adams to Richard Henry Lee, 21 March 1775, *Letters of Delegates to Congress* 1:321.

20 Anon., *Proposition for the Peace*, pp. 18–19; Anon., *Experience preferable to Theory*, pp. 95–96; [Sheridan,] *Review of Three Questions*, p. 36. Contrary, see Speeches of Lord Suffolk and Lord Lyttelton, Lords Debates, 20 January 1775, *American Archives* 1:1499, 1500; Speech of Charles Jenkinson, Commons Debates, 21 February 1766, Ryder, "Parliamentary Diaries," p. 305.

21 Speech of Alexander Wedderburn, Commons Debates, 3 February 1766, *Proceedings and Debates* 2:149.

22 Speech of Lord George Germain, Commons Debates, 16 November 1775, *Proceedings and Debates* 6:272; Speech of Governor Thomas Pownall, Commons Debates, 19 April 1769, *Proceedings and Debates* 3:155.

23 A different question than whether Parliament should exercise the "right" to enforce obedience, something petitioners in Great Britain frequently requested Parliament to do. Bradley, *Popular Politics*, pp. 72–73.

24 *Virginia Gazette* (Purdie and Dixon), 14 March 1766, p. 3, col. 1 (reprinting a New York newspaper of 20 February 1766).

25 Worcester County Resolves, 10 August 1774, *Massachusetts Provincial Congresses*, p. 630. Also, see Plymouth County Resolves, 26 September 1774, ibid., p. 622; Hamilton, *Farmer Refuted*, p. 91.

26 Resolutions of Provincial Congress, 10 July 1775, *Georgia Revolutionary Records* 1:245–46. The Continental Congress avoided stating this doctrine, but it was implicit in its demand for legislative autonomy. Consider how Galloway paraphrased that demand: "That the Colonies are entitled to a *free* and *exclusive* Power of Legislation in their several Provincial Legislatures, subject only to the Negative of the Crown." Letter from Joseph Galloway to Samuel Verplanck, 30 December 1774, *Letters of Delegates to Congress* 1:284.

27 Letter from George Grenville to Commodore Samuel Hood, 30 October 1768, *Grenville Letterbooks*; Letter from Francis Maseres to the Quebec Committee, 19 March 1774, *American Archives* 1:1846; Anon., *Defence of Resolutions*, p. 35; Abercromby, "De Jure," p. 2; Kammen, *Rope*, p. 170.

28 [Jenings,] *Plan*, p. 11.

29 Anon., *Address to People of Britain*, p. 32.

30 Speech of Lord Shelburne, Lord Debates, 8 April 1778, *Parliamentary History* 19:1052; Fox, *Speech of 2 July*, pp. 22–23. See also Letter from Earl Camden to the duke of Grafton, 4 October 1768, Thomas, *Townshend Duties*, p. 97 (for different wording see Tucker & Hendrickson, *Fall*, p. 253).

31 Letter from Samuel Adams to Arthur Lee, 4 April 1774, *American Archives* 1:239; Carl Van Doren, "Introduction," to Franklin-Jackson, *Letters*, p. 21 (quoting Speech of Richard Jackson, Commons Debates, 5 February 1765);

Speech of John Wilkes, Commons Debates, 10 December 1777, *Parliamentary History* 19:565.

32 [Jenings,] *Plan*, p. 11.

33 [Jenings,] *Considerations*, p. 21; Speech of the duke of Grafton, Lords Debates, 5 March 1776, *Proceedings and Debates* 6:444; Ryerson, *Revolution Begun*, p. 168 (quoting *Pennsylvania Ledger*, 27 April 1776).

34 Speech of John Wilkes, Commons Debates, 2 March 1778 and Speech of Earl Camden, Lords Debates, 9 March 1778, *Parliamentary History* 19:806, 862.

35 See *Authority to Tax*, pp. 250–59.

36 Votes of 22 April 1778, *Journals of Congress* 10:377. For the motion of February 1775, see *Authority to Tax*, pp. 250–55.

37 Votes of 22 April 1778, *Journals of Congress* 10:377.

38 Dobbs, *Letter to North*, p. 12.

39 [Sheridan,] *Review of Three Questions*, p. 18; [Sheridan,] *Observations on the Doctrine*.

40 For the Irish Act, see *Authority to Legislate*, pp. 38–50.

41 [Sheridan,] *Review of Three Questions*, p. 47. For a reply arguing that an Irish declaration of Rights would be valid, see Anon., *Reasons For*, p. 45. For the Irish Declaratory Act, see *Authority to Legislate*, pp. 38–50.

42 [Sheridan,] *Review of Three Questions*, p. 36; Anon., *Reasons For*, pp. 37, 36–37. Sheridan explained his theory: "It has been already determined by the Conduct of the British Parliament, in the Course of the last two Years. That Parliament surrendered the *Exercise* of the Authority they had hitherto assumed, when they repealed those Laws by which they had hitherto bound us, and from the Moment of that Repeal, the exclusive Authority of our own Parliament was, if not in *Theory*, at least in *Fact* restored to us." [Sheridan,] *Review of Three Questions*, p. 27.

43 [Sheridan,] *Review of Three Questions*, p. 35.

44 Anon., *Answer to Sheridan*, p. 10.

45 Anon., *Reasons For*, pp. 30–31. The repeal statute was 22 George III, cap. 53.

46 Speech of Henry Flood, Irish Commons, 11 June 1782, *Celebrated Speeches of Flood*, p. 3. Also, see Speeches of Henry Flood, Irish Commons, 11 June 1782 and 14 June 1782, ibid., pp. 3–4, 20, 29. For the same rule of law stated in the British Parliament in relation to the American controversy, see Speech of Lord Beauchamp, Commons Debates, 10 December 1777, *Parliamentary History* 19:576.

47 Speech of Henry Flood, Irish Commons, 11 June 1782, *Celebrated Speeches of Flood*, p. 4.

48 Speech of Henry Flood, Irish Commons, 11 June 1782, ibid., pp. 3–4. "A Declaratory Act *gives no Rights;* it is only of Specification of Rights presumed to be *antecedently* existing." [Sheridan,] *Review of Three Questions*, p. 35.

49 Speech of Henry Flood, Irish Commons, 14 June 1782, *Celebrated Speeches of Flood*, p. 30; [Sheridan,] *Review of Three Questions*, pp. 35.

50 Speech of Henry Flood, Irish Commons, 14 June 1782, *Celebrated Speeches of Flood*, pp. 20, 26.

51 Speech of Henry Grattan, Irish Commons, 19 July 1782, *Speeches of Grattan,*

p. 159; Speech of Henry Flood, Irish Commons, 11 June 1782, *Celebrated Speeches of Flood*, p. 6.

52 Speech of Henry Grattan, Irish Commons, 14 June 1782, *Speeches of Grattan*, p. 145.

53 Speech of Henry Flood, Irish Commons, 14 June 1782, *Celebrated Speeches of Flood*, p. 28.

54 Poynings Act, passed in 1495, provided that all bills introduced in the Irish Parliament first had to be approved by London. It was repealed by Yelverton's Act of 1782, which is 21 and 22 George III, cap. 47, of the Irish statutes at large.

55 Speech of Henry Grattan, Irish Commons, 19 July 1782, *Speeches of Grattan*, pp. 166, 157.

56 23 George III, cap. 28, sec. I.

57 Blackstone, *Commentaries* 1:90. Also, see Chambers, *Lectures* 1:141; Hutchinson, "Dialogue," pp. 401–2.

58 Jenkins, *Lex Terrae*, pp. 108–9. For the rule stated early in the eighteenth century, see Anon., *Old Constitution*, p. 24.

59 Speech of Lord North, Commons Debates, 20 February 1775, *Parliamentary History* 18:321. For the tax Conciliatory Bill, see *Authority to Tax*, pp. 247–55.

60 [Erskine,] *Shall I go to War?*, p. 12.

61 Anon., *Experience preferable to Theory*, p. 98.

62 *Maryland Gazette*, 2 May 1775, p. 2, col. 1 and cols. 1–2.

63 Ibid., p. 2, col. 2.

64 *Concept of Liberty*, pp. 68–73.

65 *Authority of Rights*, pp. 34–38.

CHAPTER ELEVEN: PREROGATIVE SOLUTIONS

1 Tucker & Hendrickson, *Fall*, p. 179.

2 Petition of Virginia Council and House to the King, 18 December 1764, *Journal of Burgesses* 10:302; *Gazette & News-Letter*, 21 March 1765, p. 2, col. 1; Petition to the King, 26 October 1774, *Journals of Congress* 1:119, 120.

3 Resolves of Granville County, North Carolina, 1774, Rakove, *Beginnings*, p. 32.

4 "To the Inhabitants of New-York," 6 October 1774, *American Archives* 1:826.

5 Letter from Benjamin Franklin to Samuel Cooper, 8 January 1770, Franklin, *Writings* 5:260–61. Americans made this argument even though they knew they had grievances against the king as well as against Parliament. Greene, *Quest*, pp. 445–46; Maier, "John Wilkes," pp. 391–93. One whig who wanted the colonies to be linked to Great Britain exclusively through the crown wrote: ". . . although I detest the principles of George III, and shall think it my duty at all times to oppose his unjust encroachments, yet I mean to preserve the constitution by restraining the King." "Hampden" in *Virginia Gazette* (Dixon and Hunter), 27 April 1776, p. 2, col. 3.

6 Hamilton, *Farmer Refuted*, p. 90; Price, *Two Tracts: Tract One*, p. 68. Besides

regulating trade and superintending the empire, the Parliament would have conducted the colonies' foreign affairs. [Dickinson,] *New Essay*, pp. 94–95.

7 Marston, *King and Congress*, p. 38.

8 *Concept of Representation*, pp. 119–27.

9 Instructions of the London Livery to Representatives, 4 July 1775, *Remembrancer for 1775*, p. 108.

10 Petition to the King, 28 March 1763, *Addresses of the Common Council*, p. 43. For the constitutional grievance against the cider excise, see *Authority to Tax*, pp. 277–78; *Authority of Rights*, pp. 4, 56, 195.

11 [Macfarlane,] *George Third*, p. 320.

12 Petition of Lord Mayor, *et al.* to the King, 26 March 1773, *Scots Magazine* 35 (1773): 162–63. This petition, like similar ones, was reprinted in colonial newspapers. See, for example, *Boston Evening-Post*, 3 May 1773, p. 1, col. 1. Besides being printed in British magazines and newspapers, this petition was circulated through pamphlets. For example, *Addresses and Petitions of Common Council*, p. 38.

13 Petition to the King, 24 June 1769, *Addresses and Petitions of Common Council*, p. 8.

14 Petition of the Citizens of Bristol in Guildhall assembled to the King, 25 July 1769, *Political Register* 6 (1770): 116.

15 Remonstrance and Petition of the Lord Mayor, *et al.* of London to the King, *Hibernian Magazine* 5 (1775): 287; "Address and Petition of the Merchants . . . concerned in Commerce of North-America" to the King, 23 March 1775, ibid., p. 285 (asking veto of the Fishery Bill).

16 Petition of the Lord Mayor, *et al.* of London to the King, 22 June 1774, *American Archives* 1:215–16; Sainsbury, *Disaffected Patriots*, p. 60.

17 Address, Remonstrance, and Petition of the Lord Mayor, *et al.* to the King, June 1775, *Scots Magazine* 37 (1775): 338.

18 [Macfarlane,] *George Third*, p. 320.

19 [Basset,] *Equal Representation*, p. 16.

20 [Macfarlane,] *George Third*, p. 339. Also, see Speech of Sir George Yonge, Commons Debates, 25 January 1770, *Parliamentary History* 16:794.

21 Address, Remonstrance, and Petition of the Lord Mayor, *et al.* to the King, and the Answer of the King to the Address, 23 March 1770, *Town and Country Magazine* 7 (1770): 128.

22 Similarly, see the "radical" Sergeant John Glynn make a much more royalist argument than the "conservative" Attorney General Edward Thurlow. *Authority of Rights*, pp. 154–55. Also, when George III did invoke the prerogative to embargo the export of corn, it was Lord Camden, "to the astonishment of his old friends," who "defended the late exertion of prerogative, not only from the peculiar circumstances which occasioned it, but as a matter of right. He contended, that the crown has a legal, inherent right, founded on necessity, to suspend an act of the legislature." Anon., *Candid Thoughts*, p. 61 footnote.

23 Anon., *Address to Junius*, p. 18.

24 "A Revolution Whig," *Scots Magazine* 37 (1775): 646.

CHAPTER TWELVE: CONCLUSION

1 Speech of Sir William De Grey, Commons Debates, 25 January 1770, *Parliamentary History* 16:796–97.

2 Speeches of Charles James Fox and Lord North, Commons Debates, 26 October 1775, *Proceedings and Debates* 6:118–19.

3 Speech of John Dunning, Commons Debates, 6 April 1780, *Parliamentary History* 21:347.

4 It is a guess, but available evidence indicates that very, very few constitutional observers in Great Britain were willing to have Great Britain and the colonies united only by the crown. The exceptions were: Pulteney, *Considerations on Present State*, pp. 5–7; "A draught for a bill . . . ," [Cartwright,] *Letter to Burke*, pp. 34–35; Cartwright, *Legislative Rights*, p. 240.

5 *Boston Evening-Post*, 26 July 1773, p. 1, col. 3.

6 Anon., *Some Reasons for Approving Glouster's Plan*, p. 27.

7 For example, "A draught for a bill . . . ," [Cartwright,] *Letter to Burke*, p. 38. Contrary, see argument that parliamentary taxation of the colonies infringed the king's "just prerogative" and that the crown had a "right" to obtain revenue directly from America "in the same constitutional manner your Majesty receives supplies from the *kingdom* and from *Ireland*." Petition of 150 Inhabitants and principal Manufacturers of Taunton to the King, 26 September 1775, *Remembrancer for 1775*, pp. 306–7.

8 Markham, *Sermon Preached*, pp. xxii–xxiii. "It is the desire of the Americans only, to throw the whole Government into the Hands of the Crown, which would undermine the Principles of the Constitution. The Regal Power would then infallibly rise on the weakness of the other Parts of the Legislature." Anon., *Remarks on Conduct*, p. 34.

9 Letter from James Duane to Samuel Chase, 29 December 1774, *Letters of Delegates to Congress* 1:279.

10 Anon., *Remarks on Conduct*, p. 35.

11 Address of Lord Mayor, Aldermen, and Livery of London to the Electors of Britain, 29 September 1775, *Addresses and Petitions of Common Council*, p. 121. It was a frequently stated theme that for Great Britain to conquer America would endanger British liberty by increasing the wealth of the executive. Speech of George Grenville, Commons Debates, 5 March 1770, *Proceedings and Debates* 3:223.

12 Anon., *Free Thoughts on the War*, p. 17.

13 Guttridge, *English Whiggism*, p. 103. Earl Gower insisted the war continue because of "the repeated provocations they [American whigs] gave, by disclaiming the legislative power of this country, and endeavouring to alienate the mind of his Majesty from his parliament, and render the regal power independent of the other two estates of the realm." Speech of Earl Gower, Lords Debates, 30 May 1777, *Parliamentary History* 19:322.

14 Letter from Thomas Northcote to the Irish Reform Committee, 15 October

1783, *Collection of Irish Letters*, p. 95. Also see, Robson, *American Revolution*, p. 181 (quoting Franklin).

15 Letter from William Samuel Johnson to Governor William Pitkin, 20 October 1768, *Trumbull Papers*, p. 296.

16 Johnson, "Parliamentary Egotisms," p. 348. Contrary, see Greene, "Origins," p. 41.

17 Pemberton, *Lord North*, p. 236.

18 McIlwain, *Revolution*, p. 118. A discussion of Mansfield's use of the concept of sovereignty is not pertinent to the theme of this book. It is thoroughly treated elsewhere. See, for example, Bailyn, *Ideological Origins*, pp. 198–229. It was best expressed in the colonies by Hutchinson. Surrejoinder of Governor Thomas Hutchinson, 6 March 1773, *Briefs of Revolution*, pp. 146–47. What must be understood is that Mansfield's doctrine of sovereignty and the maxim that there could not be two sovereignties (or two legislative authorities) in one state, were by no means universally accepted law or unambiguous law. For contrary principles, see Johnstone, "Speech of November, 1775," p. 89; Letter from a Gentleman, *Boston Evening-Post*, 5 April 1773, p. 1, col. 1; O'Sullivan, "Philosophy of Common Law," pp. 127–28.

19 McIlwain, *Revolution*, pp. 118–19.

20 See, for example, Maccoby, *English Radicalism*, p. 219.

21 De Lolme, *Constitution: New Edition*, p. 521.

22 Greene, "Origins," p. 52.

23 Greene, "Plunge of Lemmings," p. 144 (quoting Namier). Also, see Donoughue, *British Politics*, p. 9.

24 *Annual Register 1776*, p. 141.

25 Maccoby, *English Radicalism*, p. 219 n. 2 (quoting the *Annual Register*).

26 Anon., *Reflections on Critical Situation*, p. 4.

27 *Annual Register 1772*, "preface."

28 Ibid., p. [46].

29 Ibid., pp. [51]–[*70].

30 "An Anti-Despot," Address to New York, 2 June 1775, *American Archives* 2:884.

31 Speech of John Moreton, Commons Debates, 2 March 1778, *Parliamentary History* 19:803.

32 For example, Estwick, *Letter to Tucker*, p. 108.

33 *Authority of Rights*, pp. 151–52, 155–58.

34 *Authority to Tax*, p. 278 (quoting *Scots Magazine*).

35 Anon., *Considerations on the Imposition*, p. 1.

36 *Authority to Tax*, pp. 242–44, 247–50.

37 "Extract of a Letter from London, to a Gentleman in New-York, Dated December 10, 1774," *American Archives* 1:1037.

38 Contrary, see Carysfort, *Letter to Hungtingdonshire*, p. 8 (". . . it may be numbered among the causes of the degeneracy of Parliament from its original

institution, that the attention of the people has been too much engrossed by their jealously of the regal power, while the very basis of their freedom has been silently undermined.")

39 Letter XXXIX, 28 May 1770, Wade, *Junius* 1:376.
40 Greene, "Plunge of Lemmings," pp. 159–60.
41 [Knox,] *Considerations on the Present State*, p. 50.
42 Wright, *Fabric of Freedom*, p. 81.
43 Donoughue, *British Politics*, p. 44.
44 Entry for 1 May 1775, *British in Boston*, p. 40.
45 Speech of Thomas Powys, Commons Debates, 4 December 1778, *Gentleman's Magazine* 49 (1779): 165; Abingdon, *Thoughts on Burke's Letter*, pp. lxviii–lxix.

INDEX

DESIGNED BY IRVING PERKINS ASSOCIATES
COMPOSED BY TSENG INFORMATION SYSTEMS, INC.,
DURHAM, NORTH CAROLINA
MANUFACTURED BY BOOKCRAFTERS, CHELSEA, MICHIGAN
TEXT AND DISPLAY LINES ARE SET IN CALEDONIA

Library of Congress Cataloging-in-Publication Data
(Revised for vol. 4)
Reid, John Phillip.
Constitutional history of the American Revolution.
Includes bibliographical references and indexes.
Content: [1] The authority of rights — [2] The
authority to tax — [3] The authority to legislate —
[4] The authority of law.
1. United States—Constitutional history.
2. United States—Politics and government—1775–1783.
I. Title.
KF4749.R45   1986   342.73'085   86-40058
ISBN 0-299-10870-8 ([v. 1])   347.30285
ISBN 0-299-11290-X ([v. 2])
ISBN 0-299-13070-3 ([v. 3])
ISBN 0-299-13980-8 ([v. 4])